PSYCHOLOGY OF A GANG BANGER

Le'Taxione (a.k.a. YoYo)

Outskirts Press, Inc.
Denver, Colorado

The opinions expressed in this manuscript are solely the opinions of the author and do not represent the opinions or thoughts of the publisher. The author represents and warrants that s/he either owns or has the legal right to publish all material in this book.

Original Diamond Boy: Psychology of a Gang Banger
All Rights Reserved.
Copyright © 2008 Le'Taxione (a.k.a. YoYo)
V3.0

Cover art by Randy "Big Ran" Dixon and interior art by Joseph Brassy-Apodaca for N'STEP's Diamond Culture Art.

This book may not be reproduced, transmitted, or stored in whole or in part by any means, including graphic, electronic, or mechanical without the express written consent of N'STEP except in the case of brief quotations embodied in critical articles and reviews.

Outskirts Press, Inc.
http://www.outskirtspress.com

ISBN: 978-1-4327-2450-4

Outskirts Press and the "OP" logo are trademarks belonging to Outskirts Press, Inc.

PRINTED IN THE UNITED STATES OF AMERICA

Introduction

The following is not an attempt to glorify or romanticize the violent gang mentality.

It saddens me that I've played a role in the proliferation of the miscreant aspect of the gang mentality, but as it is in any process of psychological healing, one must revisit the trauma that gave rise to the behavior in order to begin the atonement process.

My book, "Original Diamond Boy: Psychology of a Gang Banger" was written not out of a desire to further proliferate the miscreant aspect of the gang mentality, but rather to give words to those currently suffering from that mentality in order to aid in their transformation; and also to give civilians who stand on the periphery of this subculture a bird's eye view of the adverse psychology and behavior that is woven into our social fabric.

I've dedicated my life to eradicating violent gang behavior and have authored the Nine Steps to Empowerment Process (N'S.T.E.P.)™ Gang Violence Prevention and Intervention Curriculum to facilitate that endeavor.

Society must overstand that there are intrinsic dynamics procured by the trauma of violent gang experiences that perpetuate gang violence and until we effectively deal with the psychological aspects of violent gang behavior, we'll never be able to ameliorate the behavioral outcomes.

"Original Diamond Boy: Psychology of a Gang Banger" is a dramatization of pivotal events that represent a gang banger's distorted ability to perceive reality. It also gives an insight into that mind set that is needed to create a panacea for this destructive social ill.

"Original Diamond Boy's" characters and events may have been dramatized and/or embellished for this purpose.

Acknowledgements

I want to thank Ajali for her unmoving support and inspiration. You have always been there for me through feast as well as famine. You believed in me when no one else did and you dared to believe in my vision, becoming essential to its manifestation. I've never loved as I love you and it has always been a rise, never a fall. You are the essence of a true Black Queen, strong, smart, intelligent, spiritual, independent, compassionate, humble, authentic and sensual. Your love for me procured this commensalistic union ordained by God, nurtured by our belief in the Christ and sustained by our desire to truly become as one in struggle, love and success.

Before there was sun, moon, or stars, I loved you and because time did not initiate our love, time does not dictate our love. I love you selfishly, wholly and intensely. I love you eternally!

I want to thank my father, Rip and my mother Mzazi who in diametrically opposite forms prepared me for life's trials and tribulations and instilled in me characteristics that would allow me to live on two diametrically opposite planes.

Rip who gave me those raw lessons on urban society greatly enhanced my chances of being alive today. Without

Rip's raw advice and keen insight into the worst aspects of humanity, I would have never survived in the murderous inner city streets of West Fresno or any other states that I've resided in.

My mother, Mzazi, who's lessons though they were given to me as a very young child became essential in my transformation and are even today bearing fruit in my endeavors. Without Mzazi's lessons on intellect and analytical thinking, I could not have developed the N'STEP™ curriculum and the science it espouses.

I want to thank my beloved daughter, Special Divine Faith (RIP) who even in her departure had such an influence over me that she initiated my transformation.

I also want to thank my brother, Willie, who had the vision to see the potential of N'STEP™ when it was unpopular to do so.

But most of all, I want to thank God for blessing and protecting me and using my daughter as an instrument of change and I want to thank my Savior, Jesus for sustaining the change.

Dedication

I dedicate these memoirs to all of the Six Duce Diamonds and 62 East Coasts from Fresno to Boston that kept it a hundred and stayed true to the principles, code of ethics and constitution that made us not only homeboys, but comrades. Though I no longer subscribe to the miscreant aspect of the gang mentality, I have not abandoned you.

Time dictates actions and it is time for us to clean up this mess we made and once again, become the vanguards of the communities that we've tattooed into our skin and swore to protect with our lives. We've completed the phase of killing and dying for the hood, now let's revive and live for our communities.

I also dedicate these memoirs to the fallen soldiers whose blood, sweat and tears saturate the concrete streets and alleys of our inner cities across America and to the soldiers confined behind the steel curtains of the prison industrial complex.

To all of the comrades caught in the silence of demise: Rest in peace.

One love.

Le'Taxione (aka YoYo)
Diamonds are forever

Foreword

What you are about to read is a rare insiders view into the psychology of the gang banger, which, if not effectively assessed and addressed will continue to thrive within gangs, to the detriment of our communities, our families, our children and our future.

For more than thirty years, we as a society, have striven to address the problem of gangs in our community. We, who are outsiders to this culture have tried our hand at prevention, intervention, and suppression; and in spite of the millions of dollars spent and the thousand of lives lost due to death and incarceration, gang violence persists and in many areas is on the rise. This book, authored by an insider to the gang culture, is a critical look into why, in spite of all of the steps heretofore taken, we have not ameliorated gangs and gang violence continues to grow, in numbers and intensity.

"Original Diamond: The Psychology of a Gang Banger" is a companion piece to the Nine Steps to Empowerment Process (N'STEP) ™ – Gang Violence Prevention and Intervention Curriculum, also authored by Le'Taxione (aka YoYo). It identifies the strength of the belief in and commitment to the gang; a commitment that neither the threat of incarceration or death has historically negated. It illuminates the original love for the "hood", one which at its inception was honorable, but one which over time, due to a variety of societal issues was bastardized and then prioritized above love for family and for life. It defines the closed nature of the gang culture and how that nature makes positive change almost impossible if the impetus for that change comes from the outside of the gang. It illustrates why any effort, no matter how sincere, to address the gang violence problem cannot and will never be successful if it does not incorporate the gang member and if it does not come from inside of the culture, from inside of the gang.

"Original Diamond Boy" is a study that walks it's reader through the development of a gang banger, from childhood, to male hood and from male hood to manhood. It analyzes the role of those charged with the care of our at risk youth and the reaffirming role of incarceration as well as a plethora of other inputs that create and then promulgate the phenomenon we call gang banging. But it is not only that. It is also a testament to change and transformation. From the change of language (nigga to brother) and the consideration for women (broads to sistahs), this account proves that the gang banger can learn to Recognize Identify and Transcend© his or her own gang violence induced thought processes and the destructive actions which results.

Finally, for its insightful reader, "Original Diamond Boy" begins to educate us on the new paradigm we must utilize to define and then address the gang violence problem; one that relies on the gang member as part of the solution; one that considers the elements that make up the unique psychology of the gang banger.

Gangs are here to stay. They have been in existence in one form or another since the beginning of time. While we fight with our youth about how low they wear their pants, they continue to die. Given this, isn't it time that we change our focus from gang prevention to gang violence prevention; from gang denunciation to gang reformation? Since what we've been doing hasn't worked, can we dare to try something new? Can we be courageous enough to help the gang banger change their own reality; help them to help us change gang behavior from the inside out ™?

Thank God and His Dear Son, Jesus Christ for now utilizing the brilliance for good, that was previously used for wrong.

A.L. Whitfield, Attorney at Law

For more information on the Nine Steps to Empowerment Process – Gang Violence Prevention and Intervention Curriculum:

contact N'STEP at

n-s-t-e-p@hotmail.com

or

http://outskirtspress.com/9-STEPS

or write to

N'STEP
P.O. Box 58994
Renton, Washington 98058

Open Letter to the Hood

First and foremost, allow me to extend my salutations to every one of you who's Converse' stay stuck to the turf...I am honored to have the chance to address the most important generation that has lived since the beginning of time.

I come to you from my assigned cell in the prison industrial complex. Before you discount what I have to say because I am in prison, let me ask you...when was the last time you took notice of your own personal prison out there in so called 'free society"???

Though the word 'prison' is a descriptive term used to describe physical incarceration, the term is also a descriptive word to define mental incarceration. I say this because those of us who choose to represent a 'set' or 'hood' have imprisoned ourselves, restricting our ability to move beyond the parameters of that hood without consequences that may cost us our lives.

Let me say at this time that this is not to belittle or degrade you. I too love my hood, for these are our 21st century tribes and tribal identity is conducive to community responsibility because the tribe has laws that govern the way we conduct ourselves, the way we relate to one another and serve our communities. But our tribal laws have been lost and our responsibility to the community forsaken, creating an environment of lawlessness and chaos in our communities. So much so that we are being called 'domestic terrorists" and legislation such as HR 1279 - the Gang Buster Bill, Operation Nutcracker, Operation Hammer and the Gang Abatement and Prevention Act of 2007 is being created and enforced to incarcerate the most important generation since the beginning of time. That's you!

It is our faces that are flashed across the television screen when gang violence is described and our community is afraid of us due to the senseless violence that we perpetrate in the name of our hood. And since there is a disconnect between the elders and the youth, the elders look outside of the community for help, which subjects us to police brutality, unjust laws, and in some cases, our own death.

We are no longer the vanguards and protectors of the communities that we tattoo on our chests, backs, arms, faces and hands. We've become the number one destroyers of the very same communities that are tattooed in our skin.

This is not the reason that our street organizations were started! Does it make sense to you to destroy the very same community that we are willing to kill and even die for?

Our responsibility is to protect, serve and build the communities that we live in, but we are doing the direct opposite!

We are destroying our communities from the inside out! We have become savage in our thirst for blood, eliminating ourselves at a magnificent rate of speed!

There is a price to pay for those who thirst for blood…

There is a story of how hunters destroy blood thirsty wolves in the colder regions of this nation…The hunter would place a very sharp blade upright in the snow. Then he would place a morsel of raw meat on the blade to camouflage it. The blood thirsty wolf would come and begin to eat the raw meat and in doing so cut his tongue on the sharp blade and even when the meat is gone, the wolf can still taste blood so he continues to lick the blade until he dies. He unknowingly, in his thirst for blood, dies off of the taste of his own blood.

We have become wolves in our communities and often times we die either from the thirst for blood or in puddles of our own blood…

Like Pac said "it ain't them that's killin' us off, it's us that's killin' us off".

This has to change.

If we love the hoods that we've tattooed in our skin, let's protect and build them.

If we love life, let's preserve our lives.

If we love our children and our families, let's take on the responsibility to nurture and cultivate them, because if you don't, you leave them unprotected in a society that's gearing them for the graveyard or the prison yard.

It's time to stop just existing!

Choose life comrades and live!

Choose life comrades and live!

– Le'Taxione (aka YoYo)

"Mama's Most Ruffest Pup"

64 gave birth to this young black Nigaroe
One of 6 kids project dwella deep in Fresno
Po fo sho didn't have the shit that you others had
Rough double tough society's outcast
Born into chaos I adapted to them city streets
Young as a mutha fucka and Fresno was testing me
Definitely sweated me but it brought out the best in me
Now all that you niggas see is that wicked West in me
In the night I stay docked in them back streets
Strap fat black kaks cause I'm on the fuckin' creep
Steep peepin' niggas in my when they tryin to slang
Ski mask dash on that funky ass at his fame
And if he test it that niggas gonna rest respected
Life is sho hectic so I choose to live mines aggressive
Pistol play is mandatory so I run amuck
Why should I give a fuck I'm Mama's most roughest pup

Chapter 1

"Don't ever let me hear that something happened to your brothers or sister and you didn't help."

- Rip

I was born Ernest Carter on December 15, 1964 at Valley Medical Center in Fresno California. Though this was one of the happiest days of my parent's lives, on this very day, I was subjected two violence by a Caucasian doctor who found it necessary to slap me on my ass even though I already showed signs of functional life. Can you imagine a baby coming out of darkness into light, the fear that was prevalent, then being subjected to the pain of a violent spanking? Though I was not aware of the future that would be the first of many spankings.

I grew up in west Fresno, California in the projects called Pole Cat Alley, on Fairview, across the street from Edison High School.

We were poor and couldn't afford the things that other

Le'Taxione (a.k.a. YoYo)

people took for granted. My mother was a very strong, opinionated, beautiful Black woman named Mzazi. My father was a Gangsta whose values were loyalty, honor, respect, and integrity. He earned the nickname 'Rip' from his violent exploits and his weapon of choice...the knife. His skin was very light and though he lived some of his younger years in Richmond California, he was a native of San Juan Puerto Rico. His adoption by a man he called "Old Man Carter" is what brought him to the U.S.

Rip was a very violent, street smart cat that fell in love with the hustle that eventually would cause the separation of him and Mom's and his "either you're with me or against me" mentality would cause his absence in the home.

Now Mom's was a native of Tulsa, Okalahoma. They – my grandma Artha, grandfather Garnett, aunts Laura, Thelma, Rachael, my uncles, Jeffrey, Roger and Germaine and my mother Mzazi traveled to Fresno after It was rumored that my grandfather killed a racist police officer in Tulsa, Okalahoma.

At the time we lived in Pole Cat Alley, in a 3 bedroom project, I had two brothers, Duce and Soldier Boy and one sister. We called her Ben. Though we were all a year or two apart, I can't remember any part of my life without either one of them.

We all had very distinctive personalities. Duce was a Mama's Boy but in no way soft. He was accident prone but his threshold for pain was very high. Duce was light skinned like my father with very full lips and big round eyes. He didn't cry much and was as stubborn as the Taurus zodiac sign he was born under.

Soldier Boy was different. He was a loner and was the smallest of us all. He too was light skinned. He was very thin and built like our father Rip. Soldier seemed to always

Original Diamond Boy

feel it necessary to prove himself. He was the most creative of us all and as complex as the zodiac sign, Gemini, that he was born under.

Ben was a very dark, beautiful girl with a mean streak. Her father was a man called "Goat" who was known for his mean streak. My sister Ben was very intelligent and artistic. She could draw, sing and dance and though none of us could out draw or rap Soldier boy, Ben could out dance anybody. Ben was the big sister in every sense of the word and every bit as honest as the Sagittarius zodiac sign that she was born under.

As for myself (YoYo), I was the golden child. I excelled in everything I asserted myself in. I was excellent in sports: football, baseball and track. My mother always said that I was a born leader but that I needed to learn how to control my temper and quail my propensity for violence. As many black children who don't have the proper social skills to facilitate their advancement, I resorted to violence to hide feelings of inadequacy.

I was the darkest of my siblings; so dark that my father questioned his paternity. I was told that at one point I being my father's son was a major issue of dissent between him and my mother. That fact fed my feelings of inadequacy but I kept it on the say-low as a Gangsta 'cause I'm supposed to. I kept a lot of things on the say-low. I was always reluctant to share my feelings because I didn't want to seem weak because being weak was not acceptable around Rip. He couldn't stand weakness.

Rip always told me that I had to protect the rest of my siblings and in his words "don't ever let me hear that something happened to your brothers or sister and you didn't help". He verbally seared that into my brain at a young age and to this day its words that I live by and have passed them on to my children. I was as intelligent, passionate, driven and

Le'Taxione (a.k.a. YoYo)

violent as the Sagittarius sign that I was born under.

We lived in the average project home. Three bedrooms, one bath, no grass in the front or backyard, a clothes line, a shed and a swamp cooler that you had to squirt water on from the outside to fight the 100+ degrees of Fresno summers. For the most part we ate generic cereal that came in large plastic bags with pet milk (you know, the milk in a can with a cow on the label that you had to add water to) or powdered milk, spam, tuna, syrup, bologna and sometimes mayonnaise and sugar sandwiches. Those were the good ole' days.

For fun we would make bow and arrows out of branches, nails, and rubber bands and shoot each other or we would play red light green light, hide and go get it, wild tackle or tag in the streets. When we got tired of those games we would throw rocks or broken glass at each other. I remember one day we were in the parking lot of our projects and I threw a piece of broken glass at my brother Duce. It hit him in the back of the head and cut him wide open. He bled like a hog. Duce didn't even cry but after Mom's finished doctoring on him she got the ironing cord and tore my ass up. I think she whooped me for I it seemed an hour. I had welts where the ironing cord met my skin and that was everywhere but the bottom of my feet.

On another occasion Mom's had went to work and gave Ben specific instructions not to allow us to jump up and down on her new leather couch. Everything was cool until I started jumping on the couch. Duce and Soldier Boy went next. When Duce's turn came back around he jumped on the side of the couch that had a newspaper on it. His feet hit the paper. He lost his footing and busted his mouth on the corner of the wood coffee table. Though he knocked a hole in his upper gums, he didn't drop one tear. He just looked at us with those big ass eyes bleeding like a hog; tough as nails.

Chapter 2

"Fear is stronger than love...Love puts you in a position to have to watch people...but fear puts people in a position to have to watch you."

- Rip

Moms and Pops weren't getting along too well. There were constant arguments about how Pops disciplined us and how he conveyed life's lessons to the boys. You see Rip was a realist and he was street poisoned so though the life lessons that he conveyed were beneficial, they were tainted by a street piety© that Mom's didn't agree with.

Rip had been to prison and his mannerisms and character made that evident. One day I had a fight with my friend Alonzo who lived across from us. Rip watched the fight and coached me through it like a trainer would a boxer. For the most part of the fight, Alonzo was hitting me so fast that it felt like I was fighting three people. I threw a punch

Le'Taxione (a.k.a. YoYo)

out of desperation and caught him on the chin. Alonzo hit the ground and I walked away victorious.

When we got back into the house Rip gave me a stick and told me to go and beat him until he begged me to stop. Without question I went back outside and did what Rip told me to do. I beat him until he cried "Please stop!" This time Rip watched from the front door. When I came back into the house Rip said "You done good Son."

He began to philosophize about why it was important to beat my friend until he begged me to stop. He said "YoYo, I don't want you to start any fights, but every time somebody starts one with you, take it to the extreme". He said "fear is stronger than love...love puts you in a position to have to watch people, but fear puts people in a position to have to watch you."

One day Rip, Moms, Duce, Soldier Boy, Ben and I went to the meat market on Elm. As we were on our way into the meat market, a Mexican man was coming out and as he passed us he spoke Spanish to Rip. Rip became furious. He screamed "I ain't no Mexican mutha fucka!" You could tell that the Mexican man didn't understand why Rip was so angry but we knew. Though Rip looked like he was of Mexican descent, he couldn't stand Mexicans. Being Puerto Rican, he probably heard every Mexican joke there was.

As the man walked away, Rip turned, went back to the car, got an iron bumper jack, walked up to the man and busted his head wide open. Blood squirted everywhere. Mom's got us back in the car and we left before even going into the meat market. When asked "Why the Hell did you do that?" Rip replied "Fuck that donkey rider!"

That's how Rip got down. Rip ended up back in the pen and with no man in the home and Mom's working, we ventured out into the darkness that engulfed the projects.

Original Diamond Boy

Duce, Soldier, my friend Man-Man and I formed a little click called the Dragons. I was only 8 or 9 years old, but I had been exposed to the wiles of the projects. All of us had and we were street tough. We would all go to a store on California and Fig next to Marcus Bail bonds and steal. On this particular day, Ben went with us. We did what we'd done many times. We'd send Soldier boy to the counter to get the cashier's attention and we'd steal cookies and cupcakes. On this day, Duce and I almost got caught and Ben ran home and told on us. By the time we got home Mom's was waiting for us. Once we got there she told us what Ben had told her and Man-Man immediately said "I stole everything and gave it to YoYo to hold for me. Man-Man hadn't stolen anything that day but he was trying to cover for me. It didn't work. Mom's got an extension cord and as she used to say "broke my back" but from that day forward Man-Man was my lifelong homeboy.

Chapter 3

"...in the projects gunfire was as natural as the birds chirping in the wee hours of the morn."

- YoYo

Moms & Pops separated more so for personal reasons than anything else. Rip chose another lifestyle after being released from Soledad Prison. While he was incarcerated, he joined a prison gang called the Black Gorilla Family (BGF) and enhanced his political awareness along with his vocabulary but the lifestyle that he chose made evident the fact that he had not changed his criminal mentality. He chose to become a pimp.

He had all of the attributes that would appeal to young, black, lost females. Because of his Puerto Rican descent he was very light skinned. He was tall, had long hair, an immaculate conversation and because he was a two time golden glove in Soledad, women knew that he could protect them. Though I didn't dig his lifestyle, he was still my Fa-

Le'Taxione (a.k.a. YoYo)

ther and I loved him all the same. At this time Mom's was basically on her own and though Rip provided financially as requested, Mom's bore the bulk of the responsibility of raising four children in a hostile environment such as Pole Cat Alley.

I was nine years old, going to Franklin Elementary school on Fresno's notorious West Side, along with my sister Ben and my brother Duce. My teacher was a beautiful, pudgy, black woman named Ms. Williams and my principle's name was Mr. Collins. I loved school and though my reading skills were, in my opinion below normal, I excelled.

School had never been my problem but living in the projects was challenging to say the least. As children, we were exposed to things that no child should ever be exposed to. For example, one day Duce, Soldier boy, Man-Man and I were walking to Cal's meat market located on California Street, across from Franklin Elementary. Though the walk to Cal's market was littered by the reality of drug deals, prostitution, violence, and death, this was the store where poor welfare recipients shopped and Mom's would send us there with food stamps to purchase lunch meat.

Anyway, we were on our way to Cal's market and before we made it out of Pole Cat Alley we saw a man lying by one of the many big dumpsters that was strategically placed throughout the projects for people to dump their garbage.

At first we thought that the man had overdosed on heroin like we'd seen a neighborhood fiend named Harry Hippy do so many times. But as we approached the body we could see a small hole in the side of the man's head and I knew that he had been murdered but that didn't bother me. What bothered me was that he'd been there probably for several days stankin', and though many people had either walked by or dumped their garbage, the man was left there, flies all over him, to rot.

The projects were like that. You could lose your life and nobody gave a Fuck because life was not cherished life was not revered, life was worth less! Niggas died in and around the projects all the time so death was a constant companion of those residing in West Fresno.

I couldn't wait until Rip came by so that I could tell him about what I saw. When he finally came through, I ran out to his car and told him. He took a long draw off of his favorite cigarette, a Winston, and said "YoYo, death is a part of life." That's how Rip interacted with me. He would say some of the seemingly coldest shit but it was always real.

I told Rip a lot of things that I wouldn't tell moms. They were so different in their application of knowledge to circumstance and in their explanation of circumstances. Rip would give it to you raw, uncut and real. Moms would do the same but offer some hope at the end. I was more drawn to Rip's method.

I remember so distinctively the summer of '73. It was Fresno hot and later that day, Mom's was planning one of her "get togethers" which consisted of a group of her friends, music, alcohol, and as they called it back then "herbs". I remember that morning, it was about 5:30-6:00 a.m. and duce, Ben and I were up. We always got up early in the morning, catch rats and watch cartoons.

On this particular morning, we tried a different kind of trap for the rats than our usual wood and spring trap that would be set the night before. The rats had got hip to that trap and we would find in the mornings that the cheese would be gone and no rat would be in the trap.

Anyway, our new trap consisted of a ruler, string, a box, and peanut butter. We used peanut butter instead of

Le'Taxione (a.k.a. YoYo)

cheese because it seemed as though the rats couldn't resist it. It didn't matter what time of day it was if you'd set a trap with peanut butter, the rat would come to get it. It was something about peanut butter that would cause an otherwise night creature to come out in broad day light to get it. We tied string to the end of the ruler and stood it up inside a box leaning it approximately one inch high off the ground.

We put a spoon of peanut butter on the piece of paper and set it in the back of the box. We'd pull the string to the back of the box so that when a rat went in to get the peanut butter, we would pull the string causing the box to collapse with the ruler, string, rat and peanut butter trapped under the box.

We set the trap and sat very still and like clockwork, the rat came and went under the box. I pulled the string and like planned, the box collapsed on the rat. Duce then got a piece of newspaper, pushed it under the box, folded it upwards and taped it to the sides of the box so that the rat couldn't get out. We then took the box outside, placed it right side up, soaked it with lighter fluid and set it on fire. That's project recreation.

So Mom's planned her get together and it started around 6:00 p.m. Moms' best friend was named Mona. Mona as a very dark skinned black woman with long silky black hair and pearly white teeth. I was in love with Mona. Mona would always be the first person at the house and we were allowed to stay in the front room while Mona and Mom's were the only ones there, but when the other friends came, Moms would tell us to go in the room and stay there.

There was another door to the hallway that separated the front room and kitchen from the bathroom and other rooms so Moms would also close that door. We would, after the hallway door was closed, come out of the room and lie on the floor at the bottom of that door and listen to Moms and her friends talk, Laugh and play music on the record player.

Moms' friends were allowed to use the bathroom but they were not allowed in the rooms. The only people who were allowed in the rooms were family. On this particular night, my favorite Auntie, Lou and her boyfriend, Jimmie was at the get together. Jimmie was also a friend of the family. Jimmie was cool people but he couldn't hold his liquor and every time he drank, he and my Auntie Lou ended up arguing.

Well, the guest came and we were ushered into the room. Later on that night we heard Lou and Jimmie in our Mother's room arguing. Lou was a very beautiful full figured woman and from what we heard Jimmie was upset because Lou gave someone too much attention. The argument obviously became physical because we heard rumbling in the room. All of a sudden Moms busted into the room where Lou and Jimmie was at which was across from Soldier Boy, Duce and my room. When we heard Mom's scream "Jimmie get off her" we ran to the door and saw that Mom's had her snub nosed .38 special revolver.

When Jimmie got up, Lou rolled out from under him and came to Mom's side. Mom's then screamed "Muthafucka I told you about this. Get the fuck out of my house!" Back then everybody wore afros and Moms and her friends were no different. As Mom's said "get the fuck out of my house" she pulled the trigger. The gun was loud and Jimmie ran out of the house with his hair smoking.

The bullet from Mom's .38 had gone through Jimmie's afro and into the wall where he was standing. Though that was the first time that I had witnessed a shooting up close, it would be far from the last time and served as a form of

Le'Taxione (a.k.a. YoYo)

desensitization to gun violence.

In the year 1974 I began claiming Crip. I'd heard stories about cats like K-Tempt and True Boy and beefs they'd had. Duce, Soldier Boy, Man-Man and myself already had a click called the dragons and we'd been involved in gang fights and petty crime but the violence that we were participating in was about to escalate.

One day Duce and I was walking back from Cal's market. We walked through Edison High School, our normal route to get home. We walked up on some older cats who were arguing over a drug deal gone bad. The smaller cat pulled out a gun and shot the other cat.

It seems as though he shot him out of fear because once he realized that he'd in fact shot the man, he dropped the gun and ran. The man that had got shot clutched his stomach and stumbled away.

I told Duce "let's get that pistol Cuzz". While duce began to look around to see if anyone else had saw what we saw, I ran and picked up the pistol.

It was a chrome, pearl handled .22 revolver. It was my first heater and I fell in love with it. I'd told myself that the next time that we had beef with anybody; I was going to blast them.

Due to me flashing the pistol in the hood and vowing to blast anybody that we have beef with, most cats tried to extend me their friendship. Two months had passed and I hadn't got the chance to use my pistol on anybody. I had become anxious to do what I saw the man at Edison High School do but I wouldn't do it out of fear, and after I'd done it I wouldn't drop the pistol and run. I'd walk away.

One night it was very hot and Moms had told us to come in the house. The street lights had just come on. I don't know what it was about Moms, but as soon as the street lights would come on, she'd come to the screen door

Original Diamond Boy

and scream "YoYo, Duce and Soldier, it's time to come in!" It's like she had an instinct that told her exactly when the street lights would come on.

Anyway, we had to come in and because it was so hot, I couldn't sleep so I pulled the metal latch that secured the window up, unlocking it and grabbed the handle rolling it to the right, opening the long upright rectangular window. When the window was opened I grabbed my deuce deuce from its hiding place in our dirty clothes hamper, put it in my pocket and jumped out of the window into the night.

Though I tried to kill the thought in my mind, I knew what I wanted to do. I'd watched it so many times on TV. I'd seen my mother blast on my auntie's boyfriend. I'd seen the man by the garbage can lay slumped. I'd watched the man at the Edison High school point and get off leaving his victim to die all alone, and in the projects, gun fire was as natural as the birds chirping in the wee hours of the morn.

I was raised on gun violence. It had become a normal part of my daily experiences so I was desensitized to its criminal aspects and life ending results. I was tired of watching my real life experiences which played like a movie on the reels of my mind. I wanted to shoot somebody. Anybody! Anybody that said the wrong thing. Anbody that got in my way. It was time that I took my place center stage in this movie called life and act my part in this melodramatic theatre. So – lights, camera, action…Enter YoYo!

As I jumped out of the window clutching my little .22 revolver, I knew the exact location I wanted to be in. There was a dimly lit parking lot where all of the pimps, hoes, hustlers and players met. It's like it was the launching pad of every criminal idea in the projects.

Once I got to the lot, it wasn't as densely populated as usual. It's my guess that everyone had come and gone. It was like they did this in shifts but the reality was that the police would come through and run them all off but after they'd left, the world would slowly trickle back in.

At the entrance of the route leading to the lot there was a couple of cats gambling and a dope fiend lie in wait of his next fix. Dope fiends were the most unpredictable of the criminal element in Pole Cat Alley. They had no morals, no code of ethics, and no sense of discretion. They would take advantage of anyone, young or old, man or woman. They were at that time, the lowest form of life on the criminal totem pole.

I paused for a minute to see if my homeboy Man-Man would appear out of the darkness. He too would sneak off into the night and frequent the parking lot. He was the one that had told me tales of what transpires there. Five minutes passed and there was no sign of Man-Man. I made up in my mind that I was going to go in, just stand around and watch, but if this dope fiend approached me in any way fowl, I was going to blast his ass.

As I advanced, on cue, the dope fiend approached me and said "where you going young blood?" I immediately reached into my right pocket, pulled out my heata, eased it down to the outer right side of my thigh and cocked it. The dope fiend was so high that he didn't see it. I continued to advance. As I was passing him, he extended his hand as if to grab me saying "Where you going Young blood?" As his hand touched my right shoulder, I spun, faced him, said "Fuck you nigga!" and pulled the trigger, all in one motion.

The deuce deuce erupted sounding like the crack of a bat when a major league baseball player hits a homerun.

"AAHHHH! You little mutha fucka!" the dope fiend screamed.

I let off again. I hit him two times and watched as he clutched his wounds and winced in pain. No sympathy, no remorse! If I had to use one word to describe the experience, it would be "liberating".

Yes. Liberating. Without any excuses, I was hooked on the adrenaline that intoxicated me when I let off. The sound of the gun, the smell of the gunpowder and the pain in the face of my victim were all the things that I would long to experience again.

Chapter 4

"I was a gangsta now and I would act like one."

- YoYo

The next day, my Mother's friend, Mona came to the house while my Mother was on one of those weight loss machines. It was the one that looked like it had an outboard motor attached to it with the belt that goes around your waist. To use it you would place the belt around your waist and then the motor on the belt would then gyrate in an attempt, to shake the fat off.

Mona came in, but I didn't run up to her like I used to do. I was a Gangsta now and I would act like one.

"YoYo, go outside and get out of grown people's business." Moms said.

Duce and Soldier were already outside. As I walked out of the door, I brushed up against Mona's butt. She looked down at me and smiled. She knew that I liked her and thought it was cute. She used to say stuff like "I can't wait

Le'Taxione (a.k.a. YoYo)

till you get old enough. I'm going to kick P.B. out and you gonna be my boyfriend." P.B. was an older cat that was always beating Mona up. He was neither of her children's real father and they couldn't stand him. Sometimes Von, Paul and Thomas, Mona's children, would spend the night at our house because P.B. would be in a violent rage about something that wasn't right when he got home.

It seemed common for the women who lived in the projects to have abusive men. So common that I thought it was normal for men to hit women. I thought that that was what a man was supposed to do.

Once I got outside, I called Duce over to me. I told him "I shot that dope fiend Last night". He smiled real big

"What he do when you shot him?" he asked.

"He screamed like a broad".

We started laughing.

Rip had started us equating anything deemed weak to a "broad". If you cried, you cried like a broad. If you couldn't fight, you fought like a broard. If you fell cowardly, you fell like a broad. If your voice was high pitched, you talked like a broad.

"Let's go get Man-Man and tell him" Duce said.

Man-Man was known for being in the streets at all times of the night. His father was not in the house and his mother worked two jobs trying to provide for Man-Man and his two sisters. They didn't live in the projects. They lived in houses next to the projects so in all reality they were financially better off than we were, yet they too were sucked into the dynamics that surrounded every black single parent home that existed in the projects.

I didn't want to tell Soldier because when we were little he used to cry all of the time. So much that we used to call him "Crying Ivory". But he came with us anyway.

We got to Man-Man's house and I yelled his name from

the sidewalk outside of his fence.

"West Up YoYo?" he said with a big smile as he came to the screen door.

"West Up Homie."

West up was a term we used to describe the fact that we lived in West Fresno and we were proud of that.

Man-Man came out of the house to the fence and I blurted out "I popped that dope fiend last night".

"For real?" he asked as he placed his hands on the fence and jumped up, pulling his legs together over the fence, landing on the side we were standing on. Once he landed he said "West Up Duce & Soldier".

"West Up!" they replied in harmony.

As we walked off together, I told him what happened then we all swore not to tell anybody else.

Man-Man had some cousins that had come up from L.A. and they were Crips. He began telling us about cats from Fresno who were also Crips. He mentioned True-Boy and two other cats that I'd never heard about. He was telling us that Crips wore blue and say "Cuzz" all the time. Their enemies were cats that wore red and said "Blood" all the time. At that instant I said "I'm a Crip"

"I am too" Man-Man said.

Chapter 5

"The project had a way of making the softest person hard."
- YoYo

That night Man-Man came over and tapped on the window. I went to the window.
"Monica's Auntie is naked." He whispered.
Duce and I snuck out of the window and went to the adjoining project where Monica, Tyrone, Ted, Rita' and their mother, Ms. Tate lived. They had an auntie named Tamika who was what we called a dyke (Lesbian). She was actually a pretty female, about 20 years old, with caramel skin and very short hair and a very proportionate body. Tamika used to baby-sit Monica and the other kids when Ms. Tate was gone.
Tamika was mean with a fowl mouth or at least that's the perception that she gave. The projects had a way of making the softest person hard. Anyway, Man-Man, Duce and I, we went to Tamika's window. When we got there

Le'Taxione (a.k.a. YoYo)

she told us to line up. We stood outside of the window peering in. She had the light off but she went and stood by the light switch and flicked it on and off real quick but we were able to see that she had on a bra and panties under her negligee'. We were jumping up and down so excited that we couldn't control ourselves.

She turned the light on and off about 10 times, all while we were watching for new developments. Then the light came on and went off again, but this time she didn't have any panties on.

We got quiet and stood real still. It was dark for a while, then the lights came on and went off again but this time she was naked. We didn't know what to do. Then she said "come in" so we climbed into the room through the window. Once we got in things got serious. Tamika lined us up again and said "All of ya'll pull out your dicks". I was scared but Man-Man and Duce pulled theirs out fast. It was evident that Man-Man knew what he was doing, but duce and I were virgins. We played Hide-and-Go-Get-It but all we did then was simulate the act of sex with our clothes on then tell everybody else "I humped her". But Man-Man wasn't no virgin.

After fondling us, Tamika laid down on the bed and opened her legs saying "Come on". Man-Man was the first one to try to lie on top of her but she said "I want YoYo". Now I'm scared as hell but what was I going to do? Everybody was there and I couldn't "act like a broad" and not lay on top of her. The cold thing about it is I was the one always talking about koochie. I was a little nasty boy. When Mona would wear a dress to our house, I'd wait until she got ready to leave and lay on the floor face up by the front door so that she would have to step over me and as she did, I would look up under her dress. But now, here was my opportunity to experience a female sexually and I'm scared as hell.

Original Diamond Boy

I pulled my pants down and lay on top of her. She could see that I didn't know what I was doing so she grabbed my member and put it in her and started moving her hips in a circular motion. She was very wet and my member kept coming out, but she kept putting it back in. I was 10 years old and no longer a virgin. I got me some koochie!

The next day I woke up and went outside before it got real hot. Summers in Fresno stayed about 100 degrees and the summer of '74 was no different. I saw this girl named Lisa. I was in love with Lisa. A lot of cats didn't like her because she was so black. They used to call her names like "black African", "tar baby", "black spook", "African booty scratcher", etc. (I would find out later in my life that these were names that white people called us). But I liked Lisa's dark, smooth skin. Lisa was skinny with long black hair, white teeth and the most beautiful smile. I was in love with that girl for most of my life but I never told her.

One day in '94 I saw her in a club near the Old Spaghetti Factory restaurant on Fresno Street and I almost told her then, but I didn't. Anyway, I saw Lisa outside by herself as usual. I walked by and said "West Up?" She said hi and I kept walking.

I used to just watch her. She was very graceful and won all of the races at Franklin Elementary on play day but I couldn't bring myself to tell her how I felt about her, so I just watched.

As I got to the back of the projects, I saw Man-Man and we greeted each other with "West Up". We were Young Crips now and though it was only in our minds, we acted in accord. Man-Man suggest we go to the Edison swimming pool. I couldn't swim but I said "Let's go". Every Summer Edison High School would open up the swimming pool for people to swim and since it was in the vicinity of the project, we felt that we should always be there. That was the

Le'Taxione (a.k.a. YoYo)

beginning of our turf issues.

Once we got there, there was some cats that we didn't know at the pool. As we came closer, Man-Man Said "West Up Cuzz?" to about three cats. The other cats were just there to swim, but Man-Man asked "Where ya'll from?" They said they lived in the Pottle projects. Man-Man took off on the cat (socked him) and I took off on his friend. The other guy ran. There wasn't much of a melee. A couple of blows were thrown and it was all over. As the other guys walked away I screamed "Crips Cuzz!" We were practicing.

Chapter 6

"...look at this boy's head...its perfect. This boy is going to be a genius."

- Daddy

'75 rolled around and for some reason we had to move. Whatever the reason was, Mom's didn't discuss it with us. We were children and that was grown folks business. We moved in with Momma. We called our grandmother "Momma" and our grandfather "Daddy". We called our parents by their first names or in my father's case, by his nickname "Rip". Momma was a country woman who dipped Garrett snuff out of the white container with the silver top. She ate rocky road candy bars, peanut brittle (the pink kind), drank Squirt soda, cooked every holiday and raised all of the children in the family at one point or another. Momma held the family together (may she rest in peace).

She had all kinds of country sayings like "fire don't ride

Le'Taxione (a.k.a. YoYo)

no lazy horse" and "don't fatten frogs for snakes". Now, "fire don't ride no lazy horse" was a saying she used to explain the fact that if the situation gets intense enough, anybody will react. "don't fatten frogs for snakes" was used to warn people against instigating.

Momma was about 5'2", 190 lbs, with grey hair, fat cheeks and an angelic smile. Whenever Momma was asked "how old are you? she would say "19", so the grandchildren never really knew how old Momma was. Momma lived in a three bedroom, two bathroom house in an area that is now called "The Dog Pound". She lived on E. Calwa and had had eight children: My mother Mzazi, Thelma, Lou, Rachael, Terry, Jeffrey, and Roger & Germaine. Momma's demeanor was mild and she was very old fashioned.

Now Daddy was the diametric opposite (may he rest in peace). Daddy was a Gangsta. It was rumored that he had killed a police officer in Okalahoma so they moved to Fresno. Daddy wore suits, Khakis, Pendletons, the very best Stacy Adams, derbies and packed a .45 semi-automatic.

Daddy was dark skinned and had a short grey natural (Afro). He had no teeth. I knew this because he used to keep them in a glass in the bathroom. Though Daddy used to drink, I never saw him drunk. He too used to dip snuff and chew tobacco. They used to call Daddy "Mr. Williams", but Momma called him "Garnett". When men spoke of daddy they spoke of him in tales. Like "I remember one time Mr. Williams was gambling at the shack up on Fruit and a man tried to cheat him and Mr. Williams shot up the whole place."

I remember one time Daddy got into it with the Dolphin as he called him. I watched as he pulled out that .45 and slapped him with it. Daddy used to sit me next to him while

Original Diamond Boy

he drank and say "Mzazi look at this boy's head...its perfect...this boy is going to be a genius". They always said that I was Daddy's favorite grandson but I think that was because everybody else was scared of Daddy.

'75 was a hard year for us. I heard Momma and my Mom's talking and Mom's was saying that she wanted to get us out of the projects. The crime was too high and it was so depressing. She said she wanted more for her children and herself.

Times were so hard that I can remember Mom's and my Auntie Lou used to get us up late at night, drive us to the white part of town (as we called it) and lower us down into the Salvation Army donation shacks and have us push clothes back up out of the slot that we were lowered through. Moms would say "White people donate these clothes for those in need and we are in need." One time as we were lowered into the little Salvation Army shack at the side of the road, the police pulled up.

"What are you people doing on this side of town?" I could hear them saying to my Mother and Lou.

'Donating clothes like everybody else", Mom's retorted.

"Are we breaking the law?" Lou chimed in.

The officer shot back "Are you finished" with one of those racist southern drawls.

"We are now" Mom's interjected.

"Please move on" the officer then said.

Ben, Duce and I could hear Mom's and Lou get into Mom's Belair, close the door and drive off. We sat in that shack for about 45 minutes, and then we heard a car pull up and Mom's whispered "Minna?" (That's what she called my sister Ben. We all replied "huh?"

"Ya'll start pushin' them clothes up out of there and let's go"

Le'Taxione (a.k.a. YoYo)

We got everything we could up out of there. I pushed a radio up through the slot but Mom's said "we don't need no music...we need clothes". I wanted that radio but Mom's was right.

One thing for sure though, though we would get hungry sometimes, we would never starve in Fresno. If the hunger pangs got too severe between meals Momma would say "Ya'll better go get something off of those trees". Momma had a peach and a plum tree in the back yard and we would go get peaches, put mud all over them to take off the peach fuzz, and then wash them off with the hard green water hose. If that wasn't enough, we'd walk around the neighborhood and pick almonds, cherries, oranges, pomegranates, loquats, black berries, walnuts, apples, lemons, limes, grapes, etc. Sometimes we'd have to jump over people's fences into their backyard and we did with their disapproval. Momma stayed in what we called back then "the Country". Things were slower, everybody knew everybody and they kind of talked different, not much, but different.

The neighborhood was made up of older husband and wives with children. Whereas, the projects was made up of single parent homes for the most part and the mother being the principle parent in the home. Another thing that was different is they had grass! We didn't have grass in the projects. All we had was rocks, sticks, steel bars, and glass. But I loved the projects! I loved the chaos, the danger, the sirens, the gunshots, the violence, the tension. I was street poisoned.

I transferred schools and ended up at what was then called Fresno Colony. I didn't like it at all. These people reminded me of the slave characters on television and I wasn't a slave. Mom's instilled in us that no one was better than us and that white people had no right to treat black people the way they did. Even then Mom's was an activist and her spirit was instilled in me. I had a profound love for black people which at first made it hard for me to perpetuate the violence that I became known for, but environment has a way of turning you into itself and that's what happened to me.

Man, I missed the projects. I missed my homeboy Man-Man. I missed seeing Lisa and watching Tamika get naked. But most of all, I missed my deuce deuce revolver. When we left the projects, I left my heata with Man-Man. He promised to keep it for me but most of all, he promised to use it.

Chapter 7

"I didn't like my new environment and I didn't like the country ass Niggas that I had to be around."

- YoYo

I had started getting in trouble at Momma's house. I started sneaking off and walking across town to the projects to hang out with Man-Man. The last time that we kicked it, he told me that the cats from the Pottle Project caught him slippin' and jumped him. I asked him why he didn't blast them. He said that the heata was for grown men. I told him that the heata was for anybody that got in the way. I had gotten bitter from being displaced like I was. I didn't like my uncles. I didn't like my new environment and I didn't like the Country Ass Niggas that I had to be around.

I couldn't stand my uncle Terry. He tried to be more than an uncle to me. I remember he whipped me for being disrespectful and Mom's let him do it. At that moment, I

Le'Taxione (a.k.a. YoYo)

lost trust in Mom's and I told myself that once I got old enough, I was going to get down (fight) with all of my uncles.

My Uncle Germaine was different though, at least that's what I thought. Germaine respected us and spent time with us. Even when we lived in the projects, Germaine would ride his ten speed all the way across town and give us rides. Germaine was very good at martial arts and he got all of us boys karate gees and started teaching us. Duce and myself excelled, but soldier kicked like a broad.

After I got good, I started using what my uncle taught me on other children. I used to walk up and do a spinning hook kick over their heads just to establish my dominance. (I was a trip.)

Chapter 8

"The hardest thing in the earth is a Diamond."
- Big Oso

I'd begun to hear more and more about the Crips. This homie, True-Boy was one of the most notorious Crips in Fresno at that time. He didn't have a specific hood. He was just a West Side Crip. True-Boy stuttered and I guess that's why he had a lot of fights. He was way older than I and known for biting people when he fought. True-Boy was a killa. Between '76 and '77, it was rumored that True-Boy stabbed some Mexicans to death and walked around the next day in the blood soaked clothes. I don't know how true the whole story was, but fact was that True-Boy did stab them.

In '76, a lot of us began to hang out together. The oldest of us was Big Oso. Big Oso used to direct our agenda with military precision. Everything we did was planned and structured. True-Boy was in the pen for multiple murders and Big Oso stepped up to replace him as one of the most notoriously known cats in Fresno and when my time came, I too would wear that title.

"We're going to start our own gang." Big Oso said one day.

All of us were with that but we needed a name. Big Oso said "it's got to be something hard."

"The hardest thing in the earth is a diamond" he said.

Right then, we became Diamond Boys.

Now you may be thinking "Damn, he skipped a year, but if you'd done as many drugs as I've done, such as PCP (Sherm), Angel dust, sniffing paint, smoked primo's (weed mixed with cocaine) and Lovely (weed dipped in Sherm), you'd skip some time too. But let me get back to this Diamond Boy!

"We Crips Cuzz" Man-Man exclaimed after our meeting with Big Oso in the privacy of his garage.

"Cuzz, We Diamond Crips", I said.

Man-Man never liked the title Diamond Boy but that's how Man-Man was. I don't care what anybody said, Man-Man would only agree with half of it.

The next day was initiation. Oh, I know you didn't think that just because Big Oso said we were going to start our own gang that that was it? Not with Big Oso. I told you everything was run with military precision. Big Oso had us line up in two lines with an isle down the middle. You started at one end and tried to make it down the isle with cats hitting, punching and kicking you if you fell down. Those who made it to the other end were Diamonds; all others were crystals.

After initiation, we'd all kick back and lick our wounds. At that time, none of us drank or smoked and Big Oso liked it like that. He said that you can't protect your hood when you're high. There was no bloods at that time at least none that we knew of and we weren't on that anyway. Big Oso taught us community responsibility, respect, discipline, loyalty, honor, integrity and a code of ethics governed by a real constitution. We went shopping for the elderly; we raked yards and swept sidewalks. We cut grass and emptied garbage cans. We took pride in our communities and when we had parties we protected the females in our communities. When we had disputes with one another, we would put on the boxing gloves and handle it.

Big Oso liked us to be clean and creased. Some of the homies had mothers who couldn't afford new clothes for them. Big Oso would pay for all of us to get on bus 30 and ride across town. We'd go into a department store, steal stacks of 501 Jeans and Khakis and run out. He used to call it "take and break". If any grown ups tried to apprehend us, Big Oso would knock they ass out, straight like that. We'd get back to the west side and Big Oso would issue out the pants and tell us "go to the store and get you some Niagara starch with the yellow top and iron your clothes before you come out of the house".

If we were caught with wrinkled clothes, Big Oso would discipline us without the gloves. I've watched Big Oso make most of the homeboys cry. See, Big Oso was somewhat of a bully. Don't get me wrong, he loved the homies, in a drill sergeant kind of way.

Big Oso was known for knocking people out and taking their guns from them. I'd watched him do this in dice games when cats tried to set or stick the dice on him. Though we weren't allowed to gamble, we would all watch Big Oso gamble. If he thought you were trying to cheat him, he would scream "This Diamond Nigga" and take off (sock) on the culprit. After the cat lay unconscious, Big Oso would go through his pockets.

There were a lot of things that Big Oso didn't allow us

Le'Taxione (a.k.a. YoYo)

to do, but the things that he didn't want us doing was the things that would destroy us. Big Oso was the father figure that wasn't in the home. I'm sure if we'd had fathers in the home, Big Oso's style of life wouldn't have been so attractive, for Homies would have had fathers to look up to but they didn't so Big Oso became our surrogate father.

One day, the majority of the homeboys were at Frank H. playground when we got the news Big Oso had been shot and was dead. We couldn't believe our ears, Big Oso couldn't be dead is what my mind screamed. The homegirl KK pulled up and confirmed the news. It happened at Edison high school. The Homeboy Danger's little brother was being disciplined by Big Oso. He pulled out a .38 revolver out of fear. Big Oso said "Little nigga, I'll take that gun and whoop your ass." Danger's little brother was speechless. Big Oso reached out to grab him and he let off one shot. Big Oso fell in disbelief and died. We cried for days. Big Oso was dead. –Rest in peace Homie – Diamonds Forever.

Chapter 9

"We used to sneak back and forth to the West side though Moms didn't like it."

- YoYo

Mom's moved us off the West Side to the other side of town. She had us going to school with white children. I hadn't ever interacted with white children and I didn't like how they looked at me, as if they were so much better. Young white girls liked me, but I wasn't interested in them. I remembered the slave movies that Mom's would catch us watching and turn the television channel. Black men with white all around their mouths. This was supposed to be comedic but it wasn't funny to me.

I used to sneak back and forth to the West Side though Mom's didn't like it. Mom's wanted more for her children, but all I wanted was the West Side. I did very well in school. I knew that if I didn't I wouldn't have enough freedom to sneak to the West Side, but I didn't like it. I didn't

Le'Taxione (a.k.a. YoYo)

like the white teachers teaching all of the glorious contributions that all races except blacks had made to the world. I didn't like that every time we talked about black people; we were described as savages with bones in our noses or slaves. I couldn't endure the remarks that the white children would make so I waited until after school and took off on the biggest one of them. That was a trick that Rip taught me.

"Bust the biggest cat in the nose and you won't have to worry about the rest." He said.

It always worked.

I'd wait until after school because if I got in trouble during school, I wouldn't have the freedom to sneak to the West Side. Everything I did at school or around the house was based on my ability to get to the West Side. So I excelled in the miseducation offered in the Eurocentric school curriculum.

Mom's had a library of books at the house. She made it mandatory that we read something twice a week. At first I didn't like reading. I felt that it was a waste of time, but I got a hold of a book called "The Miseducation of the Negro" by Carter G. Woodson and that opened my mind. I picked the book up because it had the name Carter on it and that was my last name. After reading that book, I became hungry. I now had a veracious reading habit that I hid from my Homies.

There was only so much that I could hide though. As one reads his vocabulary becomes vast and I began to advance concepts that the Homies had never heard (but after they'd listen, they'd agree with my premises).

Chapter 10

"Soon after being instrumental in initiating the Godfathers, Terrell died in a car accident."

- YoYo

Word was going around that a pop locking dance group called the Electronic Boogaloos had turned blood and they called themselves Godfathers headed by a cat named Terrell Jones. I remembered taking karate lessens from Terrell. He was a cat that everybody liked and he did a lot with the youth in our communities. Soon after being instrumental in initiating the Godfather's, Terrell died in a car accident.

After Terrell Jones's demise, we began to clash with the Godfathers. Most of these cats were 19, 20, and 21 years old. I was now 13. Though I was present at the inception of the Diamond Boys, others were there that were older than I was. Cats like Slim, Yellow, Oldman, Danger, K-Bone, C-Boy, Tyson, Wolf, Insane (RIP), etc. They were older than

Le'Taxione (a.k.a. YoYo)

most of us and some felt that that should have earned them the respect of the younger Homies, but I only respected those that carried themselves in the likeness of Big Oso.

Because I was sharper than the young Homies, I didn't subject myself to the subservient role that most of the older Homies wanted to superimpose on the young Homies and most of the older Homies didn't like that. They felt like I was bucking the structure when in reality I merely didn't respect their abuse of perceived authority. After all, before any of these cats held a gun, I had a shooting under my belt and I carried myself in that manner.

The dynamics of gang life are strange and sometimes contradictory. Inside the hood there were Homies that like specific Homies and only rotate (hang out) with those specific homies. There's even Homies that don't like each other for various reasons, whether it be jealousy, envy, or just hate. But if an outsider attempts to harm that Homeboy that you don't like, he has to deal with all of us because all of us are coming.

Word spread that K-Bone, one of the homeboys that I didn't like, got into it with B-Dog, one of the Godfathers and his brother jumped in. Slim, one of the homeboys that lived in our projects, that I loved, called a meeting.

We met in big V. Villa, a low income housing complex on Fig behind King Elementary School. The plan was to meet the Godfathers at Edison High School and get down with them. Old Man said "I don't want the little Homeboys there". Old Man always looked out for the Diamonds as a whole. At 8:30pm, I showed up on time. The older Homeboy, Danger asked "What is you doing here YoYo?" I said, Cuzz, I been here from the beginning. I ain't one of the little homeboys".

The Godfathers arrived and Slim did all of the talking.

"Cuzz, I don't like how you jumped the homeboy."

"You know how that goes." B-Dog said

B-Dog was one of the most feared of the Godfathers. He was fat, black, with a long perm and he had major hands, but his weight hindered him in a fight if it was drawn out. Slim told us to pick which one of the slobs you want to get down with. Then he said "I want this nigga B-Dog!"

"These are one on one fades." Slim told B-Dog. (Meaning two people get down by themselves".

B-Dog replied "This time Blood."

Slim and B-Dog was first.

Old Man said "Cuzz I've seen this slob get down and when he gets tired he grabs your clothes and tries to hang on." Slim took off his blue and black checkered Pendleton, stepped out from us and said "West Up Cuzz?"

"Get some Blood" B-Dog said as he stepped out from amongst the Godfathers.

It was on!

B-Dog ran up and Slim shot a stiff jab at him that caught him right in the forehead and sent him back a couple of steps. I immediately screamed "Knock that slob out Cuzz", as loud as I could. Another one of the Homeboys screamed "Fuck that roosta!" And the Godfathers were screaming "Fuck that crab up!"

Slob, roosta, lobsters and other terms were used by Crips as a show of disrespect to Bloods and crabs was a term used by Bloods to disrespect Crips.

B-Dog swung a left hook and caught Slim on the right side of his head, but it only grazed him as he ducked to slip the punch. Slim came back with a left cross that caught B-Dog on the chin and dazed him. Just like Old Man said, B-Dog began to reach for Slim out of desperation. Slim was tall with long arms and he used this advantage masterfully to keep B-Dog at a distance and we won the first fight.

Le'Taxione (a.k.a. YoYo)

Old Man and Danger won the next two but the Homeboy Chocolate lost miserably. I was so little that no one picked me making me feel that I wasn't worthy. From that day forward, I made up my mind to give the Godfathers the blues every time possible. How dare they look past me!

We would go on to meet the Godfathers at the Hinton Center, Frank H Playground, Ivy Center, Fink White playground, Carver Hole, and at Neilson playground and get down, one on one fades.

Chapter 11

"Never look at a situation for what it is. Look at it for what it can be. If you do that, you'll stay ahead of the average cat."

- Rip

In '78, I had formed a click within our street organization which consisted of the young Homeboys. We would get together and at night, travel the West Side and scratch Diamond Crips in the Godfather's low riders. These slobs contacted the Homeboy Wolf who in turn tried to tell the little Homeboys to quit scratching up these niggas' cars.

"Fuck them roostas Cuzz. All is fair in love and war!" I told him.

The Homeboy Dub, one of the homeboys I never liked because He was more of a weed dealer than a banger, chimed in with "If they start scratching our cars, I'm coming to get your little ass". Dub was about 5'11", big, black and bald headed. At least he looked big to me then.

He was known for jumping on the little Homeboys.

Le'Taxione (a.k.a. YoYo)

"So this shit is about ya'll cars right?" I asked.

"What about the little Homeboys that these roostas keep catching and humiliating?"

Wolf said "Nigga stop trippin!" I said, "I'm gonna keep getting at them slobs any way I can."

"Little nigga, if you do it again, I'm coming to get yo' ass!" Dub told me.

Under my breath I said "and I'm gonna pop (shoot) yo ass.

"What you say Cuzz?" he screamed

He walked up on me. I didn't say it again, but I meant what I said.

I walked off and all of the little homeboys came with me.

"What you gonna do YoYo?" Man-Man asked.

"Fuck that nigga Cuzz. All that nigga worried about is his blazer. We the ones putting in all the work" I said.

"I hate that nigga" Man-Man replied.

I whispered "I wish Big Oso was here." I had been watching our set go from what it was started to be to an avenue for niggas to sell weed. These cats wasn't putting in no work. All they did is sold weed all day, drive around in their low riders, get high, and kick it with females while these Godfathers was growing and starting to be seen everywhere.

The Godfathers inspired young cats to become bloods. The young bloods were called 4/3 (Four Trey) Villains and I was happy as hell when they started. Now we had cats our age to really bang against and in the summer of '78 we got it crackin'!

The most notable 4/3 Villain at that time was a cat named Ghost. Ghost was about 5'5", dark skinned, with long hair. He had a brother, a twin, who was a Fresno Hoova Crip named Loc'd Out. Now the Hoovas in Los Angeles call themselves Hoova Criminals but at that time, all Hoovas was Crips.

One day Ghost and his brother, Loc'd Out got into it over Ghost disrespecting Hoova. Loc'd Out took off on him and Ghost ended up stabbing him. All this took place in their mother's home. That's how serious this shit was. This Hood shit ran deep. So deep that it even separated families, including twins.

Ghost was digging a female that dug me named Sharon. Sharon was a 18 year old, short, dark skinned female with a bangin' ass body. I met her one day on bus 38. I was sitting in the back of the bus as it pulled up Cedar and Belmont. That was the Mexican side of town. Bus 38 used to run from downtown West Side all the way across town. Sharon was going to McLane High school where my sister Ben attended. I was catching the bus up there to be around my sister Ben and her friends.

Sharon got on the bus as it began to pull off. Three Esses, as we called mescans (Mexicans), started coming to the back of the bus where I was. We had been beefin' with them since the Homeboy True-Boy killed a few of them on the Westside back in the day.

I could see in their faces that they wanted funk (a problem). As soon as one of them said "Que paso vato?" I jumped up, grabbed the overhead rail in hand, lifted my lower body up, legs together and kicked him with both feet in the chest sending him back into the other two.

"It's Diamond Cuzz!" I hollered.

It was customary to holler out your hood while engaging in acts of violence so that everybody knew "West Up".

When they stumbled back, I ran toward them knowing that if I allowed them to reset, they were going to have me. I jumped on the first one who seemed to be the leader.

"AAAHHH! She stabbed me! This fuckin mayata (nigger) stabbed me!" was all I heard.

The bus driver stopped the bus and Sharon and I got off and ran to her mother's house who lived right across from the bus stop where she got on. I didn't know where I was. I just followed Sharon.

After we got to her house she said "West Up?" I said "West Up!"

"What's your name?" she asked.

"YoYo" I answered

"Where was you goin?" she asked

I told her I was headed to see my sister and told her my sister's name was Belinda, but we called her Ben.

"I know Belinda" she said.

That was real, what you done for me." I told her

"Fuck them Esse's…this West Side."

Sharon was a West Sida who had been in juvenile. Her mother also tried to relocate from the West Side in an attempt to keep her out of trouble. I could tell that she was lonely out there on the East side because she kept talking.

"You a Diamond?"

I responded "Can't stop, won't stop, don't want to stop."

She laughed and I asked her "What the fuck you laughin' at Cuzz?" We called everybody Cuzz no matter who they were.

"You a cute little nigga." She said.

I smiled.

After that encounter, Sharon began to pop up everywhere I was at. I'd be at Fink White Park and her and her homegirls would pop up. I'd be at Frank H. and they'd pop up and when I went to the house parties, they'd be there too.

One day the Diamonds gave a party in Big V. Villa. All of the Diamonds were there, Slim, Yellow, Chocolate, Danger, Old Man, West, T-Dre, Pit Bull (RIP), Nutty Boy,

Original Diamond Boy

K-Bone, C-Boy, Bone, Cat, Wolf, Insane (RIP), J-Bird, T.T., Young-C (crazy), Man-Man, Katz, K.B., Duce, Solo (RIP), myself, etc. and the homegirls, Shay Shay, Lady Tyson, Tisha, KK, etc.

After the party, some of the Homeboys was walking to the Homeboy Chocolate's house. I was walking with K.B., Solo and Man-Man. I heard a female say "YoYo!" I turned around and it was Sharon and her homegirls. They called themselves Gangsta girls.

"West Up!" I said.

Sharon asked if she could talk to me for a minute.

"Who's the dame?" Man-Man asked.

"The one that stabbed the mescan on the bus?" I told him.

As I walked toward her, she asked "What you fis' to do?"

"I'm going to my Homeboy Chocolate's house." I told her.

She came closer and I could see that she was higher than a giraffe's pussy and that's way up in the trees.

I could hear her little friends in the near distance giggling. She asked "who you wit YoYo?"

"I don't have a dame. I'm wit this Diamond." I told her.

"You want to be with me?" she asked.

I responded "You intoxicated Cuzz. Ask me that when you ain't lit."

She walked off and I proceeded to Chocolate's house.

When I got to Chocolate's house, Slim, Old Man, Danger, Chocolate and his sister's Tina and Tonya were all in the front room. There were a few other homeboys there that I didn't know. The Diamond boys were growing fast and we had new Homeboys everyday. Everybody was smokin' weed and drinking Magnum, Mad Dog 20/20 and thunderbird with Koolaid. Everyone except Tonya; she was too young.

Le'Taxione (a.k.a. YoYo)

Chocolate's sister, Tina was very light skinned, with really long hair and a face like a model. Her body wasn't very well proportioned though. She was skinny and her ass was flat. She, Chocolate and Tonya all looked like they were half Mexican. I came in and sat on the couch. The Homeboys started offering me Mad Dog and weed, but I passed on both. The Homeboy, Danger made a crack about me acting like "I was too good for the drank". I told him Big Oso didn't raise me like that.

"Cuzz I'm tired of hearing you making them Big Oso statements. Big Oso is dead Cuzz" he stated.

"And that's why a lot of niggas is misrepresenting this Diamond!" I shot back.

"What Cuzz? Who the fuck you think you talkin' to?" he asked me.

He walked up on me but stopped outside of arms length. He said, YoYo, I'll beat you ass Cuzz." I didn't say anything.

"Leave the Homie alone Cuzz." Old Man said. "You can't make him get high."

Danger smiled and went back to drinking.

About then Tina's drunk ass came and sat next to me on the couch. Tina was said to have let most of the Homeboys hit those panties (have sex with her) at least that's what they said. But in all reality she was a beautiful dame, not my type but beautiful. This was our first time meeting.

"So you the notorious YoYo?" she said

"Without a doubt, West Up." I responded

"Who you wit?" she asked.

"I ain't got no dame. I'm wit this Diamond.

"Why you talk like that?" she asked. "Like you always serious and shit?"

I told her "Big Oso taught me." Before I could finish, she interrupted.

"Fuck what Big Oso said. What you say?" I asked.

Original Diamond Boy

Then I stated "Get the fuck up away from me Cuzz!"
Now at the same time I'm watching Danger play with a .32 caliber revolver. He was pointing it at the Homeboy Old Man like that shit was cool. He had never blasted anybody so he didn't respect the heata like he should have.
I can see that this nigga is drunk and exercising this false bravado. Don't get me wrong, the nigga could squabble (fight), but he wasn't no killa. I never liked this nigga for what his little brother did to Big Oso and he didn't like me because I was always pointing out the deviation from the instruction that Big Oso gave us, so it was only a matter of time before he would turn his heata on me I thought.
Rip taught me "never look at a situation for what it is. Look at it for what it can be. If you do that, you'll stay ahead of the average nigga". Just as I expected, this nigga turned the heata on me and started talking shit.
"This nigga right here (referring to me) always got something slick to say".
I said "Cuzz, I always got something real to say".
He walked up and pointed the gun at my head and said "you scared?"
"Quit playin Danger." Old Man said.
He asked me again "Is you scared Cuzz?"
"Live or die, Crip or cry." I responded.
That's when Tina told Danger he had to go.
He immediately started smiling and said "I'm just testing Cuzz. YoYo know I'm not serious, huh YoYo?"
"I know Cuzz. It's Diamonds forever." I responded.
At that very moment, I thought to myself, *I'm gonna kill Cuzz the first chance I get. This nigga done scared the shit out of me and he got the nerve to think it's cool? I'm gonna kill this nigga!"*
He turned and the gun went off and shot Old Man in the foot.

Le'Taxione (a.k.a. YoYo)

"AAHHHH!" Old Man screamed. "Cuzz you shot me!"

Danger said, "I'm sorry Cuzz! I didn't mean to do that!"

"I told your dumb ass to quit playin!" Old Man said. "AAHHHH! I'm shot!"

We carried him to the bathroom and sat him on the toilet. Chocolate called the ambulance and reported that someone had got shot. Before the ambulance came we rehearsed our story.

"When they get here, we gonna tell 'um that some Mexicans drove through while we were in the front yard and shot me" Old Man explained.

And that's what we told the ambulance workers and the police when they came.

After they took Old Man to the hospital Tina walked me down the block to Fig Ave and said "Don't trip on Danger. He likes me, but he's too old for me."

I told her "I ain't trippin and flashed a smile, but in the back of my mind I said *"I'm gonna kill that nigga as soon as I get a chance."*

The next day I told myself "It's back to basics. I got to get another heata." The violence in the streets was elevating and niggas wasn't fighting as much. Niggas was blastin'. I talked to my little brother Soldier and his crew, Little T-Dre and my cousin Bass and told them to be on the lookout for some heat while they were breaking into houses. These little niggas was terrorizing hoods using cat burglar tactics. That was their hustle and at that time they were the best. I would never do the burglary thing because it left too much to chance. Are the people home? Will they come home while you're in the house? Do they have dogs in the house? It was just too much to think about for me. I was a banger!

Chapter 12

"I don't care what you want to be in life, just be the best at it."

- Rip

I remember Rip told me "YoYo, I don't care what you want to be in life. Just be the best at it. If you want to be a ditch digger be the best. If you want to be a wino, drink the finest wine. If you want to shovel shit, have the biggest shovel! Whatever you do, be the best at it! I chose to be a diamond Crip and I was going to be the best, even if it cost me my life. I chose this shit for a reason, not for a season and it was till death do us!

A week later, I saw the homeboy C-Rag. It was rumored that he too had eyes for the dame Sharon. C-Rag was known for not talking much. He too was a killa. Somebody had spread the rumor that Sharon and I was together and I thought that C-Rag and myself was going to beef for this fact but all he said was "West Up YoYo." and kept

Le'Taxione (a.k.a. YoYo)

strollin'. Next thing I heard was that he got pinched (locked up) for cutting a cat named Bony Face's throat. As the story goes, C-Rag and Bony Face was gambling and Bony Face was winning. C-Rag caught Bony Face trying to stick the dice (set them on a particular number) and he gave him a California smile (cut his throat from ear to ear). C-Rag was a technician with a razor and Bony Face found that out the hard way.

Chapter 13

"...I love these young Niggas."

- YoYo

"**J**ackpot!" is what Lil T-Dre said when I saw him. He, Soldier Boy, and Bass had hit a house in the Zephler Holmes across Fig, and came up on a .38 special snub nose revolver, plus they had a bag of shells. I gave them $50 for it and they boned out. Those little niggas was some of the most hustling ass cats I'd ever seen and they kept it a hundred (100% real) with each other. They'd split the proceeds down the middle; all the way to the Last penny. After the purchase, I walked off and smiled saying to myself, *"I love these young niggas"*.

From what I understood, the nigga, Ghost was with the dame Sharon, yet every time I saw her she was trying to get at me. I saw her at a block party on Weller near the mini park and she was at me.

"YoYo, when you gonna give me a kiss?"

Le'Taxione (a.k.a. YoYo)

"You fuck with that slob nigga" I told her.
She asked "who told you that?"
I answered "a Bluebird Cuzz."
She said "I ain't with him" and I told her 'Yeah, fish ain't biting. Water's too deep" (I'm not going for that. I'm too sharp). I boned out.

I was on my way to Tahas market to get a can of Niagara starch, some chips and a Suzy Q cupcake when I was approached by this dame named Tiffany, the Dolphin's daughter. She asked if I had heard that Man-Man got pinched. I told her I was just with him and she explained that they had got him the previous night for battery. Man-Man had been stealing eight track tapes from J&C House of Records on Fig and California and when he attempted to exit the store, security apprehended him. Man-Man fought back and broke one of their noses in the fight but he couldn't get away. That sounded just like Man-Man.

I made my purchase and boned. I got back to Momma's house and began to iron. I started with my 501's. I laid them across the ironing board with the left leg on the board, reached on the inside of the pants, pulled the pocket out, pulled the right leg back over the top of the pants, lined the outside seam up and began to iron. I sprayed the leg with the starch until it was white with foam then I rubbed the foam in with my hand until it disappeared and lightly passed the iron over it so it wouldn't stick to the pants. It was a science and you had to do it like this lest the iron would stick to the pant leg and make a flakey impression of the iron on the pant leg. I ironed the inside of the left leg until it was dry, then I started on the outside of the right leg. The process was the same as far as pulling the pocket out of the pants, but on the right leg of all 501's, the outside seams don't line up properly. If you line the outside seams up like you did on the left leg, you won't get a straight crease down the middle of the leg, instead your right crease will end up on the outside of your leg. So, you have to line your right outside seam up so that it is in front of the inside seam. The whole process took over an hour.

Then I put what we call a California Crip cuff at the bottom of the pants. I took my blue and white checkered Pendleton and ironed two creases down the front, two down the back and one down each arm. I laid all of my clothes across the bed and waited for Ben to braid my hair. After she finished, I put a shower cap over my head and took a shower. After I got out of the shower, I ironed my blue rag.

At about 5:00 pm I began to get dressed. We had a meeting at Wolf's house and I couldn't wait. I loved being around the homeboys even though there was a lot of them that I didn't like. I put on my 501's, my Croakasack shoes, my hairnet, suede baseball cap (which ad two golf clubs crossed in the front with a golf ball in the middle), my white slingshot (wife beater tee-shirt) and Pendleton and buttoned it all the way up to the top button. I put my blue rag in my back left pocket making sure to let it hang, put my .38 in my right front pocket, then put on my locs (dark shades). You couldn't tell me shit! I was saggin' and blue raggin"!

I got to the meeting but the whole get down (environment) was different. It wasn't festive as it usually was. Something had transpired and whatever it was, it was serious.

"West up Cuzz?" I asked.

"These 4/3 niggas is trying to claim turf" Tyson said. They trying to claim the Villa."

"What? We been strollin' and controllin'" the Villa for the longest."

"These niggas want the Villa." Tyson said.

I said "fuck them slobs, let's go to war!"

Tyson simply responded "We are at war."

Chapter 14

"My adrenaline was flowing so hard I could feel my heart beat in my throat and hear it in my ears."

- YoYo

We had many skirmishes that year and just on the strength, I started messing with the dame Sharon which exacerbated the beef between the Villains, Godfathers and the Diamonds. A new blood gang called the Bounty Hunters sprang up through this nigga named Chukie and we went to war with them too. As the beef went on, a lot of cats that I called "mascots" (meaning that they dressed in the uniform but didn't put in work), fell off (stopped representing diamond.) This shit was very serious now. Niggas was getting caught slippin' and getting beat with bats, golf clubs and getting stabbed. That year slobs carved out their Turf. They controlled the California court projects, Cooley Plaza and Nielson playground. That was the year we also lost the Vill to the 4/3's.

Le'Taxione (a.k.a. YoYo)

Right before the summer of '78 ended we met again and tempers flared. Our numbers were up so as a demonstration of strength it was decided that we walk the West Side from California street all the way to Roeding Park, blue rags flyin', but with no heat and we did. All except me. We stopped at Fink White playground and picked up some more Homeboys and started out on our way to the park.

Once we got there, we positioned ourselves across from the rides which was the most sought after spot by anybody who came to the park. But that day it belonged to the Diamonds. There were new faces in the crowd though. A cat from Los Angeles named Big Flux who was cool with the older Homeboys was there. We stood around for a while. Cats were drinking, smoking weed and Crip walkin' (a celebratory dance Crips used to challenge our opponents). We saw the 4/3's off in the distance coming our way. As they got closer, we saw the God Father's caravan coming up the street. The 4/3's were getting closer and the Godfathers parked and got out of their cars and met the Villains and began walking with them.

As they got closer to us and B-Dog said something to Wolf. Wolf walked with his torso bent at a forward angle due to a back injury he sustained. Wolf began to walk forward to meet him and we all followed. We met in the middle of the street and cars were parked on both sides of the street where civilians left them and positioned their picnic materials next to barbecue grills.

I watched families grabbing their children in anticipation of the drama. They were 3 feet apart when B-Dog said what's up blood and Wolf took off. Wolf was killing' him from the shoulders and this became evident to B-Dog so he grabbed Wolf. When he did, Wolf let out a scream. Ahhh! He felt pain in his back. He then screamed "Cuzz get this nigga off me!" At that time Insane (RIP), Wolf's brother, came out of the crowd and sprayed B-Dog with mace causing him to let go of Wolf and holler as he grabbed his eyes. After that it was pandomonium. Everybody was fighting.

I happened to look to my right and I saw Ghost. The Villains had flanked us and he had a sawed off shotgun in his hands. He held the short but of the gun in his right hand and his left hand was on the top of the sawed-off barrel, thumb toward him, palms down in order to manage the kick of the gun when he fired. I pulled out my .38 and as he raised the barrel of the sawed off I pointed the trey eight at him. This all seemed as though it was happening in slow motion but it only took a matter of seconds.

I got off (shot) first. Then he got off. The civilians began screaming, scurrying and hiding. The Homeboys too ran for cover. It was all over in a matter of minutes.

My adrenaline was flowing so hard I could feel my heart beat in my throat and hear it in my ears. It sounded like someone in a band was hitting a big drum. I fell in love all over again with the feeling.

Chapter 15

"There was soon to be a shift of leadership inside the set and I was positioning myself to take it."

- YoYo

The fog crept into Fresno as it does every year and all that winter I put in work. I would put on an all grey dickie suit, tie my blue rag around my face and hunt red rags all night. There was soon to be a shift of leadership inside the set and I was positioning myself to take it. As the banging got more violent, the elder Homeboys hooked up with dames and fell off but me? I loved this shit. Live or die – Crip or Cry!

My actions were becoming far more brazen and unpredictable. I had been to juvenile twice for assault and battery and once for brandishing a weapon. On one occasion my brother Duce walked into an Arco mini mart on the Eastside across the street from Mosqueda center and jacked the teller. That's how Duce was. Duce's hustle was jackin' and

Le'Taxione (a.k.a. YoYo)

there wasn't an establishment that he wouldn't rob. After the jack he came to me and let me know what he had done. As we were standing in Butler Park talking to dames, the police rolled up with the clerk in the back of the car. He made me stand and face the patrol car with his spotlight shining in my face. I didn't run because I hadn't done the jack and this was just a formality.

I figured after this I would call him all kinds of punks and laugh at him as he rode off. His partner turned off the light, stepped out from the passenger side of the car and said "cuff him".

"What the fuck you cuffin' me for?" I asked.

"You've been identified as the perpetrator".

I asked him "What the fuck did I perpetrate?"

"A crime."

They put me in the back of the police car while the other car with the clerk in it drove off. As they were taking me away, Duce just looked at me and laughed. Though this was the first time that I did time for something I didn't do, it wouldn't be the last; but I rode it like I was supposed to.

Evil Seed

Now I was only 15 addicted to crime
I was smokin angel dust at my Momma's house in the blind
She never knew or had a clue what I was going through
I kept it on the under as a youngsta cause I'm supposed to
I'm clocking G's in the breeze on a summer's night
Looking for another lick before I greet the morning light
And if I'm right I'll catch a sucka slippin with his bitch
And shut him down like an addict on his first fix
I got no tricks up my sleeve and I don't believe
In fallin' to my knees when my babies got to have their cheese
So nigga please count your blessings
Cause niggas that I know is facin' death when they pull up in that intersection
Some anorexic livin numb smokin hella crack
Claimin' they my homies acting like they got my fuckin back
But you can scratch all that dumb shit
Cause nigga I can picture mutha fuckas trying to get next to this bomb shit
But see I'm slicker than yo average fuckin playa
Cause every time I hit the block yo bitch is plotting trying to share
Go everywhere by myself cause I'm livin cautious
Rollin in my Benz by my lonesome when I want to floss it
And when I toss it nigga passin' Hennessy and weed
But this is only just a curse from my evil seed.

Chapter 16

"Everybody stopped, but I couldn't. I was in a rage."
- YoYo

While in juvenile, I went to school. They held co-ed classes so it wasn't that bad. I stayed in for three months and was released. Moms had kicked me out of her house years earlier behind my stepfather, Darren.

Darren was an alright cat but because he wasn't my real father, I didn't give him the chance he deserved. One day I came home and Soldier boy told me that my stepfather had whooped him. I immediately brought it to him. Rip had told me the last time that his girl Sandra took us to Soledad to visit him "Don't let nothing happen to your brothers. If something happens I better not find out that you didn't do nothing".

"You're not Soldier's father" I told him. "If he does something you let me know and I'll discipline him but you keep your hands off of him"

Le'Taxione (a.k.a. YoYo)

After that Soldier told me that Darren tried to whoop him again. Duce, Soldier and I jumped him and Mom's kicked me out. Her exact words were "YoYo, one of ya'll got to go and it ain't Darren". So I put all of my clothes in a green garbage bag and left.

So after my release I couldn't go back to Mom's house. I began staying with my Auntie Rachael in the Fink White Projects. I was always very athletic so I started attending Sierra High School in '79. I played football and ran track averaging 2 touch downs a game. That was the same year that the movie roots came out. Sierra was a predominately white school across town and the new busing policy was in effect in order to integrate the schools. There were a lot of stoners (racist white kids that stayed high) that went to Sierra and there was much tension between us and them. We would all congregate at the donut shop across from the school. After the movie Roots was televised we were subjected to older stoners riding by screaming "Nigger" out of the window. We would of course yell back but they never stopped.

One day we were tired of it and once we got to the donut shop my friend Curtis said "I'm tired of this nigga shit!" Him and his friend Dale lived out in what we called the country around the corner from my grandmother. I said "the next mutha fucka that hollas nigga or that Kunta Kinte' shit…we gonna tear this mutha fucka up!"

As before, the white boys rode by and screamed "Toby" (a character in Roots) and I yelled back "Yo Momma". The white boys came back and it was on. We got into a brief scuffle and Curtis knocked one of the white boys on his back. They picked him up, got in the truck and pulled off but the adrenaline was pumping now. We went off inside the school grounds. The first cat that I saw dressed like a stoner, I jumped and did a spinning round house kick that

Original Diamond Boy

landed on the side of his head. I hadn't done that karate shit in a long time and I was rusty but it served it's purpose. We ran through the halls of the school jumping on stoners. We got all the way to the principle's office. Everybody stopped but I couldn't. I was in a rage. I ran into his office, assaulted him and tore his office up. Needless to say, the police came and though four of us were arrested, I was the only one that stayed in Juvenile.

When I went to court the judge said that he was considering sending me to CK Wakefield, a juvenile facility where cats did 18 months or more. But I only ended up being sentenced to 45 days. I was there for a week when duce came in. I laughed my ass of when I saw him. I was happy to see my brother. A couple of homeboys came through too. Black, D-dog, Loc'd Out from Hoova and West.

Loc'd Out and I weren't friends at first because I had beef with his brother Ghost but we became homeboys over a ping pong game. Loc'd Out was on his way to the California Youth Authority (CYA). We all attended the juvenile co-ed classes and wrote notes back and forth to the broads. There was a Mexican broad named Lorraine that wrote to me and Loc'd Out had her sister.

Duce didn't give a damn about no broads and Black was ugly as hell so no broads gave a damn about him. I could see that the Esse' cats didn't like this and when Loc'd Out brought it to my attention I said "Fuck them mescans nigga this 62 Diamond." We added the "62" taken from Big Flux's 62 East coast and called ourselves "62 Diamond Crips".

Chapter 17

"If there's a problem, make sure that you are the aggressor and once it starts, go to the extreme."
                                                    - O.G. Nighthood

I was good in class and they had started up a program where those that did good in school could get furlough passes to leave the facility and go with our teacher Tamika to her church. I went twice. The first time I went Tamika started speaking in tongues and scared the hell out of me. When I got back I told everybody.

The Homeboy Craig, Duce and I stayed in an area called the honor rooms. One day Craig was saying that his hair was longer than mine (which it clearly wasn't). I said "Nigga you crazy. You look like a Platapuss". Loc'd Out and Black started laughing. Craig jumped up and said "Nigga what you say? Nigga you can't fade me."

"Cuzz, I didn't stutter." I'll fade you all day" I said as I rushed his ass. I got him on the floor and started bombin

Le'Taxione (a.k.a. YoYo)

(punchin) on him.

Black told us the counselor was coming so I got off him and started doing push ups. The counselor didn't trip and that was the last time Craig ever challenged me.

Loc'd Out turned me on to a Homeboy named O.G. who was locked up in Tracey State Penitentiary and was writing him. O.G. was a Fresno Nighthood Crip. Nighthoods were one of the first Crip Hoods in Fresno. He reminded me a lot of my homeboy Big Oso. I started writing him and he became one of my closest homies. He wrote me weekly and gave me words of wisdom and even instruction.

While I was in juvenile I took pottery classes. I made my Moms some black stallions with blue eyes that she still has today. I also created her a black vase with red drips of color on it. Little did I know that the same vase would be used to hold my sister Ben's ashes after she passed in 2002.

The next furlough I got, Tamika was supposed to take me back to church but instead she took me to her apartment. Once we got there she sat me down on the couch and we talked about what I was going to do after I got out of juvenile. I told her that I wanted to play football and besides crippin' that was the only thing that I was good at. She said that she would help me realize that goal. She asked me if I wanted anything to drink and I told her kool-aid. When she came back to the couch she sat closer.

For some reason broads had become very attracted to me.

"YoYo you are so cute. Do you have a girlfriend" she asked.

I told her that I was in love with this Diamond and she laughed. Then she threw her right leg up across my lap revealing her big thighs. I began rubbing her leg and she asked "Do you want to have sex with me?"

"For real?" I asked.

Original Diamond Boy

She stood up, pulled her panties down to her ankles and stepped out of them. She didn't take off her dress, but she raised it up, stood in front of me and showed me her koochie. Then she sat back down, laid back, spread her legs and said "come here".

I pulled my pants down, taking only one leg out as I did when I used the toilet in juvenile in case anyone came in and tried to bomb on me and I climbed on top of her. She grabbed my swipe (penis), put it in and started gyrating. I started pushing in and out of her until we both climaxed. I felt her thighs quiver and knew she had had an orgasm. I had sexed a 30+ year old woman and couldn't wait to tell it.

When I got back to the facility, I decided not to tell anybody. Loc'd Out told me that he had got at one of the Mexicans and their big Homie Indio had a problem.

"Let's take it to they ass." I told him.

The homie O.G. had written to me and said "YoYo if it's a problem, make sure that you are the aggressor and once it starts go to the extreme". I'd been told this by Rip before.

So we got at Indio.

"West Up Cuzz" I said. "You got a problem with me and my Homie?"

"Yeah, you binchy ma..." But before he could get "mayate' out of his mouth I bombed on him and the riot was on. We faded their asses but I ended up getting stabbed with a pencil. They sent all of us to lockup unit. Staff came to my cell door and asked me who stabbed me.

I responded "Fuck you peckawood, I ain't no snitch" loud enough for the whole unit to hear me.

Chapter 18

"I caught him with his mouth open and knocked him out."
- YoYo

I got released from A unit. By the time I hit the bricks (got released) my reputation and my ego were big. The first thing I did was get a perm. My hair dropped past my shoulders and all of the females were telling me how fine I was. Duce got out a while after me.

I went to Grandmom's house and saw the nigga Ron. This nigga had punked out on us when we got down with the stoners and I wasn't going to sleep on that (let it go). I stood on the corner and waited for him. When he got close enough I said "West Up Cuzz?" He said "what's up YoYo?" Ron was a civilian but he should have helped in the riot. I said "Nigga, why you didn't help us in the riot?" When he tried to answer, I bombed on him.

I caught him with his mouth open and knocked him out. He hit the street, regained consciousness and jumped up

Le'Taxione (a.k.a. YoYo)

running. His mother called the police and I was put back in juvenile. Ron and his mother showed up in court to testify. Once the judge saw that his mouth was wired shut and heard that I broke his jaw in five places it was over. I was sent back to juvenile for 90 days.

    I studied hard and got excellent grades while I was in juvenile. One day a football coach from Mclane High School came to see me. He asked me what I was going to do when I got out. I told him that I wanted to play football. He said that if I was serious I could come play at Mclane. I played quarterback at sierra and ran the I-formation with ease but they wanted me to play running back and safety at McLane.

Chapter 19

"Niggas that slip, sleep."

- Big Oso

I got out and started messing with Sharon. Before I knew it I had a few females. I had Sharon, Tina, Tasha, Joyce and Tisha. All of them knew about each other and all of them bought me things like clothes and shoes. I truly liked Tasha and the rest I just charged. Sharon was the most possessive of them all. She felt that she had more rights to ownership because I'd been with her the longest. Tasha was a very dark short female with an athletic body. She was my good girl. Tina was my freak. Joyce had beautiful brown skin and long hair and she was my fashion model.

Tisha was my Homeboys C-Dog and T-Dog's (RIP) sister and she was my sex any time. I was tired of the others. I was attached to Sharon because she was a Gangsta girl. She had tattooed YoYo on her arm and represented herself as such. Sharon was very jealous and had beat

Le'Taxione (a.k.a. YoYo)

Tina up a couple of times for claiming that she was my girl. Tina had been pregnant by me and had a miscarriage so we did have history but I wasn't the only one hittin' those panties.

Sharon had gotten pregnant and was unbearably possessive during her pregnancy. During the early trimester she poisoned me. She never admitted it but I knew it was her. One time I ate at her mother's house and ended up at Valley Medical Center getting my stomach pumped. The next time (yes it happened twice) she cooked for me at my Auntie Rachael's house and I felt like I was on fire. I had to get my stomach pumped again. After that I never ate anything that she cooked again. Needles to say, I shook her (broke up with her).

I played for McLane that year and we only lost one game. I averaged one touchdown and one interception per game. I was always in the newspaper and on the news. The varsity coach tried to get me to move up and play for him but I was a sophomore and wanted to play at that level. At one game, Tina was in the stands screaming "that's my man!"

"You with YoYo?" Sharon asked her as she walked up on her. She said "Yeah" and Sharon beat her up. Tina was a very pretty girl but she couldn't fight and everybody knew that so they took advantage of her.

That year I won MVP but that gang shit followed me. I used to go to school with my sawed off shotgun in my gym bag and when I got there I'd put it in my locker. My East side females were Joyce and Kathy. Joyce was my age but Kathy was a senior. She was dark chocolate with a short curl and a very distinct nose. She ran track and played basket ball so her body was tight but she had a baby by this fool named Tommy that was obsessing over her. She got at me through my sister Ben who was also a senior. Ben liked

Original Diamond Boy

Kathy but knew that Tommy was a fool over her so she told me to watch that Nigga.

It was the end of the school day and Joyce came and told me "Them Godfathers are out there lookin' for you". It was the thing for gang members to go to the high schools and try to catch rival members out of their element slippin but Big Oso taught me better than that. He said "Niggas that slip, sleep".

I wasn't never slippin. I went to the locker and got my sawed off pump and went out to the front of the school to let off on them but they had left. A week later I went over to Kathy's house. She cooked me dinner. We smoked a joint and laid in the bed. I took my pants off but kept my shirt, socks and boxers on and of course I kept my sawed off on the night stand. That night we didn't have sex. We just kissed and explored each other's bodies. Her skin was so smooth it reminded me of silk.

As we lay there caressing each other, I could feel her stomach quiver. She had been locked into an abusive relationship and had tried to make it work for their daughters' sake. This nigga was beatin' on this beautiful girl when all she wanted to be was loved and held. I would do that tonight but tomorrow wasn't promised. I placed my hand between her legs and she moaned. I kissed her again and we laid back.

All of a sudden I heard something outside of the window. I rose up slowly and put my pants on. Somebody was tampering with the window. I picked up my heata and placed one finger over my lips gesturing for her to be quiet. I raised the barrel with my left palm on top of it. As I pointed at the window she screamed "No!" and reached for my arm. I fired once and pumped it to reload the chamber. When I realized that she was trying to save whoever it was outside I knew that she wasn't ready to shake that Nigga. I

Le'Taxione (a.k.a. YoYo)

put my shoes on and bounced (left) and never looked back.

When I saw her at school, the next Monday I acted like I didn't know her. A couple of weeks later she was back with Tommy.

Chapter 20

> *"I could hear my heart beating loud as hell and that shit felt good."*
>
> - YoYo

The summer of '80 came quick and I had began drinking and sniffing paint. We would all meet up at the Fink white Park, get some Old English 800 Malt Liquor, some socks and gold paint. We would turn the socks inside out, spray the foot of the sock with gold paint, roll the sock up and put it in our mouths and inhale the fumes.

After we'd done this, we'd fight each other all night. The Fink White homeboys were Diamonds but just in a different part of the West Side. The Fink White Diamonds consisted of Lil Bobby, Snow, T-Mike, J-Bone, Ice, C-Dog, T-Dog (RIP), Coast, Doc, Drop and Ran.

Lil Bobby told us that there was a party in the Vill and that "He didn't give a fuck who was going to be there, Fink White was going". We all got drunk and went to the party.

Le'Taxione (a.k.a. YoYo)

Once we got there, some of the people started leaving. We had got the Vill back from the 4/3s who had moved out across Jensen where my Grandmother lived. I had my trench coat on with a shoe string tied at both ends of the sawed off and had it hanging across my shoulder where it wasn't visible from the outside. The nigga Danger came to the party and it eventually turned into a diamond party with Diamonds from all over the West Side in attendance.

I was talking to the homegirl Candy, Lady Slim's sister, when I saw Danger leave the party. I'd been watching him all night and made up in my mind that night that I was gonna kill that nigga. Yes, three years later I still wanted to kill him for putting that gun in my face. I didn't forget a mutha fuckin thing and he had to pay for that shit that he did.

He left the party with some bitch and I thought "I'm not sparing none". If that bitch chose to stay with him she could lay with him. I let them get out of range of the street lights and I slipped out of the party and followed them. I waited until they hit a dark spot and I said "West Up nigga?" When he turned around I blasted on both of them – boo yaw!—chick chick—boo yaw! – chick chick—Boo Yaaw!

Because I was so far away I only hit him with buckshots. I could hear my heart beating as loud as hell and that shit felt good. I jumped two fences and came out on another street. The next day everybody said that the Villains tried to lay that nigga down (kill him). The Villains took responsibility and I let them. I told myself again *"I'm gonna kill that nigga as soon as I get a chance"*.

Chapter 21

"I seized the opportunity to give them my vision."

- YoYo

A new drug was on the scene. Well, it was new to me, but apparently cats had been smoking it since '77 or '78. It was called by various names such as cliff jumper, superman, butt naked, wet, water, brake fluid and Sherm. It was PCP or formaldehyde, a chemical used to embalm dead bodies. It was a hallucinogenic and it made it's user do all of the things that it was called. They were truly embalmed.

Sherm took a lot of otherwise good brothers out of the rotation. Some cats caught murder beefs and other's behavior became so unpredictable that they were ostracized. One way or another, they were taken out of the rotation (active duty). Though some of my homeboys like Wolf, Tyson, Insane (RIP), Ice, Black, C-Boy, Bone, T.T., Young C and a few others got wet, it mostly affected the Godfathers and Villains because they were the ones that were cooking it,

Le'Taxione (a.k.a. YoYo)

giving them ready access to a seemingly endless supply.

A meeting was called and I'd planned to address this issue then. There were a lot of young homies, 13, 14 and 15 years old getting put on (initiated on the hood) and I didn't want them experimenting with Sherm. I had put a lot of them on the hood myself and felt a sense of responsibility to instruct them properly in the gang demonstration.

Duce, Soldier, Shorty, T-Dre, Nutty Boy, Lil T-Dre, the homegirls Patty, Maisha, Lunatic, Tiny Girl, and Carrie had reclaimed what they called the country as a Diamond Hood. We ran Pistol, Tim-Dog and three other red rags, the last remnants of the 4/3s out.

On the day of the meeting we all got dressed, got our heatas and marched to Wolf's house. We were a little late, well, a lot late and upon arrival the homies let me know of their disapproval through sarcasm. Wolf said "Well if it isn't the notorious YoYo"! I said "ease up Cuzz".

"You act like you run this Diamond" he said.

I could tell that he was wet by the look in his eyes, the way he talked and the smell in the house. Wolf never really liked me and the feeling was mutual.

"Somebody needs to run it since you niggas stay wet." I said.

He screamed "Nigga, I run this shit!" He was hallucinating.

"Nigga, how you gonna run anything when you can't even run yourself? I shot back. "For the past three meetings you niggas ain't been strategizing or planning a thang. All you want to do is get wet and fuck a bitch while we out here puttin' in all the work. You niggas can't direct me no more. From here on out nigga, I'm doing this shit like gangstas are supposed to do it! Duce law!"

I took the young Homies and we left. I hated that the young Homies had to see these well respected cats in the

Original Diamond Boy

state of mind they were in but I had to denounce how they were getting' down in order to deter the young Homies from that sort of insubordination. All the way back to the hood I lectured them on how this Diamond was set up by Big Oso and the vision that he had for us and at the same time I seized the opportunity to give them my vision. In the Fink White area, Lil Bobby was doing the same thing but I took it a step further.

"Tear Drop"

I was a young nigga up in Big V. Villa
Game laced with that paper chase but my skrilla
Now who'd a figured that a little nigga from West Side
Would grow up from the flo up, make that Diamond shine
A steady grind but keep in mind it's 2-0-9
Let the reason that I'm livin be the reason that I ride
On these punk mutha fuckas that I've grown to despise
If death is your desire nigga look in my eyes
But realize there's no mercy nigga no remorse
Overcomin' all the obstacles in my course
And of course I eradicate erasin the drama
Revenge is swift when I dip nigga that's on my Mama
Cause I'll be damned if I let you niggas take my life
I'm already frustrated by the struggle and strife
And there's a price to be paid while you're stuck in this game
Cause there's some niggas that'll kill you just to taste yo' fame
But they lame if they thinkin' that I'm gonna drop
Cause I ain't never been accused of not squeezin' the glock so pop
And when yo body drop lock livin life has stopped
Remember the face that's pasted with a teardrop.

Chapter 22

"Son, leave a nigga the back door or you'll make him kill you."
- Rip

We put in work every night, all of us, because those who blasted together lasted together. I promoted unity and military precision as did Big Oso. I enforced an everyday workout regiment which ended with us putting on the gloves and boxing each other. I created hood patrols where two homies would walk the whole hood and report back.

I wanted to know who was gambling on every corner or who was trying to sell weed in our Hood. It was time for reform. I remember when the elders used to be happy to see us. Now they turned their faces in disgust when we walked by.

I wasn't naïve. I knew that it would never be the same between us and the elders. The shootings and killings had become too many. The hatred, vengeance and thirst for

Le'Taxione (a.k.a. YoYo)

blood ran too deep between the hoods. The beef was too thick! All I could do now was to make sure that the homies respected the elders while we protected what we perceived to be ours.

By this time the nigga Dub had become a full fledged sherm head. We called those that stayed wet everyday shermheads, meaning that they were addicted. I guess he'd heard about what I said at the meeting and he took issue with it but I didn't give a damn. What I said was duce law.

He sent word that he was gonna fade me when he saw me. I wasn't trippin'. There was a house party in the hood and almost all of the Diamonds came including Dub. Sure enough, while I was talking to some female, the nigga stole (punched) on me from the back. At least that's what I was told when I woke back up. He had knocked me out and got on (left).

The next morning I got up and tricked my uncle Jeffrey into driving me around to look for this grown ass nigga who stole on me. I told my uncle that I wanted to fade him one on one but I had my trey eight and I'd planned on killing him. We caught the nigga in the Vill up under his car changing the oil. My uncle drove up, parked and got out saying "My nephew want to get down with you. I don't think you can see him (whoop him) head up (one on one)". I stayed in the car until I recognized Dub.

When I saw that it was him, the adrenaline started pulsating. I jumped out of the car and started dumpin' buck, buck, buck, buck. I kept two shells because the homeboy O.G. told me always keep some ammo for your get away.

Jeffrey froze. He was scared as hell The nigga Dub wasn't moving. I said "Get in the car nigga!" Jeffrey ran back to the driver side.

"This Diamond nigga!" I screamed.

We got back to Momma's house and the news had already got to the little homeboys and homegirls. As we drove up, I could see them posted up (gathered) on the side of the fence where we met every morning. I hopped out of the car. They were there smiling and saying "what that Diamond like?"

I had to retaliate first lest I would have shown weakness to the younger homies but in doing so I did something that we weren't supposed to do and that was blast on a homie. I changed the rules and where we were just blood killers, we became anybody killers. Anybody that transgressed the limits and boundaries opened themselves up to retaliation. No more sit downs to resolve beef between the homies. If a nigga got at you, you got back at him with the quickness. Retaliation was mandatory!

Little did I know that almost three decades later this mentality would serve as the main element in the destruction of solidarity between Diamonds.

The nigga Dub didn't die but he retired. He withdrew into the shadows of irrelevance and I kept soldiering.

I got word that the nigga Dub was telling people that he didn't know who had got off on him. You have to understand the cat was a fighter but I was a killa. These niggas had made reputations in this life for jumping on cats and selling drugs. I didn't mix anything with my crippin'. If saying he didn't know who had got off on him was the way he chose to swallow it, then nigga have it your way. All it told me was that he didn't want no beef and I left him the back door (a way out). Rip always told me "Son, leave a nigga the back door or you'll make him kill you".

Chapter 23

"...He was on some I need some money shit."

- YoYo

I made it mandatory for all of the homeboys and homegirls to not just attend school, but to excel in school. I'd begun to hang out with the Fink White Diamonds on a daily basis. I had major respect for Lil' Bobby and I liked how he ran his hood. The Homeboy O.G. had got out and sent word that he was looking for me. I quickly got on my beach cruiser and rode over to the King of Kings low income housing complex where he was rumored to be living.

When I got there I saw this gunned in (muscular) cat standing out in front of the housing complex as if he was on patrol. I'd never seen O.G. personally but this nigga looked like he'd just got out of the pen. I said "West Up Cuzz?" and he responded accordingly. I asked him "What that diamond like?" He asked me "What that Nighthood like?" right then I knew it was him. I told him who I was and he

Le'Taxione (a.k.a. YoYo)

smiled and said "Homie, I been looking for you for two days."

I dropped the bike and hugged him. This cat was huge. I was only about 150 lbs and he was every bit of 210-220 lbs. and about 6' tall. At least it seemed like he was that tall.

"I been hearin' about you Cuzz" he said to me.

Before I could reply he said "You know the slobs at yo ass."

"They supposed to" I stated. "They hate you too Cuzz". We laughed.

I left my bike at his house and we walked to my hood. I introduced him to all of the little homeboys and homegirls. O.G. was fresh out so he was on some "I need some money" shit. O.G. was the last of the Nighthoods so he didn't kick it with anybody but me.

Duce had been selling weed in the hood and tried to give O.G. a gang (lot) of it so that he could check some money.

"I don't sell nothing Cuzz. I jack (Rob)." O.G. said

After we talked for a while he said "Stroll to the Vill wit me."

"You heated?" I asked

"Fo sho" he said

I said "Let's go" and we walked off.

We went to some female's house that he'd been with prior to getting locked up. He said that he had left some money there and wanted to get it back. The female answered the door and was very happy to see the Homie. He walked into the house and I stayed outside so that we couldn't get crept on. After a minute O.G. came out, kissed her at the door and we boned. After we hit the corner he gave me a C-Note ($100) and I asked "what's this for?" He said "Just on the strength that you the Homie."

Original Diamond Boy

I watched how O.G. got down (carried himself) and his style was truly Gangsta. I stayed rotating (kickin' it) with him. He didn't get down like my other homies. He had that military mentality like I had and I dug that. His hustle was jackin' and I adopted that hustle. I didn't want females doing nothin' for me because they felt that that obligated me to them. So we hit one lick (crime) together, split the loot and hustled on our own terms.

O.G. gave me the jackin' game and when he did he told me never to rob businesses.

"Rob dope dealers. They can't tell that they were selling dope because they are in this lifestyle." he said. (At least they couldn't then).

There was one thing that I did different than my homeboy when I hit licks. Instead of slapping them with the pistol, I would pop (shoot) them in the leg to let them know that I was serious and that it was not a game.

Chapter 24

"This is the life I chose Cuzz...Live or die...Crip or Cry."
- YoYo

Sharon had had my son and that added to our bitter interaction. She played games with the visitation after I'd took him from the hospital. He was born with meningitis and I blamed her for that. When I saw him at the hospital with all of those tubes hooked up to him I cried. When he got better I took him from the hospital. She called the police on me who in turn threatened to take me to jail for kidnapping if I didn't give my son back to her. After that night I never fucked with her again.

I stayed Crippin' and jackin' to support myself. I played football at Hoover high school and as a quarterback averaged a touchdown per game. One day Sharon came up to the school looking for me. Tasha came to my class and told me "that girl Sharon is up here looking for you". I told her "I don't give a fuck, fuck that bitch". A little while later we

Le'Taxione (a.k.a. YoYo)

heard sirens. Sharon had went into the girl's bathroom and heard Joyce's sister saying that Joyce was with me. Sharon confronted her and she checked Sharon verbally. Sharon pulled out a blade and cat the girl. That's how the story was given to me.

The ambulance came and the police swarmed the school but somehow she got away. They ended up catching her and sentencing her to jail time for the assault. I helped her financially while she was locked down but I didn't want to be intimate with her any more.

I started messin' with my homegirl Maisha. Maisha was caramel colored, had long hair and exotic eyes. Her body was nice and her personality was infectious. She had a beautiful smile and she loved me.

She was the only female outside of my sister that I would let do my hair. She wanted to be a cosmetologist but her mother was a shermhead which forced her to take care of her little sister Mia. Mia was a hand full. She was 13 and sexually active. We constantly heard stories about her having sex with multiple partners at the same time. She was known around the hood as an easy lay but she was a very pretty girl. She drank and smoked weed and I think that that added to her promiscuity.

Maisha also had a brother named Larry. Larry was a square that tried to fit into the gang lifestyle. I remember one day some Mexicans came through the hood. At the time I had a .45 semi automatic. As they attempted to creep through Larry was standing on my right side as I dumped on them. One of the shells discharged out of the side of the heata and hit Larry in the head. He started running down the street screaming "I'm hit! I'm hit!"

"That's the shell casing that hit you nigga" I yelled.

Maisha and I put in work together and hit licks together. She was a Gangsta girl who stayed down for me through it all. We often talked about leaving Fresno and starting over again. We would do that later in life but then we felt "Diamonds-R-Us".

One night Maisha and I were outside sitting on my 74 Cadillac Brougham De Elegance.

"Yo Yo do you ever regret that you didn't go to college and play football?" she asked.

She knew that colleges were interested in my ability to play football and had offered me scholarships.

"This is the life I chose Cuzz. Live or die, Crip or cry! After this is death baby and death is a part of the life cycle." I told her. We went inside, got into bed and went to sleep.

The next morning we woke up to fire trucks in the front yard. Someone had thrown a malatov cocktail onto the car and burned it up. I was furious. I had just bought that car. The rumor was that this other female that I called One had done it. Though I couldn't see her doing such a thing, I couldn't dismiss it.

Chapter 25

"We hid the heat in a garbage can and went back to check on the homie."

- YoYo

It seemed as though Mexicans had started moving to the West side and I didn't like it. We had reignited the beefin' with them at the Fresno fair the previous year. The next incident happened at the downtown bus terminal.

For some reason the mescans tried to make a stand as though they were claiming the downtown area but this was too close to the West Side and we could not allow that potential breach of our security. Duce, Soldier, West, Solo, Lil T-Dre, J-Bird, Young-C and several other homeboys and homegirls made a conscious decision to start strollin' and controllin' the downtown bus terminals across from the Fresno County jail. Esses got off of bus 38 where we were posted at.

Duce immediately took off on one of the esses and it

Le'Taxione (a.k.a. YoYo)

was on. All of the homies got active that day. The esse that Duce took off on hit the ground face first and as soon as he hit the ground I jumped up and landed both feet on his head. I looked over to my right and Solo had one of the esse's shirts pulled over his head so he couldn't see and he was upper cutting him. Then we heard Boo Yaa! And saw West bend over. He had been hit with the buckshot from a gauge so I busted in the crowd buck—buck—buck! Then silence. After we saw that West had just caught buckshot we had to go. The homegirls stayed with him.

    We hid the heat in a garbage can and went back to check on the Homie. He was being placed in the ambulance. All of this happened across the lawn from the police department.

Chapter 26

"Never pass up the chance to totally smash your enemy. If you do, he'll be back and you may not live to talk about it."

- YoYo

As we were walking and talking about the need to secure this West Side the rolos (police) pulled up four cars deep and jumped out. They said "Hey YoYo! Come over here. We want to talk to you". All the while their hands were on their guns.

"It don't look like you want to talk to me. It looks like you want to kill a nigga." I said to them.

Soldier Boy was drunk and lost his composure.

"Ya'll always over here sweatin' us. Why don't you go across town and sweat some of them stoners – oh yeah—I forgot, that's your children" he said. He stepped out onto the street and in my mind I said *"damn he fucked up."*

They got Soldier and used excessive force to do it so I walked forward and said "that's my brother Cuzz. You

Le'Taxione (a.k.a. YoYo)

don't have to do him like that".

"Get back or we're taking you too!" One of the officers said.

They got Soldier in the squad car and all I could think about was what Rip said about not letting anything happen to my brothers. I pulled the heat and blasted. Buck—Buck—Buck! They all jumped in their squad cars and almost crashed trying to get out of the hood. We all went into Maisha's mother's house and cut off all the lights.

I knew that they would be back with reinforcements so I took Maisha into the room, laid her down and sexed her one last time. In a matter of minutes we heard the ghetto bird (police helicopter) over the house. It sounded like they were trying to land on the house. Then the banging came on the door as police surrounded the house shining their lights through the windows. Bam—Bam—Bam!.

"Open the door! Fresno Police Department!"

"Open the door or we'll kick it down."

I was cocking the gun when duce snatched it out of my hands and put both mine and his in the freezer.

Boom! They had kicked the door in, breaching the perimeter. "Let me see your hands"! I was lying in the bedroom with Maisha playing like I was asleep (as if that was going to work.)

They drug us out of the house and cuffed me. They pulled my pants down in front of all the onlookers. As I scanned the faces in the crowd I saw the elderly people cheering but I saw the homeboys and homegirls fighting back tears. Their fearless leader was captured and it looked like they were thinking 'what are we gonna do?' I smiled and said "This is the price for this Diamond life! Fuck em all!"

I was transported to the County jail and as I sat in that holding tank there was a white man with a gold and dia-

Original Diamond Boy

mond cluster ring. I took it and said "Nigga this Crip!" When they booked me I turned the ring over, Diamonds facing my palm and told them it was my wedding ring.
After five hours I made it upstairs and it was packed. People under bunks, under tables, by the toilet, everywhere. So I placed my bunk on top of a table and went to sleep.
I woke up to people all around me watching the news. The reporter said "Last night police took on fire in the area of Calwa and Clara in West Fresno. They were responding to multiple reports of homes being assailed with gunfire. They contacted a group of young men and women. When they took one of the men into custody, they were fired upon. "Ernest Carter has been arrested and booked into Fresno County Jail on charges of assault on a police officer with a firearm." They plastered my mug shot across the screen.
Everybody looked and said, "That's you" and began shaking my hand. Out of one of the cells came my Homeboy Pit Bull and said "West Up Cuzz?" I responded and he told me to bring my mattress and myself into the cell. We sat and talked all day about the hood. I told him about the time that Coast got down with this cat at the playground. The cat approached Coast while he was playing pool. A verbal confrontation ensued. Coast took off on the cat like he was supposed to and stayed at him the entire fight. Coast had long arms and used them properly to keep the cat off of him hitting him with straight left jabs and stiff right crosses. After the cat retreated, Coast felt dizzy. Only then did he realize that the cat had stabbed him in the throat. The ambulance was called and Coast was rushed to the hospital. When the story reached me I called the hospital to check on the Homeboy even though we were not the best of friends. Coast was given the phone and I asked "Cuzz, you alright?" he told me he was and went on to say "Cuzz, I'm

Le'Taxione (a.k.a. YoYo)

not bangin' no mo!" I hung up on him.

I told Pit Bull 'Cuzz these niggas be banging this Diamond under false pretenses. While it's the adversary's blood being spilled, it's all good, but as soon as a nigga see his own blood he has a spiritual awakening and abandons the hood that he's sworn to protect and perpetuate." The same nigga that stuck him jumped on me when I was 14 or 15 years old in front of Coast and some other squares. The nigga was a grown man then! After he couldn't dog (humiliate) me like he thought he would, he went to his trunk on me. Self preservation took over and I boned out (smiling). Pit Bull gave me a pound (hit each others fist) and said "That's right!"

The point was that if we would have exercised that true Diamond love then and all stomped him out, this would have never took place. I had learned early on that you never pass up the chance to totally smash your enemy. If you do, he'll be back and you may not live to talk about it.

Pit Bull was anxious to hear more. He sat at the edge of the bunk like a child listening to his father tell him about life.

"I heard them Godfather's shot you" he said.

"Yeah but Crips don't die, we multiply" I said He asked me how I got caught slippin' like that? I told him that we got into a gang fight with the Godfathers at Roeding Park and that afterwards we went back to the hood. I went on to tell him that they tried to creep through the hood on us in William's car and I lit they ass up.

"Real talk, I let them have it and they got up outta there with space shuttle speed" I told him. We both laughed.

"Now you know the alley behind Tip's house?" I asked him

"Yeah." He replied.

"Well they came back later on that night when it was

only Duce, Nutty Boy, my uncle Germaine and me out there and got off with a shot gun – Boom! The Homie Nutty Boy got back at them with the .38. If it wasn't for Nutty Boy them Niggas would have run up on us. After it all happened Duce, Nutty Boy and I went in G-Mom's house and duce noticed that I had blood on my light blue sweatshirt."

I went on to tell him that duce said 'Cuzz you drippin'. Then I felt the pain in the back of my head and my right shoulder. G-moms said 'call the ambulance". I told her that I was alright and that I wasn't going to the doctor but she said 'Boy you going to that doctor. I told her "I'm cool Cuzz". Yes, I even called G-Moms Cuzz. She said "yeah you cool, but your goin to the doctor". Needless to say I paid a visit to the doctor that night.

I went on to tell him that I was cool when I got there, the first thing that they asked me was "who shot you?"

"Some mescans" I told them sharply. We always said that it was Mexicans. We didn't want the police to get our enemies; we wanted to get them ourselves.

They took x-rays and told me that I had buckshot pellets in the back of my head and in my shoulder. They said they could take them out if I wanted. I told them they could take them out of my shoulder but that they weren't going to cut my hair. My perm was down my back and Maisha had just dyed it blue black two days earlier and when the sun hit it, you could see hints of blue.

G-Moms asked whether the ones in my head would cause me a problem later on and the doctor told her that they may move but that he didn't see them being life threatening. That was all I needed to hear so they took them out of my back and I still have them in my head to this day."

"Let me see" Pit Bull said.

Le'Taxione (a.k.a. YoYo)

I placed his hand on the back of my head and let him feel them.

"They sho' is in there" What did you do? He asked

"The next day I came back to the hood with a blue rag around my head, my neck, my left arm, in my left pocket and around my face!" Pit Bull laughed and said "Crip crazy".

I thought I'd save some for the next day so we talked about females for a while...who was sexin' who, who was a freak, who was pregnant, who had that fire cock (gonorrhea).

After that, since it was my first time in jail Pit Bull began to give me the grapes (information) on who's who and rules as they apply in that atmosphere. He said "Don't fuck with nobody but Diamonds, respect everybody, and stay on point because the mescans is sneaky. And if anybody disrespects you handle that shit right then."

"Fo sho nigga!" I said.

It was only Pit Bull and myself that were truly soldiers in the tank at that time so the esse's ran the tank but Pit Bull had established a two hour TV. time slot for us to watch what we wanted to watch.

That night I witnessed one of the most brutal beatings that I'd ever witnessed at that time. There was an esse who was exposed as a rata (snitch). They beat that cat from sun up to sun down and made him live under the bunk. If he had not been called by the Sheriff for a court day he surely would have died. They beat him for a week straight. He was broken and almost dead when the sheriff called his name and no one reported to the front of the tank. Because there was no answer, they came in and found him under the bunk laying in his own urine, feces and blood. When they took him out he was unresponsive but he lived. The funny thing about it was that he didn't tell on none of the esses that beat him.

    Pit Bull and I being the only Diamonds in the tank had to sleep in shifts. We had beef with the esse's on the bricks (streets) and it was only a matter of time before that beef would be ignited inside the tank. Pit Bull chose to sleep at night so I was on deck while he slept. This worked out for me because I had just come off of the bricks where we were up all night strollin' and controllin' the hood. Plus most people in jail stayed up all night and slept throughout the day so everything that was going to happen, happened during the night and I preferred being the one on deck during that active time.

Chapter 27

"Crush your enemy totally in order to prevent any attempt at retaliation."

- Rip

A week later they brought in this stoner named Nigretti. He and I had major beef since my days at Sierra Freshman high school. Nigretti was a racist and bought into the age old white male dominance and aggression ideology and he would try to superimpose that ideology upon weak cats. I'd faded Nigretti several times for his indiscriminate use of the word "Nigger" but no matter what I did to him, after all was said and done he would pick himself up and call me a nigger. I was determined to beat this word out of him and when he arrived I saw the opportunity to make another attempt at doing so and at the same time exhibit the violence that is concomitant with respect in these dungeons called jails.

I could see Nigretti waiting outside the tank for the

Le'Taxione (a.k.a. YoYo)

doors to open to come inside. He had the standard jail issued accoutrements, a towel, two blankets, two sheets, a pillowcase and a bag of hygiene articles. The gate opened and he entered. I told Pit Bull "I'm fis'ta fade this peckawood."

"I got yo back" Pit Bull said.

Before he could put his bedding down, I came out of the cell and said "West Up Cuzz!" and attacked him. I couldn't afford to loose this battle; not in front of the homeboy or in front of the tank so when I took off on him, I stayed on him. He tried to fight back but he was overwhelmed by the barrage of blows that were landing on him with full force. I could hear Pit Bull shouting "Fuck that peckawood up Cuzz! Show him what that Diamond like!"

I dug deeper and when he hit the ground I stomped him until he was unconscious and unresponsive. He was bleeding like a stuck hog. When it was over, I pulled my swipe out and pissed on him. Rip always told me to crush your enemy totally in order to prevent any attempt at retaliation. I did just that.

Later that night the Sheriff brought dinner and noticed Nigretti's injuries. His lip was split, he had a cut above his right eye and his nose was visibly broken. They took him out and I never saw Nigretti again in my life.

About two weeks Later, Wolf and a couple of the cats came into the tank. Our numbers were growing and though only five of us were Diamonds, there were approximately 15 brothers in the tank. This automatically started a power struggle between us and the F-14s which consisted of Parkside, Eastside and Calwa Park esses. F-14 stood for Fresno 14s. These were the esse gangs that we had beef with on the bricks. Though we had got down with Calwa Park and East Side 14s, we had never got down with the Parkside 14s, but we knew that when it jumped off (happened), all of them would be active.

Tension was so thick that you could cut it with a knife. Though we couldn't speak Spanish fluently, we caught bits and pieces of their conversations. The cat that was running the F-14 car (group) was an esse named Boxer. Boxer was on his way back to the pinta (penitentiary) as they called it, for murder. He didn't like the fact that we had secured more TV. time and that at the times that he wanted to watch channel 21, the Spanish channel, we were watching channel 47.

Boxer was a boxer and in most instances that gave him the upper hand. I'd watched him take off on a couple of esse's with precision and he was physically fit, but I remembered a while back when O.G. got into a fight with a known blackbelt. That cat was known for winning karate tournaments so he was no novice. I asked O.G. "Cuzz how you gonna get this cat when he knows that shit?" O.G. said "If I hit him first, he'll forget all about that karate shit!" Sure enough, O.G. walked up on him and took off – Pow! And just like he said, this cat started trying to wrestle him, so I knew that even though Boxer knew how to box, that if I took off on him first, I would even out the playing field.

That's how I thought. I'd put myself against all odds because I trusted me. That's why I wanted to be on deck on the night shift. I wanted to be the first line of defense and that kept me on the front line.

Chapter 28

"Gato picked up a steel mop ringer and walked up behind the brother."

- YoYo

One day we saw the esse's congregating and I knew that Wolf slept on (was unaware of) the tell tale signs but I was on deck and I caught it all. I said "Cuzz it's goin' down" (it's about to happen). One of the civilians were in the esse's area after we'd been clear that we were to move in twos to prevent cats from being caught with their ass out (by surprise).

"Get your heatas" Pit Bull said. We called our shanks (makeshift knives) heatas in the absence of our guns.

I saw this black Parkside 14 named Gato. As he picked up a steel mop wringer and walked up behind the brother. I, with my shank in hand made a bee line for Boxer, but before anybody could get to Gato, he had busted the brother in the head with the mop wringer and blood shot everywhere.

Le'Taxione (a.k.a. YoYo)

I aborted my mission to get Boxer and stuck anybody that I could stick. The little Homeboy, Shorty dropped his shank in the middle of the fight but he held them at bay. After the melee, five Mexicans and two civilians were stuck. And though the sheriff came in with their riot gear on faster than I'd ever seen and neutralized the situation, we called it a victory. All of us were transferred from the 4th floor to the 3rd floor where they housed people on their way to the pen or people coming back from the pen for court, and guess who was there...? None other than my father Rip.

Chapter 29

"Walk slow and drink plenty water."

- Rip

I was happy to see Pops. We talked about the riot and reminisced all night. This was after I'd called him on the phone after I got busted for the shooting and he told me "Nigga, get it all. You chose that life and prison is a part of it, so get it all."

That's just how Rip was. He was a realist and he didn't waste time candy coating anything he had to say. Rip was abrasive, curt and had not tact, but he was real.

He had come in on a violation but he was on his way back out. He was only there with me for a week. When he was getting released I asked him "are you going to come see me?" He said "Naw, but anything that you need, call me and I'll make sure that you get it." Rip had been doing time most of his life and he said that it was bad luck to visit a person that was locked up when you were in the game.

Le'Taxione (a.k.a. YoYo)

"It's like throwing rocks at the prison walls." He said.

I still remember his parting words as clear as if it was yesterday.

"Walk slow and drink plenty water" he said as he left.

In other words, be careful, watch and keep your mouth closed. That's the best advice that a father can give a son who is on his way to the pen.

One night I laid in my bunk pondering the night of the incident for which I was currently confined and as I began to replay the events of that night I asked myself why did it all seem as though they knew that it was I who fired the weapon? This question and many more would be answered once I got the police reports. My Public Pretender (Public Defender) came to see me with the police reports that I requested at our first meeting. I skimmed the reports looking for what or who gave the police the impression that it was I who fired the weapon. As I skimmed the report I found it. "Witness Rita states that she saw YoYo extend his arm as though he had a gun. She then heard multiple shots.

Rita and her family were the remnants of red rags left in the hood from the days that the 4/3 Villains controlled that area. She lived next door to Maisha along with her mother and sisters. I'd riddled their house before with bullets and they knew that it was me. My G-Moms told me one day "boy I've been knowin' her mother for years and I want you to leave them folks alone. As long as them folks ain't botherin' you, you leave them folks alone. Hear?" I didn't readily agree but then she said "You hear me YoYo?" I reluctantly said "Yeah Cuzz".

Now Rita had taken the opportunity to revenge the shootings. I immediately called my Homeboy O.G. who was in L.A. at the time. Though we were beefin' with some Crips from L.A.. O.G. was down there frequently and he took Latoya, my brother Duce's ex girl friend with him.

The phone rang twice. On the second ring O.G. answered.

"This is AT&T. I have a collect call from YoYo. Will you accept the charges?"

"Fo sho!" O.G. said.

We exchanged the customary greeting and I asked him if he'd heard about what jumped off. He said he had.

"That slob bitch Rita told the police it was me" I told him.

"Don't worry about it Cuzz, I'm on my way back to the No.

That's how O.G. was. He always talked about loyalty in his letters to me when I was in juvenile and the importance of keeping it real as penitentiary steel.

We exchanged sentiments and I said "Diamond love Homie". He said "Crip love, loyalty, honor and respect." After I hung up I said "Damn! I hope they didn't record that one!" Then I said "fuck it. This Crip!" out loud.

Chapter 30

> *"We used Diamond Love and Crip Love to keep from saying I love you."*
>
> *- YoYo*

A couple of females would come visit every week for a while. Tasha, Sharon and Kathy always came up. Tasha would say "YoYo when are you going to quit gang bangin' and get your life together?"

"It's Crip for life Cuzz" I'd say with all the bravado I could muster. She went to Hoover with me and watched as college scouts came to talk to me and she genuinely wanted more for me, but all I wanted to do was Crip.

As for Kathy and Sharon, they both had boyfriends and they were sneaking up there to see me and every time they came, I'd ask for some money because the next visit wasn't guaranteed.

"One day I'm gonna quit comin' up here because all you do is ask for money" Kathy told me.

Le'Taxione (a.k.a. YoYo)

I said "Seriously Cuzz, what you expect? You out there free fuckin' and eatin' fried chicken with that busta ass nigga and you come up here and expect it to be all apple lights and cherry sticks like I'm some kind of simp?" I went on "Cuzz whether you come up here or not, I still got to do this and as long as you don't stop the clock, I don't give a fuck whether I see you or not but one thing is for sho'…if you come up here, you gonna help me financially."

I remember Rip telling me "The game is cop and blow, not cop, block, and lock". He said "Never stop a bitch from leavin' you. Celebrate when she leaves because it makes room for a real bitch to come fuck wit you."

Rip was a pimp for real. He had won the players ball at least three times and as a youngster I could remember going to his house and him having six women walking around in their bra and panties giggling and catering to him.

Rip had this long perm, jewelry, clothes, cars and hoes. He was the stereotypical pimp and he used to tell me "Man, you missed yo callin'. You need to put down them pistols and send a bitch to the track". I said "Pops, I'm a Crip. Them hoes can't get me nothing that I can't get myself".

"Yeah, but it's so much easier" he said flashing a smile.

I didn't dig Rip's lifestyle and he didn't dig mine but we had a bond that he didn't have with his other children. I spent a lot of time with Pops. He wasn't very sensitive or sentimental so we never had any of those kinds of talks but I could see how much he loved me in his eyes. We'd exchange looks whenever I left his presence and in those brief glances were all of the love and compassion that wouldn't be spoken. One day as we were parting I think he knew that I caught sensitivity in his eyes and he immediately said "Get on nigga." I smiled and left.

As I sat in the courtroom for my pretrial hearing waiting for the prosecutor to present his evidence and witnesses against me, a guy walked over to the prosecutor and whispered in his ear. The prosecutor stood up and adjusted his cheap ass Sears suit jacket.

"May counsel approach the bench?" he asked.

The judge waived both him and my Public Pretender forward. They whispered for a minute and then they returned to their seats. I asked my counsel, "what's up?" She said they wanted a continuance because his witness didn't show up. The judge granted the continuance.

After the hearing I called up my G-Moms house because Duce was in the courtroom and as I was walking out he put his hand to his ear signaling for me to call him. When I called he told me the slob bitch couldn't make it.

I called the homie O.G. in L.A. After the operator did her routine spill, the Homie said "fo sho!" I said West Up Loco?" He said he was trying to keep his head above the water and below the heat. Then he told me that he had taken that trip to The No (Fresno). He said he had talked to those people and everything should be cool." He asked me if I needed any cabbage (money). But I told him I was set and I told him how I appreciated how he got down.

"I get down how I'm supposed to. I live by the code." He said.

After I said "Diamond Love" and he said "Crip Love". We hung up.

We used to use "Diamond Love" and "Crip Love" to prevent from saying "I love you". Though they meant the same thing, saying "I love you was considered weak so we used our hoods and sets to mask what we really wanted to say. It was mandatory to exhibit strength in the lifestyle we were living. Weakness lead to snitching and even jeopardized the security of the entire hood. If you were deemed weak you would be put off of the hood. Sometimes this occurred in the form of a verbal notification. "Cuzz, keep the hood out of your mouth and stay off the soil (turf)." Or it could have been physical notification in the form of the homeboy brutally beating you off of the hood. So one can see why we made every attempt to avoid any word, deed or gesture that may have been construed as weakness.

    I'm sure that this fact also played into the cycle of violence that was prevalent in our communities amongst our peers.

Chapter 31

"In the gang lifestyle, one's emotional development is arrested."

- YoYo

I had taken a polygraph test previously that came back inconclusive. I was facing eight years in prison but with an inconclusive polygraph test and the star witness unavailable, my attorney sought to plea bargain on my behalf. She suggested that I plead Nolo Contendre which meant that I wasn't saying that I committed the crime, but that I was saying that if I went to trial, I might have been convicted...at least that's what she told me. I entered a plea of guilty and after the legal jargon I was sentenced to 365 days with credit for time served and four years suspended.

When I came back from court I was told to roll up (pack) because I was being transferred to the tank where people were serving their sentences or sentenced and waiting to be transferred. Once I got there it looked like the

Le'Taxione (a.k.a. YoYo)

hood. I had ten homeboys down there serving wino (County) time.

"What that Diamond like Cuzz?" they all yelled at the same time.

"Shinin' Loco!" I responded.

It was dorm living but it looked like the block. Cats were in one corner gambling with dice made out of toilet paper, squared, hardened and numbers placed on them. There were cats that were smoking weed. Cats were lifting weights with buckets of water and other cats were drinking pruno (homemade wine). It was on and crackin'.

"We over here Cuzz." My Homie J-Bird said.

I made my way through the smoke filled, body littered dorm over to the corner where my Homeboys were.

"What you come out wit Loco?" He was referring to how much time I got

"A bullet." (one year) I answered

"That's all?" he asked.

Before I could answer he said "You know Maisha let O.G. play in her panties (have sex with her)?

"It ain't no fun if the Homie can't have none." I responded.

We all laughed but deep down inside I was crushed.

Maisha was my girl and O.G. was my homie. While my mind raced to process this information he said "She's pregnant too Loco. And she's sayin' that it's yours".

"That bitch is crazier than a road lizard if she thinks that she is gonna put that crumb snatcher on me. She better get at the Homeboy." I stated.

Though it tore at me, that was not the place or time to show concern. In the gang lifestyle one's emotional development is arrested prohibiting him or her from experiencing intense feeling of remorse or care for not only actions that he or she has committed but also actions that are committed against them. Life becomes a process through which the gang member navigates not based on society's definition of what is right or wrong but upon what those of us who have been desensitized to violence in our state of arrested development deem as real. What was real then is that my Homeboy had played in my Ex's panties. Period.

I worked out intensely to ignore the emotions I was experiencing at the time. Any place of confinement that you visit you'll find that some work out far harder than others and these men and women are labeled machines; but in all reality these are the men and women who are experiencing the most emotional turmoil. Calisthenics or weights have become their outlet, their way of dealing with pain.

I developed my body very fast. All of my life I had been thin, but during this stay, I became very muscular and packed on pounds and though I didn't grow any taller, my physique made me look taller. I was becoming a Crip monster.

"Crip Monster was a term that we used to describe those who were the embodiment of what a true Crip was supposed to look and act like. At that time it was a cat with a long perm, very muscular, aggressive, violent and hard. I was all of that with a military mindset.

Chapter 32

"I'm a gangsta sweetheart and as long as we can keep it on that level, stay at me."

- YoYo

My time in the dorm was for the most part uneventful. A few skirmishes played out here and there between the esse's but we ran the dorm.

The day came for me to be transferred to what they called "The farm". The farm was opened to relieve the population in the County jail. At the farm everybody worked either in the kitchen, on the yard crew, the field crew, weight room or on the grounds crew. The good thing about the farm was that it was co-ed and though the women had their own building, we would see them across the yard and when they came to eat chow.

Of course there were cats that had girlfriends at the farm and they would communicate by sending letters back and forth through kitchen workers or by hiding them in salt

Le'Taxione (a.k.a. YoYo)

and pepper shakers on the chow hall tables.

There was a female named Shelia that was interested in me and expressed her interest in receiving a letter from me. One day I was working in the dish tank which had windows that Faced the sidewalk where the females came in to the chow hall to eat. Shelia walked up to the open window and threw a note through. I didn't pick it up because I didn't know it was for me. This older cat named Louis picked it up and gave it to me. I put it in my pocket without even looking at it because if you got caught interacting with the females like that you would get fired.

I got back to the dorm, took off my kitchen whites and hit the shower before I read the note. Though I wanted to read it first, Black was watching me and to invest yourself in one of the females before taking care of yourself was viewed as a weakness. I'd just checked Black about the same thing. He had come back from the field crew, dirty as hell, plopped down on his bunk and started reading a letter. I said "Cuzz, you gonna read what that bitch is talking about before you wash yo ass? Get up and wash yo ass! Duce law!" He complied.

As soon as I got out of the shower and got back to my bunk I opened the carefully folded letter. The first thing that caught my attention was that there was a stick (joint) inside the letter. I put the stick in the plastic wrapper off of my camel non-filter pack and tucked it in one of the two long braids that I had on each side of my head. I began to read the letter

"What's up YoYo! How's the game treatin' you? My name is Shelia and I'm a friend of your homeboy Louis."

I thought "My homeboy?" and continued to read.

"I've been watchin' how you get down and I'm interested in writing you. If it's cool, let Louis know and we'll go from there. – Sincerely, Shelia

Louis was my Homegirl Tiny Girl's stepfather, but he wasn't my Homeboy.

I got dressed and went across the grass to Louis' dorm. He was sitting at a table playing dominoes higher than giraffe pussy.

"West up Loco? Let me holla at you Cuzz." I said to him as I walked over to the table.

After he finished the last hand he came over to where I was posted (standing).

"What's happening' youngsta?" he asked.

"West up with this broad Shelia?"

She wants to get at you. She asked me about you the other day and I told her to write you and I'd get it to you." He explained.

I said "That broad is about 35 years old. What she want with a young Crip monster?"

"Ask her youngsta. You trying to get me to think for the broad. I can't read her mind." He said.

I took the stick out of my braid and said "Here Cuzz. It's on the bitch."

I got at her that night…"West up Cuzz? I'm in receipt of your script. However I took offense to the contents. I'm not one of those young niggas in here that's lookin' for a mother figure to help me do this stretch (time). I'm a Gangsta sweetheart and as long as we can keep it on that level, stay at me. – Mr. YoYo Loc Fresno Diamond Crip Monster –

She shot back "I respect what you're sayin' and I apologize. Can I ask you a personal question? You've been here for 30 days and haven't got at any of the females. You got a girl or what?"

Shelia didn't know it but my dislike for rejection prohibited me from initiating any type of relationship with a female. Every female that I'd been with had initiated our relationship. Rip had once told me "YoYo, anytime you get at a bitch, the relationship is on her terms, but if you let her get at you, the relationship is on your terms." Though that wasn't the reason that I didn't get at females, it was the excuse that I used to hide my dislike for rejection.

    Shelia became a good friend of mine. We wrote everyday exclusively until she got released. As soon as she did, several females would write stating that Shelia would read my letters out loud to them and they liked how I talked and they wanted to write to me. I wrote all of them. I'd always loved interacting with females and I found their thoughts very interesting. I learned a lot about females at that time and the complex emotions that they displayed. Cats joked about how many females I wrote to. They tried to label me a player, but that jail wasn't a game and every day was a reminder of that.

Chapter 33

"When you get back, drink five glasses of water, throw them balloons up and get yo money."

- Rip

They brought a couple of white boys from prison that had County time left to do on their sentences. These white boys were A.B.'s (Aryan Brotherhood), a prison gang that had a long standing animosity with the BGF (Black Gorilla Family). These cats stayed to themselves and that was the best thing for them because we were layin' to move on them if they attempted to implement their prison politics there.

It was obvious that these cats had brought drugs in with them because after they arrived there was a large supply of what was then called K.J. K.J. was some form of speed and the white boys and Mexicans loved it. Brothers didn't mess with it because they didn't know what it was and after watching the motions that it sent it's users through, cats

Le'Taxione (a.k.a. YoYo)

didn't want any part of that.

I watched cats that used K.J. sell all of their property, sweat profusely and move around frenetically all day and night. As with any drug in this environment, it brought scandalous moves and unpaid debts which subsequently lead to violence.

One day a fight broke out in our dorm between one of the A.B.'s and a civilian white boy. Neither one could really get down but they were at it. The A.B. cat got the civilian down on the shower floor, bit his ear off and spat it out. The civilian screamed in pain. The other A.B. picked the ear up and flushed it down the toilet. When the sheriff came there was blood everywhere and they searched frantically for the guy's ear. Needless to say, they never found it.

I had gotten word that Maisha had her child and named him after me. This was a trip because I not only had a son named after me already with Sharon, but I didn't believe that this baby was mine. I called Rip's house and asked if he'd seen Maisha.

"She's here right now." He said.

She got on the phone and I said "So you let O.G. play in your panties, huh?"

"What you talkin' about YoYo? I've been takin' care of your son!" she responded.

"My son?"

"Yeah, Your son." She said.

I asked her why I hadn't heard from her since I fell if it was my son. She went into a dramatization of how her shermed out mother put her out because she got pregnant and she was living with her strict grandfather. I knew her grandfather. He was a mean old man that lived near the corner of Calwa and Fig.

"I want to see the baby." I told her.

"I was asking Rip if he would bring us up there because

there's no way that my grandfather will let me come if he knew and that's the only place I have for me and your son to live." She said

I told her to let me holla at Rip and she gave him the phone.

"You gonna bring her up here? I asked.

He said that he would.

"What happened to that 'I don't visit jails stuff'" I asked him.

He said "you need to see your son".

"It's like that?" I asked

Rip answered "Yeah. He's yours."

Rip asked me how I was doing financially and I told him that I was broker than the Ten Commandments.

"I'll handle it." He told me. Then he said "all right son, get off of my phone.

"In a minute". We hung up.

I waited all week to receive a money order from Rip but it never came.

Visiting was that Saturday so I got up, got my hair freshly braided, pulled my clothes from under my mattress, inspected the creases and got ready. When they called my name over the intercom my heart began pounding. I thought, *here's this female with this baby that I've never seen that Rip says is mine.*

When I got to the visiting area I had it all together. At least that's what it looked like from the outside. I came through the visiting area entrance and there stood Rip, Maisha, my son and Maisha's nephew, Tavon. I went to Rip first and said "West up Cuzzin?" with a smile so big I could feel it touching both of my ears.

"What's happenin' man? You thought I wasn't comin' didn't you?" he asked as he extended his hand and hugged me.

Le'Taxione (a.k.a. YoYo)

As we hugged he said "You done got big now, but I'll still whoop your ass." I remembered when I was 17 and I tried Rip. He whooped my ass. I hadn't tried him since and his crack was a way of warning me not to ever try him.

I looked at Maisha and shot at her "West Up loco? You remember me?"

She immediately gave me my son and Rip said "kiss her".

"For what?" I asked

He said "Nigga kiss her."

I did and as our mouths met full she pushed ten balloons in my mouth with her tongue. Rip then handed me a soda and said "Sit down and swallow them one by one." I did what he said as I examined my son. After I was done I said "what happened to that paper (money) that you were supposed to send me?"

"I didn't tell you that I was going to send you no money. I'm not yo broad." He responded

He went on "You said you were broke and I said I'd handle it and that's what I just did. When you get back, drink five glasses of water, throw them balloons up and get yo money".

Maisha told me she had 14 more for me. After about 20 minutes I was forced to swallow the rest of the balloons before I was ready because Maisha's nephew started saying "I want some balloons" loud as hell.

The Sheriff looked at me but I flashed a frown at him and he turned his attention to someone else. I told Maisha, "Don't ever bring this little nigga up here again. Duce law!" We laughed.

We talked for hours until it was almost time to go and then Rip said "I'm gonna go sit in the car and let ya'll talk".

"When you comin' back?" I asked him.

"I ain't." he said.

I said "Straight like that?"

"Straight like that. Call me man."

He didn't hug me or anything and I said to myself "This cat's a cold father". Then I smiled out loud.

Maisha and I talked for the remaining time and I came to grips with the reality that I had another son. I let that O.G. shit go and focused on my son. Right then I named him Kisasi, a name that I call him to this day.

Once I got back to the dorm I told Black to get on deck while I went into the toilet area.

"Don't let nobody come in here loco". I told him.

He posted up by the front entrance like a soldier. I drank five tall glasses of water, stuck my hand down my throat and threw up 24 balloons. I washed them off, dried them, then went to my bunk, opened them and started rolling joints.

Black said "Damn Cuzz, we gonna smoke tonight?"

"Yeah, we gonna smoke tonight, but tomorrow we gonna get money." I told him.

We sold sticks for the most part. A stick is a joint the size of a toothpick if you were lucky and they cost $5.00 a piece. We'd sell a whole balloon for $100 and cats were buyin' it up.

"I Control California"

The law of omerta I leave my victims in silence
Every since I was a young nigga addicted to the violence
Run amuck in the city streets my method extortion
Passions excited by paper pussies keep prayin for portions
I'm a soldier of fortune comrades follow my orders
First we clashed over corners now we're controllin the borders
Some beef is never forgotten federal agencies watchin'
Follow my words like the Torah blow up yo spot like Bin Laden
Now the casket is dropping I put a hit on that snitch
Execution style murder now I'm thuggin his bitch
Why you rap niggas switch you got a pocket full of fame
While you were claimin to be players I took control of the game
What's my alias name? Le'Taxione I'm the Don
With a squad of drug dealas, killas, jackers and cons
Mercenaries show no remorse confrontations deleted
Your congregation extinguished while Fresno Diamonds keep gleaming
I control California.

Chapter 34

"When I walked out of the County Jail, I kissed the street, then hugged Moms who held me tight."

- YoYo

One day Louis saw me doing business with this Mexican cat named Zapata. Zapata was a short, fat Esse from parkside. Louis said "Youngsta, we don't do business like that.".

"All money is good money" I told him.

"No it's not. You gonna have problems with that mescan cause his money ain't right." Louis said.

I told him "If it's a problem, I'm going to handle it."

"You gonna have to." Louis said.

Weeks went by and Zapata still hadn't reached me my paper (paid me) but I was checkin' so much paper that it didn't hurt my pockets. You couldn't leave business unhandled like that though so I stopped Maisha from bringing anything in and I made sure all other debts were paid. Then

Le'Taxione (a.k.a. YoYo)

I got at Zapata.

We were in the Chow Hall and I said "Cuzz, where my paper at?"

He said "I'm gonna get it to you YoYo. Cedio (serious)".

I didn't say anything else. I'd already made up my mind that if he didn't have my paper I was gonna get at him.

When he got up to leave I followed him talking and laughing with Louis. Once we got back to the dorm I took off on him. I socked him right in the back of his head and when he hit the ground I started stompin' on his ass. A couple of esse's walked in and Louis said "It's heads up" as he blocked their access to the stompin' I was putting on Zapata.

After it was over I said "Cuzz if you don't get my paper all of you donkey ridas is gonna get off the line (out of population)!"

The next day one of the esses told me that he was going to cover Zapata's debt and assured me that they didn't run their car like that. After we'd arranged for the money to be sent to Maisha, the esse's put Zapata off the line. They had to do that or they would have looked weak.

When I got released, Mom's and my stepfather were there to pick me up. Moms had supported me with letters of advice the whole time that I was down (locked up). When I walked out of the County jail, I kissed the street then hugged Moms who held me tight. She was happy to see me and asked "Boy, you gonna stay out?" "If they don't test me" I told her. She said "Monkey, come on" as we walked towards the car. Monkey was one of Mom's terms of endearment for her children. I never liked it but what could I say? It was Moms.

When I got to the house, Maisha was there waiting for me. She'd already gotten my clothes starched and was ready to perm my hair. Our interaction was still a little strange but I had planned to hit them panties upon arrival anyway. I got released at about 1:00 am so we sat around for a minute talking, then Mom's and my stepfather went into their room.

"Let's go out to the garage." I told Maisha. We did and I sexed the hell out of her.

I was still only taking one leg out of my pants during sex. Old habits die hard but this one would stick with me for the rest of my life.

Afterwards we went back into Mom's house and Maisha permed my hair. After the process, my hair lay far past my shoulders. I went into the bathroom, stood in front of the mirror with my shirt off and complimented myself out loud. As I was doing that Maisha walked into the bathroom and said "I love you YoYo."

"I love myself Cuzz" I replied as I walked out of the bathroom past her.

The hood was abuzz with the news that I was back on the bricks. The homies wanted to throw a house party to welcome me back but I was interested in making my appearance at this new club that they had on California street right across from Franklin Elementary school. It was said that this was where the red rags went to party and I wanted to make my appearance there.

Before I did that wino time in the County I was about 150 lbs. and thin. I was now much bigger and very muscular and I was layin' to see what I could do with it if I was jumped so I hit the West Side at about 10:00am and called a meeting in the hood that I controlled. My Homeboy Shoota was one of the first cats there. I'd been knowing Shoota for years and though he was a Hoova Crip, he and I had become comrades and put in work (committed criminal acts) together on many occasions. One of them resulted in a

Le'Taxione (a.k.a. YoYo)

cat's nose, jaw, and ribs being broken.

"Hoova groova blood remova" he shot at me.

"Chitty chitty bang bang, hard hittin' Diamond Gang ahha boohoo mutha fuck a piru" I responded.

These were both sayings used to glorify our hoods and disrespect red rags.

"Damn Cuzz, you got yo Yoke on!" (You got big) Shoota said.

He had just got out of Y.A. (California Youth Authority). We both fell around the same time but they shot him to Y.A. and I did County time.

Hoovas were West Siders too so I told him I was going to fade that slob club that night.

"I'm goin wit you Cuzz" he said.

The few Homeboys that had not been locked up came to the meeting but in my hood there were mostly homegirls still on the bricks. I told them of my plans for the night. They just wanted to kick it in the hood, but I had to come back like I left. With a bang! The night was set.

I had Maisha come to G-Mom's house and put my hair in Shirley Temple curls with her electric curlers. When she finished I could feel the curls hanging past my ears. When I looked in the mirror, they were on my shoulders. I began to compliment myself again and Maisha said "You so conceited."

I'm not conceited Cuzz. I'm convinced." I told her

Every time I'd turn my head, my curls would swing. I'd been told from the time that I was a child that I looked good so even if I didn't, I believed it now.

I creased my all blue Khaki suit and laid it across the back of a chair in G-Mom's kitchen, went to the bathroom, put a shower cap over my head and got in the shower. When I got out I hollered for Maisha.

"Yeah?" she answered

"Bring my clothes" I instructed her.

She came to the bathroom and knocked. When she came in she sat on the toilet and I got dressed.

"YoYo, don't get in no trouble tonight" she said.

I told her, "Cuzz you know how this shit go". She said "We need you out here" referring to herself and my son.

I told her that I wasn't goin' anywhere but I couldn't guarantee it and I knew that when it fell out of my mouth. My first day out and I was ready to get on the bang. I hadn't spent a full day with my newborn son and I was ready to put myself in a position to go back to jail and maybe even prison. That's how strong the pull of the violent gang mentality has on the gang banger. It's like it circumvents rational thought, numbing him/her emotionally, exalting itself as the primary concern, making everything and everyone else secondary.

I got dressed and began to walk past Maisha.

"YoYo, when you get back we got to talk about us and I'm serious." She said as she stood in the way of the door.

"Aigh't" I responded. "Duce law."

She knew that when I said Duce Law, we would talk. She kissed me and I walked past her into the front room where Shoota was waiting for me.

We decided to walk to the club and though most of the homies knew that they couldn't get in, they decided to bail with the homeboy. We walked from Jensen to California in uniform step. I loved that military shit. To the onlooker it showed unity and discipline. It also spoke volumes of the leadership that commands the respect of the soldiers. I watched people look on as we marched up Fig Avenue in amazement and some in disdain at our demonstration.

Once we got to the club, there were people that were congregated outside. Some immediately went in the club in an attempt to remove themselves from what they perceived

Le'Taxione (a.k.a. YoYo)

as a potential clash.

"Nobody under 18 can get in" the guy at the door stated.

That left Shoota and myself. The youngstas went to a house party that was going on down the block. I told them that we would be down there after we left the club. We had no intentions of staying at the club. Our appearance was only to let cats know that we were back and were accepting any fades from anybody that sought to get down. I took off my Khaki shirt and gave it to my homegirl Tiny Girl exposing my yokes (muscles) scantily covered by my sling shot. Shoota did the same thing.

While I was locked down there had been limited clashes between the rival hoods. A lot of people were locked up and others had quit banging so there was little activity. I felt like a general without a war. I didn't like that and I was ready to get it lit again.

As soon as we walked in you could see the red rags and the females pause and take notice. I could see the contempt in the red rag's Faces but I saw curiosity in the female's faces. I noticed that all of the cats that had looked big to me before I fell looked small in comparison now. Shoota and I went to the middle of the dance floor and started Crip walkin'. This was the challenge for anyone who had a problem with any one of us. There were no takers.

A red rag named Pele' approached me. Pele' was a cat that I used to get down with when we were very young. Pele' used to do cruel shit to animals like putting firecrackers in cat's asses and lighting them. He would get baby birds, tie them up by their feet, soak them in lighter fluid and set them on fire. He was a cold little kid.

"What's poppin' YoYo?" he asked

"You know, strollin' and controllin'" I answered.

I was attempting to bait him into an altercation. I

Original Diamond Boy

wanted to get down with anybody. He said "Let's go smoke one (a joint)". I asked Shoota if he was cool and told him that I was going out to Pele's car to smoke one. Shoota asked Pele' if it was laced. Pele' said no. Shoota's question was in reference to cats mixing weed with other drugs and he wanted to make sure that Pele' wasn't trying to serve me like that.

We got to the car and got in. He had a red rag hanging from his rearview mirror. I immediately took my blue rag out of my back left pocket and hung it on his rearview mirror. He didn't trip. We smoked, reminisced for a minute and right before we went back into the club he said "YoYo, ain't nobody trippin' right now. Cats is just tryin' to get money".

"Cuzz it's Crip wit me. Fuck just tryin' to get money." I said.

This shit was all strange to me. When I fell we were at war but now cats were talking about this getting money shit. I would investigate this the next day but right then I wanted to get Shooter and get the hell up out of that spot.

As we walked up the block, we could hear the music bumpin' and voices coming from the inside of the house where the party was. As we got closer we could see cats outside of the party trued up (in all blue). As we began to walk through the crowd there was a gang of people extending their hands saying "good to have you back Cuzz". These were cats that I didn't even know. It's funny how much things can change in just one year.

As we got inside the party, cat's screamed "West Up Cuzzin!" Shoota and I threw up West Side with our hands (four fingers, two crossed in the middle.)

The Homies rushed drinks to us and homegirls pressed up against us communicating that we had action at their panties. All of the Homegirls regardless of who they were

Le'Taxione (a.k.a. YoYo)

with at the time would try to be the first ones to get with the Homies fresh out of the pen. I sat on the couch and the female One came up and sat across across my lap.

"West Up YoYo" she said.

One was about 5'1" with a banging body, dark, with medium length hair. She was very cute but I had eyes for this female named Patricia that night.

Patricia had very dark skin, long hair, cute, but she was kind of thin. She wasn't affiliated (with a gang). She was just a female going to a party.

"Who is that?" I asked one of the Homies.

He told me that she was Apple Head's cousin. Apple Head was a female named Shonda. Shonda was black as hell, skinny and had a big ole' head.

I pushed up on Patricia and said "West Up Cuzzin."

She said "Hi" and smiled like a Cheshire cat. I asked her who she was there with and she told me she was there with Shonda.

"You got a man?" I asked.

"No" she answered.

I left the conversation right there, turned and walked away. I knew that if she wanted to fade me that she would come get at me Later on and if she did, she could never say that I got at her and it would be under my terms.

Shonda also had a cousin named Mimi. Mimi messed with a red rag named Mikola who beat her constantly. Mikola showed up outside of the party looking for Mimi. She wasn't ready to leave and this infuriated him. He began to threaten to come up into the party and drag her out. I saw a chance to get down and jumped on it. I went outside and told him "Cuzz this is a Crip party. I don't know how this shit been goin' since I've been gone, but it's back to basics now."

"I ain't got no beef wit you. I just want my female out

of the party." He said.

"Cuzz you got to catch her at another time." I told him. He left. I would hear that when he caught her the next day, he brutalized her and threw her in a dumpster.

Patricia, Shonda and Mimi were leaving the party. On the way out Patricia stopped and said "take down my number". I said "Naw Cuzz, take down mine." She did and promised to call. I said "without a doubt" and they left.

The party shut down at about 3:30 a.m. One pushed up on me again.

"I saw you talking to that square ass bitch. Don't get her fucked up." She said to me.

"Cuzz, all the while I was down I did that shit solo and that's how I'm gonna keep it" I told her. "If a bitch wants to fuck wit me, she better come with her purse wide open, mouth closed and ready to follow my directions."

"Like that?" she asked.

"Choose up or lose up" I said, and walked away.

Chapter 35

"Cats were having major money but loyalties were sacrificed; honor was subverted; integrity compromised."
- YoYo

I had no respect for women. How could I in the lifestyle that I was living? I still remember when I had a thing for this female named Darlisha. I had been wanting to fade her panties every since we were very young.

One day I went to her apartment under the pretense of doing just that. She had a portable bar in her apartment. We were sitting on the couch and after we'd finished our first glass of Hennessey, she asked that I get us another drink. As I got to the portable bar, Capone and four other red rags came out of the closet and beat me to within inches of my life. The only reason that I survived is because none of those bustas was killas and for that reason they would have to see me again.

I'd woke up the next day after spending the night at

Le'Taxione (a.k.a. YoYo)

G'Mom's house and called my sister Ben. She asked me where I was the day before. Apparently she had planned a surprise get together for me.

"I was in the hood." I told her.

"Where are you now?" she asked.

I told her I was at G'Mom's house and she told me to stay there, that she was coming to pick me up. We hung up and I went and took a shower.

Ben stayed on the East side so it took her a minute to get there. I talked to Momma after I got out of the shower. She asked me if I was hungry and began to cook some bacon, eggs and biscuits for me and we talked all the while she was cooking.

Momma told me that Ben had a boyfriend named Cane and that he was a big drug dealer. It was 1984 and a new drug called crack was on the scene. Everybody was getting their money off of crack and the money was plentiful. I didn't know it then but the crack would prove to set Homeboy against Homeboy and align those who were once enemies. I realized that crack was why things had changed and the attitude between rival hoods were so nonchalant. I didn't like that shit one bit and as I said earlier, I wanted to get it lit.

Ben finally got there. She pulled up in a brand new Caddie (Cadillac) with trues and vogues (true spoke rims and vogue tires). She got out and I met her at the door. She was genuinely happy to see me. She leaped into my arms and hugged me tight. She asked me if I needed anything and I told her I was cool. She went into the house and said hi to Momma. Momma asked her how she was doing and she told her she was fine.

"I see." Momma said referring to the Cadillac.

Ben told Momma that it was Cane's car. Ben would never let Cane buy her things like cars or jewelry. She was very independent and though she would use his vehicles, she always let him know that she wasn't for sale. That's the way Mom's had raised us.

We said our good byes to G-Moms and Ben promised to call her once we got to the house and we left. Ben stopped at White's liquor store and got me a carton of Camel non-filters and a pint of Hennessy. She told me that her apartment was located across the street from this female named Karen's apartment. Karen was a female that used to write me while I was locked up. She'd gotten my address from my mother since they attended the Kingdom Hall together. They were both Jehovah's Witnesses. Karen had also attended Hoover High School with me and had eyes for me back then, but I was with Carol.

Karen was a real cool female but I didn't dig that religious aspect of her rotation. Moms had attempted to superimpose that particular doctrine on us but I didn't dig it. Jehovah's witnesses didn't believe in the holidays and I thought that Mom's used that to deny us holiday gifts but I would come to find out later on in life that Mom's truly believed in the doctrine.

We got to Ben's house and it was very stylish on the inside which was in contrast to the outside view. From the outside, it just looked like any other apartment. Ben had the latest furniture, household appliances and television sets. It was a two bedroom and before I could sit down, she said "Let me show you your room." We'd never discussed the fact that I would be living with her but at the same time, I didn't have anywhere else to live. All I had was a few outfits. Not a pot to piss in, nor a window to throw it out of so I accepted the room. She gave me a key.

"The only thing YoYo, is you can't have your homeboys over here." She said.

I kicked back in the room and thought for a while. I

Le'Taxione (a.k.a. YoYo)

heard someone come to the door.

What's up baby" he said as he came in. "Where's your brotha?"

I came out of the back room and said "West Up Cuzz?"

He extended his hand and introduced himself.

"I'm Cane" he said. "I would like to holla at you later on".

"Without a doubt." I responded.

Ben called him into the kitchen and I watched as they exchanged money and a white substance. I put two and two together and came to the conclusion that Cane stashed his drugs and money at Ben's house. I didn't trip. That was their thing and I had nothing to do with it.

I made a few calls and put together about $500. At the same time I was investigating this crack phenomenon. Apparently this was the new hustle and it was so addictive that it sold itself. That fact turned nobody's into somebodies. Cat's that couldn't walk the hood, now road around town in Nissan trucks, El Caminos, Blazers, Caddies and Chevys on 13s (tires) McLanes, Roasters and Daytons (chrome rims). Cats were having major money but loyalties were sacrificed. Honor was subverted. Integrity compromised. The lines had become blurred between red and Blue. The cats that were soft as hell co-opted the banging and got everybody on some stay safe ass shit, making alliances across color lines and I didn't like that shit.

I spoke with Maisha extensively that day. I told her that I would be with her but that I couldn't promise that she would be my only female. The reality was that while I was down, nobody stayed down for me 100%. Everybody had their fun and now that I was out everybody wanted an exclusive relationship with me and I wasn't with that. It was my turn and I was going to do this shit like I wanted to do it. Maisha agreed to my arrangement and we began to rebuild the trust that had been lost while I was down.

Momma called and said that Patricia had called and left her number. I took it down and thanked G-Moms. I didn't call Patricia that day. I just kicked back and thought about everything. Ben threw a get together that night and invited her friend Niecy.

Niecy had a man named Herb who I became cool with for a while. She was very black, with short hair and you could tell that her body was banging before she had children, but then she was a little chubby. Niecy's boyfriend, Herb was an older Crip cat who spent too much time smoking sherm. Half the time he was so high that he didn't know what was happening.

Niecy was loose (flirtatious) and had eyes for me but I wasn't attracted to her in the least. There was another female that lived downstairs named Janet. Janet was about 5'10" or 5'11", caramel complexion, long hair with a bad body, but Janet had a lot of hoe in her. Her character and mannerisms were truly ho'ish. She messed with this red rag named P-Dog. I did time with P-Dog and his people lived down the street from my G-Moms. P-Dog was another cat known for smoking sherm but what he was most known for was smoking sherm with a community hero named Stross and ending his career. Stross was a quarterback for Edison High School who was definitely going to go pro until P-Dog smoked sherm with him. Stross tripped out and was taken to the crazy house (mental hospital) and he was never the same again.

Janet had eyes for me but she was known for stabbing her men. As a matter of fact she had just gotten out of the pen for doing just that. Janet also came to the get together.

I'd spoken to Karen that day and made plans to eventually go to her house and kick it but not that day. I planned on getting drunk that night and kicking back. Ben wanted

Le'Taxione (a.k.a. YoYo)

to do that for me so that's what we did. The get together just consisted of some of Ben's friends, drank, weed, and music. Cane came through and brought a couple of females that he'd given some drugs to entertain me but I didn't get down like that.

"I appreciate the gesture Cuzzin', but I'm cool." I told him.

I took a few applications (entertained females interested in me) but I missed the hood and wanted to be there in the midst of it all.

The next day I couldn't wait to get to the Westside and when I got there everybody was present and accounted for. Duce and Soldier had continued investing in the weed game and were now selling quarter pounds. They both had money for me upon my arrival. I didn't see them the first day that I got out because they were out of town copping' some more weed. They were happy to see me and I was ecstatic to see them. We'd always been close and now was no exception though Later on in life we would drift apart.

They tried to give me some weed to sell.

"West Up with you cats? I asked. "Last night, the nigga Cane tried to give me some crack to sell and now ya'll tryin' to give me some weed."

I turned to Nutty Boy and said "What you gonna try to give me to sell, some vacuum cleaners or somethin'?" We all laughed, but I was dead serious.

The night before, at the get together, Cane had broke down the crack business to me. He explained how lucrative it was and how a cat like me that had soldiers could get rich fast off of it and not really have to touch it. What he was really saying is how he could use me to use my soldiers to help him get rich, but I didn't see my soldiers getting rich.

"Cuzz, its Crip wit me. I know a lot of the homies have started sellin' dope but it's Crip wit me!" I told him.

Original Diamond Boy

He told me to let him know if I changed my mind. It was obvious that a lot of homeboys did.

I talked to everybody that day and I told them that none of the homies in the hood would be selling crack. I didn't care what the other homies in the Vill, Finkwhite, King of Kings, Holly, Frank H., or anywhere else were doing but we would not sell crack. I knew that cats from L.A. were bringing that shit to The No and every time we chose to get money like that, we were losing a grip on our hoods. They weren't setting up shop in our hoods but they were controlling the economics of our hood and that was just as bad. If they weren't 62 East Coast's, I didn't trust them. I could see this shit turning sour and time would prove me right.

Chapter 36

"There is a certain street piety©; a moral criminality© that gangstas are supposed to exercise."

- YoYo

The homies from the Vill would come through flossin' (show boating) in their Chevs, trucks and Caddies, but all the while those L.A. cats were getting deeper and deeper (growing in numbers) in the Vill and one day the homeboys found themselves in a gun battle for their own turf.

One of my homeboys was killed in the battle. That was a life that could have been saved. A life that was precious to our soil. A life that I loved and cherished. A life that in my opinion was not finished with it's expression.

I called a meeting to address the crack issue, but how can you ask cats to return to poverty after feasting? How can you suggest that one embrace financial destitution after he's experienced a perceived liberation given to him by the

Le'Taxione (a.k.a. YoYo)

ability to access finances that sustain his creature comforts? Needless to say, I couldn't, so I put plan C into action. Start jackin' the dope dealers!

I put together a crew which consisted of Duce, O.G., Solo and myself; naming it the M-1s

I'd returned to Ben's house and told her that I would be moving soon.

"YoYo, please don't get off into them streets and lose your life." She said.

I told her "Ben, to live is to die and to die is to live again." "I'm going to be into some things that I don't want to bring to your doorstep so it's best that I go.:"

She smiled and said "Yeah, please don't bring it to my doorstep."

We laughed and she asked me what I wanted to eat. Ben was one of my best friends. She knew what kind of life I led and that I sincerely believed in this Crip thing so she never tried to openly dissuade me, though she did so from behind the veil.

That night Ben told me "YoYo, Terry got a duffle bag full of guns in the closet." She didn't tell me to take them, but she implied it. I looked in the closet and saw a green duffle bag. Terry had been to Viet Nam and smuggled some guns back to the states and had stashed them at Ben's house. I got the duffle bag out of the closet and sat on the couch. I unzipped the bag and found five guns. A double barrel shotgun, a .38, a .45 a 30.06 rifle and an M-16 assault rifle.

You should have seen the smile on my face when I saw that M-16. No one in the hood was using assault rifles at that time and as far as I knew, I was the only one that had one.

I called the M-1's. M-1 stood for Murder in the 1st degree. We were about to terrorize the West Side.

"Cuzz, I got an M-16." I told Duce. He said "What?"

"I got an assault rifle that the army uses and at the flip of a switch it becomes fully automatic." I said.

He responded "Let's get this paper."

Our first lick, we targeted a cat that pipelined drugs into the hood but didn't stay there. Houses would be set up in our hoods by outside sources and manned by the homeboys. Shit, it was like the homies were protecting these other cat's establishments and though they were getting paper, the ultimate winner was the cat that set up the rock house and supplied it with rocks (crack).

The first places that we wanted to hit were the spots set up in the projects. We hit a spot in the Cooley Plaza. I had duce hold the M-16 and I held the .38. I wanted the .38 because of the technique that I used during jacks. I would come in and pop (shoot) my victims in the leg to let them know that this was real and that any resistance would be met with extreme force. This stopped cats from being what we called heroes during the lick. This technique, though brutal, was very effective and it saved lives.

We only came up with a few thousand dollars. We left the dope because there was nothing we could do with it.

On our next lick, we caught the supplier in the spot. He begged for his life and in doing so he offered to give up the people who supplied him. We found out that there were two sources of crack in the No. One was the cats from L.A. and the other was the Mexicans.

When I found out the extent of the esse's involvement in furnishing drugs to the hood, I was livid. We had been beefin with these cats for years and now they were putting this shit in our communities, facilitating crime and death among the homies. What I was doing was no better but there is a certain street piety©, a moral aspect of the criminal element that Gangstas exercised and drugs of that mag-

Le'Taxione (a.k.a. YoYo)

nitude, with those vast destructive properties were a violation of that street code.

I watched females abandon their children, preachers abandon their congregations, men abandon their families and homies abandon their oaths to the hood all behind crack. Still, my intentions were duplicitous. I wanted the crack out of the hood, but I also wanted to get my money. Both happened.

Our next lick was on some Mexicans that lived by Calwa Park on the East side. We went in full force. Solo kicked the door open and Duce went in first. I followed him with the M-16. We couldn't make any mistakes because we were told that these cats were heated. We tied them up and searched the house. The female that was in the back bedroom half naked showed us with her eyes where the drugs and money were. There were only two cats in the house at that time and we wanted to get out of there before anymore came.

We got away with a kilo of cocaine and $20,000. We got $6,000 a piece and bought a car with the rest. We sold the kilo for the dirt (cheap) to a cat named Styles. Styles was a pimp who had his hand in the dope game but kept his dope houses outside of the hood. This would begin a long relationship between Styles and us.

Chapter 37

"... mandatory that everyone in the house not only go to school, but that they also got good grades."

- YoYo

I moved into the King of Kings low income housing complex with my Auntie Rachel and her two children, Baby and Jason. At this time and for a long time after they were my favorite cousins. I'd lived with them in the Fink White projects and for most of that time I provided the meals for us all. Rachel was cool as hell but like a lot of people in my family, she was an alcoholic. She would never admit it but that was the reality. She spent most of the time in the clubs drinking and would be gone for days at a time but she'd always make sure that the electricity and phone stayed on and that the rent was paid. There is no doubt in my mind that she loved her children and even me at that time but later on in life that would change – at least her love for me would.

Le'Taxione (a.k.a. YoYo)

While I stayed with Rachel I was thrust into the role of father figure. Jason's father was an alcoholic and absent in his life and Baby's father was just absent. Baby was about 14 or 15 years old at that time and had a very sharp foul tongue. She was always in somebody else's business and for that reason we called her "Hot Mouth". Jason was about 10 or 11 and very playful as all children should be. He used to catch me sleeping and drag a string across my face in hopes that I would slap myself in my sleep (and sometimes I did). I can still remember tying his leg to the staircase, putting matches between his toes and lighting them.

I'd also moved Maisha and One in with me. They were both my females at the time and both understood that I was going to have as many females as I wanted. They agreed to that stipulation. I slept with both of them in the same bed but never had sex with any one of them while the other was in the bed. I enjoyed the company of females, but I wasn't a freak like that.

I made it mandatory that everyone in the house not only went to school, but that they also got good grades. Neither Baby or One was good in school so at times they would ditch classes. I had arranged with their teacher that if they didn't show up to class that the teachers would call me. At first, their attendance was cool though they would be late sometimes. Then they became problems in the classroom because they were not completing their homework. They weren't completing their homework because they were not listening in class so I began getting the absent calls. I put Maisha on the case. She and the homegirls Patty, Tiny Girl and Looney Girl would find out where they would go when they ditched school and come notify me. They would usually be at someone's house in Pole Cat Alley along with a lot of other people who ditched school. I would get my heata and a couple of homeboys and myself would go to the house pistols in hand and notify whomever's house it was that if these two females, Baby and One, were caught ditching school again at their house, that we would come, snatch them out and shoot the spot up.

I began to hold classes at the house with all of the young homeboys and homegirls everyday. We used school books, but I would also teach them about black leaders, something that was absent in their school curriculum.

Rachel didn't allow me to throw any parties at the house but we bar-b-cued all of the time. One day she came home and we were gambling in the kitchen. All of us froze when she came through the door anticipating her cussing (cursing) us out, but instead she squatted down with us and said "what they hit for?" and began to gamble with us. On top of that she broke the dice game (won all the money).

"Hold it down YoYo." (take care of everything) She told me on her way out of the door.

I always did.

Chapter 38

"Leave a nigga the back door or you'll make him kill you."

- YoYo

The word was going around that the police were making threats on my life. They would harass the homeboys and upon letting them go they would say "Tell YoYo that we are going to stick our nightsticks up his ass, and we are going to kill him when we get the chance." I knew that they were hot about the shooting incident and that they were looking for some get back (retaliation) but I didn't trip. I had this M-16 and if they tried to cross me, I would hold court in the streets!

That night Soldier Boy was in the mini park gambling. The mini park was where a lot of people got high, hung out and gambled. A lot of people also lost their lives in the mini park and it was for that reason that it was finally closed down. The mini park was on fig across from the

Le'Taxione (a.k.a. YoYo)

King of Kings. As a matter of fact, I could see the mini park from my front door.

Apple head Shonda ran to the door and said "YoYo, these dudes just jumped on Soldier Boy!" When Solo, Bass and I got to the mini park, the cats were gone and Soldier boy was being picked up off the ground by a female named Samantha. He reeked of alcohol. He had been drinking Night Train (wine). Someone told us what direction the cats were walking.

"If we travel this route we can catch them on Fruit and California." I said.

We went that way and came out on Fruit and California ahead of them. We began to walk towards the cats as they were playing their music on a boom box, walking and laughing. They didn't know that the shit was about to get real.

Solo clicked his blade open and we walked up in the middle of about 5 cats. Once we got in the middle of them I took off – Bayaaw! I dropped the one with the boom box, picked up the box and began beating him in the head with it. Solo began stabbing cats and I could hear them screaming all around me. Bass was doing what he could to aid in the fight. The other cats ran off and left the one that had hit the ground. Bass and I stomped the cat and Solo stabbed him on the strength. Solo was a rida and he too was one that would take it to the extreme.

We left the one cat lying in the street. As we walked back to the King of Kings, Solo said "Cuzz you should have kept the box!" We all laughed. When we got back, we retold the story of what transpired with sound affects and all. Soldier Boy was alright. He just had a knot on his chin where he had apparently landed when he fell.

"Cuzz, I told you about being fucked up (drunk) and gambling in that mini park." I told him.

Beef between Crips and Bloods was very light at this time. As a matter of fact some of the Godfathers had offered to supply me with sherm and we'd split the profits down the middle. At least that's the way that the message was brought to me. They knew that I wasn't with the crack aspect of the game so I guess they figured they'd try to get at me on the sherm aspect. I gave the offer no thought.

I was still jackin' and Maisha and One were also hustlin'. One was what we called a Creeper. She was very short and she would go into department stores and creep on their safes. Maisha would go with her to distract clerks and management. At the time I had a royal blue '68 Chevy and I would drop them off downtown and wait for them to call me. We were doing cool. We ate, we were clothed, housed and kicked it everyday.

From the proceeds from our illegal ventures I would make sure that Jason had lunch money everyday and that he made all of his football practices. Baby was already a Diamond Girl but Jason was a civilian. Jason would begin to claim Diamond later on in his life in another state but while we were in Fresno he was just a civilian.

Duce had committed a robbery in Bakersfield and was sentenced to time in Preston (California Youth Authorities) so I was charged with making sure his son by Kate, Lil' Duce was alright. My plate was full. I found myself taking care of Baby, Jason, Lil' Duce, the young homeboys and homegirls and running the hood. That was not counting the obligatory money that I was giving Sharon for my son Askari and now Maisha was pregnant again.

I decided to take a leave of absence on a day when Rachel was home. I went across town to Karen's house to just kick back. I had been over there once before when I first hit the bricks. On that day we had got lit (smoked a joint and drank some Hennessy), sat on her balcony and eventually

Le'Taxione (a.k.a. YoYo)

had sex. Once I got there, we did the same thing that day, except we didn't have sex. Karen was a short, full figured female with a beautiful personality. I enjoyed her company and the fact that she lived on the other side of town gave me the opportunity to rest somewhat at the house and that's just what I did.

The next day I was craving the West Side. I had her drop me off on Fig. It was something about the West side that had an attracting pull on me. I loved the West side and all of the chaos and violence that went with it. I was West side born and bred, raised and fed.

As I came through the door I could hear Rachel hollering at Maisha about something. Whatever it was, I knew that the real reason was that she hadn't had a drink and was going through withdrawals. Maisha wasn't saying anything but I've always been very protective of my females so I got at Rachel.

"Cuzz, what are you sweatin' her for?" I asked.

"I'm tired of all these people in my house."

"All these people is the ones that make sure that there's food in this house." I shot back.

"I don't need nobody to do shit for me! All of you can get out of my house!" she hollered.

Right then I told Maisha to go pack our shit. She shot right up stairs to do so and I told Rachel "You got this shit twisted Cuzz. I've always been a mutha fucka who would do this shit on my own."

"Put the shit in the car and let's shake this bullshit." I told Maisha once she finished packing.

Baby came out to the car begging us not to leave saying that "You know Mama don't mean that." I hated to leave Baby and Jason but I wasn't going to subject Maisha and my son to that bullshit. I didn't know where we were going to go but we were getting the fuck out of there.

Original Diamond Boy

We went to my G-Mom's house who agreed to rent us the back room until we got on our feet. The first day we were there, Rachel called and told me that she was sorry and that she wanted us to come back. I told her that although I accepted her apology, the fact that she would even suggest that my pregnant girl, my son and myself get out of her house made it evident that it was now time to go. She would spend the next week trying to convince Maisha to talk to me about coming back and after the second time Maisha brought it to me I told her not to bring that bullshit to me again. Duce Law! She never did.

The room G-Moms rented to us was cool. It had a bathroom with a shower in it. We bought a king size bed and a stereo system and we were cool for the moment. One had started messin' with some old man that was paying her for her company. Like Rip said, "the game is cop and blow, not cop block and lock".

Though I entertained short lived relationships with other females, Maisha was my main girl and she got solace out of that fact. Of course she didn't like that I had other females but that was the arrangement. I grew closer and closer to her and that was one of the reasons that I kept other females. It sounds contradictory but in my mind, the frequenting of other females kept me from falling head over heals for Maisha. It kept my feelings for her at bay. This was a tactic that I would use for most of the rest of my life.

One day we had awakened at the same time. She had to go to the hospital for a routine visit and I was on my way across town to visit Karen. She got into the shower first and I didn't want to wait for her to finish so I got in with her. Maisha had a beautiful body and I marveled at it while we were in the shower. I washed her and she washed me. It was very sensual. That was the first and last female that I'd

Le'Taxione (a.k.a. YoYo)

ever taken a shower with. In retrospect I think that she was the female that I'd been closest to. I can't say that I loved her because if I did, I wouldn't have had other women but she was the one that I was closest to. I really dug Maisha.

I got to Karen's spot across town. She was waiting for me with a joint and a bottle of Hennessey. I told her about the Rachel incident and she told me that I could come stay with her.

"What about my son?" I asked her

She extended her invite to both of us but I knew that it didn't extend to Maisha. I told her that I had to get Maisha straight first. I didn't close the door on the invite but I let it be known that I wasn't going to leave Maisha out in the street like that. I just didn't get down like that.

Maisha's grandfather had attempted to force her back into his home by threatening to call child custody and tell them that she was homeless. The next time he drove by the house, I stopped him and checked his old ass.

"Cuzz, she ain't fixin' to be your babysitter so you can call whoever and report whatever. I'm the hog wit the big nuts around here and you don't call no shots on her. That's my woman nigga." I told him.

I went on to tell him that if I caught him around there again it was going to be violence. The cat sped off but he wasn't no punk. Later on that day I was outside washing the Chevy and he pulled up, stopped and aimed a rifle at me. I dove over the hood of my car just as he shot a single shot – Pop! When I hit the ground on the other side of the car, I picked up a Pepsi bottle, raised up, threw the bottle and it hit his window and it busted sounding like a gunshot. He panicked and took off.

I ran into G-Mom's house, got my .45 and ran down the street to his son Leroy's house where he had parked. I ran straight up to the front door, jumped up and kicked it in –

Bam! I backed back when the door opened and busted up into the house three times – buck buck buck!

I would later on find out that they saw me running up through the window and retreated to the back room. All of this happened in the broad open day light. That's how Fresno was. It wasn't unusual to see this kind of shit. The police drove through 30 minutes later, but no one said anything to them and they left.

Maisha and I smoked a joint and laughed about the whole thing.

"Boy you just like Garnett (my grandfather)." G-Moms said.

"I'm just like Rip." I responded

She said "Him too."

The next day I got a call from Duce who informed me that there had been some problems concerning Lil Duce. He told me to go to check the broad Kate about it. I went to her house which was around the corner from G-Mom's house. When I got there she answered the door.

"Where's Lil Duce?" I asked.

"She got smart and asked me "Why?"

She started "I don't know who the…"

"Bitch, let me see my nephew!" I said as I slapped her. She closed the door.

I walked away. When I got back to G-Mom's house, her brother Bony Face, the one C-Rag gave the California smile to called and asked what had happened.

"I came to check on my nephew and that bitch got out of pocket so I slapped her ass." I told him

He said "I'm comin' to see you."

I hung up the phone, got my sawed off shotgun and stood in the front yard. Duce had gotten the M-16 took but the sawed off would do.

Bony Face came walking up the street like he said he

Le'Taxione (a.k.a. YoYo)

would. As he got closer, I could see by how he was moving that he was heated. As he approached he said "I see we got a little problem."

I pulled the sawed off, cocked it and got off – Boom! He crouched down and busted back – pow! I cocked the gauge and busted again and as I tried to cock it again, it jammed. He saw that and ran at me bustin' – pow-pow-pow. I thought on how many times he had shot and quickly figured that he had at least one shot left. As I turned to run, he busted one more time. I made it in to the house and G-Moms said "Boy, what are you doin'?"

Two shoot outs in two days. It was time to leave G-Mom's house. Later on that day my uncles had come over after they heard what had happened. They attempted to pull that uncle shit and I lit into their asses.

"Who the fuck you niggas think I am Cuzz? I been wantin' to see any one of you niggas anyway. Which one of you niggas want it?"

They backed off and began to try to speak to me correctly but it was too late. I started calling them niggas, bitches, hoes and bustas.

"If you take that and won't fight, then you'll suck my dick and won't bite!" I told them.

You couldn't melt them cats down and pour them on me so I remembered what Rip said "Leave a nigga the back door or you'll make him kill you" and that's what I did. It was clearly time to get Maisha, my son and myself a new spot. G-Mom's told me to stay until the baby was born which would be in a couple of months so we did. G-Moms liked interacting with my son Kisasi and she knew whatever happened that I would die before I allowed anything to happen to her.

Bony Face called begging me to squash the beef between us. I told him to meet me at Ivy Center so we could finish the shit. He didn't want to beef so I told him "Cuzz, stay out of my area and it's cool, but if I catch you anywhere in this area, I'm gonna get at yo ass!" He agreed.

Maisha went into labor. She wanted me to go to the hospital with her but I didn't and I regret that to this day. She called from the hospital and said that we had a girl. She asked me what I wanted to name her.

"Almasi" I answered.

"Almasi?" she asked.

"Yeah." I told her and hung up the phone.

Maisha brought Almasi home and she was so beautiful. I started calling her 'Money Honey'.

My mother had moved to Portland Oregon and had plans to move G-Moms up there. I got at G-Moms and told her to let Maisha, my children and I have the house and that way Duce could have somewhere to stay once he got out. She agreed.

There was a very pretty female named Tammy who stayed across the street from G-Moms. Tammy liked me, but was smart enough to not be with me. I was street poisoned and she was all about school. One night I went over to her house and we laid on a blanket in her front yard and gazed into the universe.

"YoYo, when are you gonna quit living like this?" she asked me.

I told her "Baby, It's Crip for life!"

"YoYo, you are one of the last true Crips left and ain't none of them niggas puttin' in work like you and when you fall ain't none of them niggas gonna help." She said.

I told her that how them cats get down didn't have nothing to do with how I got down.

"It's Crip wit me!" I said.

Chapter 39

"Someone had to pay for the life that was spent... "
- YoYo

Karen had a little girl and told me that she was mine. All of a sudden (or at least that's how it seemed) I had four children, Askari, Kisasi, Zuri and Almasi. I regularly spent time with all of them except Askari. His mother had begun to prostitute for the homeboy Snow. One day I went to the Vill where she was staying to see my son. The busta Snow had a problem with that. He pulled a shot gun on me and I chased him down the alley.

"Bitch, you knew that coward had a heata when you told me it was cool to come visit my son. You playin' both ends to the middle! I'll see my son when he's old enough to see me!" I told Askari's mother and I bounced (left).

Karen was on some 'let's be a family shit' but I didn't trust her. One day I was spending the night at her house and we got into an argument. I lay down and went to sleep

Le'Taxione (a.k.a. YoYo)

and woke up to the police shining their light into my face telling me that I had to leave. I did and my heart grew hard for her. Though I didn't stop communicating with her, I didn't trust her any more. Don't get me wrong. It's not like I treated her like a queen, but I didn't deserve that.

Word came that Solo got killed. The esse's had cut his hands off and burned him up in a vacant building. This news tore at my very essence. This was one of my true homeboys that I loved and somebody had to pay!

The code was swift retaliation. Someone had to pay for the life that was spent. A precious life that I loved and I couldn't rest until retaliation was exacted. An eye for an eye (Le'Taxione).

Duce got out at the very same time that my little homeboy Stone was becoming a factor. Stone used to be Lil'Black until his reputation far outshined Black's. He reinvented himself as Stone. Though I had great admiration for the young homie, our hustles were different so the time that we spent together was limited but not non-existent.

G-Moms and the rest of the family moved from the No to Oregon and that left Duce and I in the No together and we ran amuck. For money we began to profit off of the violence that we were known for. We started taking contracts from heavy hitters who couldn't afford to do the dirty work. If these cats were owed money, we'd be called in to collect. If other cats were stepping on the toes of those we were hired by, we'd eliminate the threat. We'd even functioned as security for hoes at times.

One day Styles called on us for a job. Styles sent six hoes to come pick us up and take us to his home. His home was lavish and we were treated like royalty; waited on hand and foot by an ethnic variety of hoes. That didn't move me though. I'd been around hoes all of my life. I was moved by the money that Styles paid for our services. He was a big spender and he appreciated our work.

In his very deep voice, flashing a smile Styles said "What's up homie?"

Styles was always genuinely happy to see us whether it was to do a job or just to enjoy a glass of cognac. We returned the greeting "West Up Cuzz?"

He'd never get straight to business. We'd talk, have a drink and laugh for a while, and then he'd present the job and the result that he wanted.

"Homie, I got this area that I'm tryin' to lock down but there's some cats that was there before me. I've extended to them an offer to pay for their cooperation. That offer was denied. I need this area. I want their leases to be terminated." That's how Styles communicated

Then he asked one of the hoes "How long do they give you to vacate the premises after your lease has been terminated?"

"30 days." She answered.

He turned to us and said "I need it done in ten".

"Give us seven." I said

Styles busted out laughing and said "That's what I'm talking about."

That night Duce and I put on sweat suits with suits on top of them. We made five flyers for the five rock houses that were owned and active in the desired location. At about 3:00a.m. we traveled to the area and quietly put the flyers on each door. The flyers simply said "Vacate". Then we chose which house we would start with.

Once the house was chosen, we knocked on the door and retreated into the darkness. Once the door opened we shot at the lower part of it and once the doorman fell back into the house, we began to fire at head range. We didn't

Le'Taxione (a.k.a. YoYo)

want to kill anybody if we didn't have to but we wanted to express the severity of the vacate request.

We hit four houses in four nights. The occupants couldn't tell the police that this was drug turf related. Not back then. So the police filed it as random shootings. On the 5th day all five houses were vacated.

We were taken to Styles' house but he wasn't there so we waited for his return. When he came through the door he smiled and said "My niggas! I thought you told me seven days?"

Duce said "That was only if they resisted." We all laughed.

"Was you niggas getting' naked after the work? Styles asked. He said "The word is that all them niggas knew was that they were findin' suits in bushes and shit".

After we'd put in the work, we'd take off the suits and leave them and walk away in our sweat suits.

"What did they expect from business men besides business suits?" I cracked.

The question was rhetorical.

The word spread that there were some cats from out of state trying to take over drug locations in the No and we left it just like that because it allowed us to continue to operate in silence.

The next job that we did was more personal. A client's family member had been beaten with bats and left in a ditch to die. Our names were given in reference to effect retribution. It had been Mexicans who committed this violent act so we would not only have to go into their hood but the client wanted to send one of his own to watch. We were given names and addresses by a third party to protect the identity of the client.

That night we dressed in all black khaki suits and went to the Mexican's house. They were having a party so the circumstance couldn't have been better to veil motivation. Duce looked like a Mexican until you got right up on him so the plan was to get him close enough to start the assault, then I would come in and sweep the place.

We spotted a specific cat that we were to get. Duce pulled his bandanna over his eyebrows and walked up in the party.

"Que paso Loco?" one of the Esses stated.

Duce returned the greeting. Then he pulled his heat and dumped (shot) through the crowd at the intended target. I came up with our client's people on my left. Duce broke to my right and I began to blast into the crowd – buck-buck-buck!

There were females screaming and crying. Cats were hitting the ground, clutching parts of their bodies. The getaway was smooth. We got in one car and drove for three blocks then switched cars. We hit the back routes all the way back to the West Side in the midst of police sirens and lights flashing. I thought to myself, *"I'll never make a move like this again and attempt to make it all the way back to the West Side."*

The next day the news flashed "Six Shot in a Gang War over Turf". The veil was perfect. They were looking for esses. I sighed with relief.

Though I was now committing acts of violence for monetary gain, I still longed for the bang. I was a gang banger in a town where most of my rivals were extinct. Duce, Kate and Lil'Duce had moved to Oregon leaving Maisha, Kisasi, Almasi and myself in the No. Styles had also took his operation to Oregon so my business was short. So was my money. Times got hard fast. I started smoking primos (weed mixed with cocaine) and got hooked.

"Evil Seed"

Now things are different it ain't quite like the past
Niggas thinking that it's safe to sag but scared to flag
I got to fade you mutha fuckas that ain't real in this game
Cause you only in my way if you ain't pure as the cain
A damn shame out on bail as I face 3 strikes
My name erased from the book of everlastin' life
How many niggas in the hood with they foot on the throttle
Resort to searching for tomorrow in a Hennessy bottle
Now soak it, and try to hold it, provoke it from takin off
Even though I got myself it's amazin' how I'm feelin' lost
But I'm a boss with that Nina Ross by my side
Finger on the trigga cause I'm cautious when I'm in my ride
My evil seed got me heedin' every word he say
But it's up to God if I make it through another day

Chapter 40

"I picked up my son and began to walk as fast as I possibly could to the train station."

- YoYo

I decided to take my family and move to Oregon when I heard that they were gang banging up there but I needed money. I wanted to expand my hood and I told myself "one more lick and I'm gone".

I knew this one cat that would at any time have at least $3,600 in his pocket but he knew I was a jacker. For this reason it would be hard for me to get up on him. I decided that if I had one of my sons with me, he wouldn't think that I was going to jack him, not in front of my son. All I needed was a split second to get up on him and a child would give me that split second.

I rationalized using one of my own children as a decoy. I told myself that this lick was for us to leave The No and get a start in Oregon. I told myself that enough times that I

Le'Taxione (a.k.a. YoYo)

believed it and though a voice inside of me spoke out against the vile act, I acted against that voice. I would find later in life that it became easier and easier to act against that voice until one day I didn't even hear it anymore.

It was Duce Law! I was going to hit this lick. I told Maisha to pack that night, make arrangements with Amtrak and to meet us at the train station the next day at 2:00 p.m.

The next day Maisha took my daughter Almasi and went to the train station downtown. It was about 12:30 p.m. when she left. At 1:00 p.m. I got my son and walked to my victim's spot. I knocked on the door. He looked out the window and saw me holding my son's hand. The curtain closed and I could hear him unlocking the door.

"What up YoYo?"

I had bought joints laced with cocaine from him before so I said "Let me get five joints" as I walked in. He turned and I closed the door and drew down on him.

"Cuzz, this is a robbery. Don't make it no murder." I said.

He started begging and I started to pop him in the leg like I usually did, but I didn't want to spook my son.

"Take what you want, just don't kill me". He said.

I asked him where the paper was. He moved to get it and I followed him with my heat trained on him. I let go of my son's hand and said "Stay right here". He got to a little lock box, pulled out a roll of money and extended it to me. When I reached to get it, he dropped the money, turned to reach back into the lock box and I popped him in the leg – pow!

He tried to turn and I popped him again. This time I caught him in the jaw. He hit the floor screaming "AAHHH! I moved towards him and picked up the money from the floor. I put the roll of money in my pocket, backed out with my heat trained on him, never taking my eyes off of him. I reached down with my left hand and felt my son's head. I grabbed his hand and cut out.

The boy stayed in the house as we left. I walked down the street, saw the first car going by and flagged them down.

"I'll give you $50 to take us downtown." I said.

I sat my son in the back seat and periodically I would turn and look at him. He never said a word, just looked at me. I smiled at him and he smiled back.

I kept the conversation short in the car. When we got downtown I had the female who was driving drop me off at the County jail, gave her a fifty dollar bill and we parted company. I picked my son up and began to walk as fast as possible to the train station. I finally saw Maisha and walked over to her.

"Is it cool?" she asked.

"Fo sho." I answered as I gave her $200.

She went and paid for our tickets. We waited for what seemed to be hours but in fact it was only about 45 minutes. The train pulled up, we boarded and we were on our way.

All we had was one suit case that Maisha borrowed from Tammy and all that was in it was diapers and some baby clothes. Maisha was breast feeding so we didn't need baby formula. Anything else we needed, we would get at the next town.

While we were on the train I slipped into the bathroom and counted the paper from our lick. I say "our" because my son had a part in the lick so he was entitled to that part. After counting I found that we had $5,100. Altogether we had come up on $5,350. I smiled and returned to my family.

Maisha never asked me about money because she knew by experience that I didn't like discussing money with her.

Le'Taxione (a.k.a. YoYo)

At the same time she knew that I would always take care of the family and protect them with my life. That was one of those ironies that played out in my life. I would disrespect her by having multiple women but I would lay down my life in defense of her. That's that street piety©; that moral criminality©.

The train ride for the most part was uneventful and long as hell but comfortable. We arrived in downtown Portland, Oregon the next day. Upon arrival I called my mother to let her know that I was there. I then contacted Rachel to arrange a place for us to stay temporarily. I tendered to her a specific amount of paper to cover our food and shelter once I got to her spot.

The first thing that I noticed about Portland was that it was very clean and there was grass everywhere. The air was clean and the city was tall, unlike Fresno which was flat. Rachel stayed in a very good community. I stayed in the area for about four days before I began to long for the hood.

"Where the hood at?" I asked Rachel.

Once she gave me directions I got my heat, kissed the children and began walking in that direction.

I lived off of beef (conflict) and without it, the monotony was driving me crazy. I got to my G-Moms house before I saw any signs of gang activity. My G-Moms stayed on 13th and Ainsworth which was in an area that was claimed by Crips so at that moment I made up my mind to make that area headquarters.

There were Imperial Village Crips (IVCs) from L.A. in that area but because of our longstanding beef with L.A... I didn't really mess with them. One day they rode by and hit me up (threw up their hood with their fingers) and I hit them back up with that West Side Diamond Crip in three hand signs. They turned around and came back. I pulled out my heat and waited for them to get back. They parked in front of the house and right then I figured that they weren't beefin'. They got out and said "Where you from Cuzz?"

"I'm from that mad ass Diamond Crip Gang. Mr. YoYo Loc, Fresno Crip Monster."

The one named Stax said "It's that IVC Crip gang, Los Angeles".

"What that do? (what's next?)" I asked.

He said "homie, we out here tryin' to get money". Then he asked if I was slanging (selling dope).

"Naw homie, I'm bangin" I informed him.

Then he got a call on his big grey Motorola phone. This was the first cellular phone that they came out with. They were big, grey, and rectangular with a three or four inch antenna. All of the doe boys (dope dealers) had one. It was like a symbol of status and success. There was no doubt that these cats were getting money and though that wasn't my demonstration, I respected it.

After he finished his call he said "Homie, I got to get this money. I'll catch you later".

"Without a doubt" I replied.

I started spending more time in the hood than I was spending with Maisha and when I was at Rachel's house I was playing with Kisasi and Almasi. Maisha got homesick and my mother, G-Moms and Rachel hatched a plan and put her on the Greyhound back to Fresno without my knowledge. Now I can see their concerns were legitimate. I was back into the gang activity and wouldn't be the father that I was supposed to be. But back then I saw it as a cross (a betrayal). And I became very bitter.

Duce was really trying to leave the bangin' behind him. He was working and doing good. He told me that he was saving his money to move to Seattle. He was doing the responsible thing, but I had no family in P.O. and my responsibility lied with this Diamond.

Chapter 41

"This is a robbery cuzz; don't make it no murder"
- YoYo

I had to establish myself in this new environment. All of the Rips from L.A. were establishing themselves with dope. I would have to establish myself the old way...through violence.

I went to the hood that had the most gang activity, around 9th and Sumner. I put on my all blue Dickie suit with my blue converse and my blue rag creased and hanging out of my back left pocket. I wore my blue derby, got my cane and my heat and strolled to 9th and Sumner. As I walked, people would break their necks turning and looking at this Crip monster and I loved it!

Once I got to that hood, I posted up on the corner like it was mine. I hit everybody that passed by up with this Diamond. It wasn't long before females began to stop and talk to me. "What's your name?" they asked.

Le'Taxione (a.k.a. YoYo)

"Mr. YoYo Locs".

"Where you from?" "What set you claim?"

Females have always been the best way to get your name out, but you had to be careful because they were also the best way to get killed.

I stayed out there for four hours with no incident then I left. I would return the next day and do it all over again.

The next day I went back with my 501s, my white Chuck Taylors (converse), my royal blue sweat shirt, my cane and my heat. I didn't wear my derby that day. I had baby braid my hair the night before.

Once I got there, there was an even larger crowd of females. It was like they were gathered to see the new Gangsta on the block and I obliged them. I walked up and said nothing. I just posted up. One of the females that was there on my debut the day before said "What's up YoYo?" I responded "West Up Cuzz." They all began to smile.

A cat approached me and said "You got them boulders (crack rocks)?" I asked him what he needed (how much did he want).

"What you got for the note ($100).

I told him to shoot the note (give me the $100). He gave me the money and I took it and said "Nigga chalk that up to the game." (You just lost that.)

"Nigga give me my money!" he said.

"Nigga you got six seconds to get the fuck up out of my range." I told him as I pulled out the heat.

He began to run but I popped him anyway. He grabbed his ass, hollered and hit the ground. I looked around to see which way I would make my exit. One of the females that had inquired as to where I was from was standing on the porch of a house near the corner. She called my name. I looked and she motioned me over to her house. I ran about ten yards to her house and dashed up the steps onto her porch.

Original Diamond Boy

From the porch I watched the ambulance come and pick up the smoker (crack user) and transport him. The female's name was Andrea and from that day forward, she was my homegirl.

"You crazy as hell." Andrea said to me.

At that moment I had established myself in P.O. as Mr. YoYo Loc the Crip Monster.

It was my intention to control that hood. That meant that I would have to man that hood by myself and that's what I did. I'd show up at about 10:00 a.m. and post up at different corners in the hood for a couple of hours at a time and made Andrea's house headquarters. Andrea lived there with her brothers Danny, Leroy, Case, her gay ass brother Stacy and her mother Ms. Andrea. I never knew her name so I called her Ms. Andrea out of respect.

Andrea was light skinned with green eyes and was a rida. She was known for using a blade when she got down and had a couple of stabbings under her belt. She was a cute female but we were never interested in each other sexually although we would drink and smoke weed together.

Before long there were a lot of young cats hanging around me but they weren't a part of any set (gang). Females started to come to the hood to peep this nigga from Cali named YoYo and as we rotated (talked) I'd introduce them to this real Crip philosophy. They'd ask "so the cats that are sellin' dope aren't real Crips?" They spoke very proper English in P.O.

"Yeah, they Rips, but we're on different levels. They are gang members and I'm a gang banger." I told them.

"What's the difference?" they asked

Instead of explaining their position, I explained mine.

"A gang banger puts in all the work." I left it like that.

My money was short and I needed to hit a lick fast.

Le'Taxione (a.k.a. YoYo)

There were a couple of rock houses in the hood and they quickly became sources of income. I walked into one under the premise that I was going to buy some dope. Once I got on the inside I pulled my heat and said "This is a robbery Cuzz, don't make it no murder". I laid everybody down and took nothing but their guns and money. I left the dope. As I left I said "Cuzz this Diamond!"

After the jack I asked Andrea "Who's spot was that?" She told me it belonged to a couple of cats named Robert and Dontay and that they owned two spots. I said to myself that I might as well go hit the other one and I did. I guess Robert and Dontay had problems because they put the word out that they were looking for me. But they couldn't have been looking too hard because I was in the hood everyday. I felt that they put the word out just to save face. This was a weakness and I exploited it.

Every time they opened a spot, I jacked it. I was walking back to G-Moms house one day and a white BMW pulled up beside me. I pulled my heat and laid it against my thigh out of sight and said "West up Cuzz?" The driver of the car asked me what my name was and I stopped walking and told him "Mr. YoYo Locs.".

"Can I talk to you?" he asked "I'm Robert."

I said "I don't give a fuck Cuzz. This Crip!"

"I'm not trippin' man, I just want to talk to you and hope that we can come to an understanding." He told me.

Robert was an older cat. He was probably about 36 then. He was very tall, slim and well spoken. All the while we talked I kept my heat pressed up against my outer right thigh. If this cat made any erratic move I was going to leave his lanky ass stretched right out there on Ainsworth and his car would become his coffin.

He said "I know that you're from Cal and I know you're hungry. I also know that you ain't wit sellin' no dope."

Original Diamond Boy

I could see that this cat had done his homework.

"Cuzz, I can look through muddy water and see dry land and I know that you have a proposition for me." I said.

Rip had taught me that after you've moved on a cat and he approaches you talking, he always has a proposition for you.

"Come work for me." He said.

"Cuzz, I don't sell dope." I told him.

"I don't want you to sell dope. I want you to protect my spots." He said.

It was an ingenious proposition because he clearly didn't have the means to stop me from hitting his spots and because of that fact, his weakness was exposed. If he didn't get some security everybody would be jackin' his spots so why not get the cat that was brazen enough to jack him to protect him from being jacked. He always respected that move and I respected his.

"Come by the spot tomorrow about 9:00 a.m. he said and I said "Right."

I knew that this cat could be setting me up to get moved on but regardless I had to accept the invitation because to not accept it would show fear and I didn't fear nothing that had two legs and an asshole that pointed towards the ground.

I got up early and made it to the hood at about 7:45 a.m. and watched as the time approached to meet the doeboy. 8:45 came and he showed up. I watched as he and another cat got out of the car and walked into the spot. As soon as they closed the door I ran up to the spot and knocked on the door.

A voice from inside hollered "Who is it?"

"Diamond Boy" I hollered back as I stepped back off of the porch.

A short light skinned cat opened the door as I stood

Le'Taxione (a.k.a. YoYo)

there heat pressed to my outer right thigh. The cat smiled and said "come in". I walked in and stood by the front door which I refused to close. Robert said "What's up and introduced me to Dontay. I motioned with my head to him but didn't speak to him verbally.

Robert got right to it.

"I'll give you $200 a night to work the door in my spot." He said.

"$200 and you buy my breakfast, lunch and dinner." I Said.

He said "cool".

"And I have the only heata in the house." I continued.

He asked me why and I told him "I don't want one of your coward ass doeboys giving one of their niggas his heata and getting' everybody killed."

I told him that when I hit his spot I took all of the heatas and that that was not going to happen while I was up in there. He said that was cool.

Robert called the boy that was to hold the dope and the boy that was to hold the money and told them to come to the spot. It took them about 20 minutes to arrive. Once they got there Robert explained that I was security and asked how I wanted the house to be set up.

I told him that I would man the front door and that I wanted the cat that was holding the dope to be in the room by himself. Also, I wanted the cat holding the money in the front room with me. I explained that the people would come in two at a time. I would check them for weapons and after the cat in the back room was notified by the money cat of the amount purchased, they would walk into the back room to get their rocks.

This system would put me in control of the buyer and the money, leaving the dope to it's own devices. Because I was letting two people at a time come in, my weapon of choice was a 12 gauge sawed off pump shotgun. Normally it shot four shells but there was a spring that if removed would allow you to store eight shells. The reasons for it being sawed off were several: by the barrel and the butt being sawed off, it made it hard for a person to grab it; it was easier to wield and when blasted because the barrel was sawed off, it would spray the buckshots from the shells covering more space. It was the ideal weapon to move the crowd.

There came a time when I had to allow more people in at a time to prevent long lines in front of the spot. One time a smoker came through and commented on the security.

"Ya'll ain't playin' up in here. I bet Jaylon and Darnell won't come in her trying to jack shit." He said.

After this cat purchased his dope and left I asked the cat holding the money "Who is Jaylon and Darnell?" He began to explain that they were two red rags that got hooked on that dope and were jackin' all the spots. I drew from his statement that though they were using this drug, they were ridas and I took the smoker's statement very seriously.

A week later Jaylon and Darnell came to the spot at about 2:00 a.m. The only reason that I knew it was them is that after they left, the cat holding the money told me. They came back the next night and when they came in the cat Jaylon said "What's up dog?"

"West Up Loc!" I responded.

Back then red rags called each other dogs and blue rags called each other loc. He looked surprised but he gave the cat $20 and proceeded to the back room. I kept the heat trained on Darnell. One false move and I would have to kill the slob and go back to Cali but everything went smooth. Smoother than I even knew.

Chapter 42

"It was imperative that I kept it Cali".

- YoYo

The next morning Robert came by.
"YoYo, come ride wit me." he said coming out of the back room.
We went to get something to eat and as we were riding he asked "Is everything cool at the spot?"
"Fo sho!" Why, West Up?" I asked.
He explained that for the past two days the count had been extremely off.
"Is that right? What the cat holdin' the sack say happened to the count?" I asked.
"This nigga sayin' he don't know." He replied.
I told him to turn around and go back to the spot.
"I'll show you how to find out."
We got back to the spot and walked in. I said nothing but Robert called everybody to the front room. Once every-

Le'Taxione (a.k.a. YoYo)

body was present I began walking around the house closing all the open doors. I then started pulling down the shades in the front room one by one. All the while nobody said a word. I told everybody to sit down and they did. I sat blocking the front door facing the money man and the sack man. I then picked up the sawed off, laid it across my lap and began shoving the shells into it. The sack boy asked "What's happenin'?" "Nigga, shut up!" I said. Those cats were about to cry.

After I got the last shell in, I told Robert to go into the room and grab a sheet off of the bed. He did and returned with the sheet.

"Spread it out on the floor" I told him.

He did.

"You niggas take off all of your clothes and stand in the middle of that sheet." I instructed.

Now they were crying like bitches. After they got naked and stood in the middle of the sheet I said "I'm gonna ask you one question and if you don't tell me the truth, I'm gonna kill you niggas and wrap you up in that sheet you standin' in".

"Why in the fuck has the count been short for the past two days?" I asked as I cocked the gauge –chick-chick.

"Jaylon been takin' it from me and tellin' me if I say anything he was gonna shoot up my mama's house." The sack man said.

I turned to Robert and said "Cuzz shoot me $3,000 and I'll make sure that those slobs won't jack another one of yo spots. Give me $1,500 up front and $1,500 after I put in work."

"Cool" he said.

I told the worker that when they came that night to go on and open the door and step to the side.

About 3:00 a.m. a knock came at the door. The money

man looked at me scared as hell and I asked "who is it?" Jaylon answered identifying himself. The money man went to the door, opened it and stepped to the side and I let them have it – boo yaw – boo yaw! They broke and I ran to the front door, stood on the porch and busted at them again while they were running.

The next day Robert came by G-Moms house and gave me my other $1,500.

"I'm through with that rock house shit." I told him, "but if you ever need some muscle get at me". We parted ways.

I had put in work on the most notorious bloods in P.O. at that time. My name and my hood was ringing on the lips of the people. War was ignited in this very act and would last for the next seven years but I loved the beef. I found peace in the chaos and embraced conflict. I had all three, beef, chaos and conflict.

I put my gauge up and started packing my .45 with three extra clips. I was in a state by myself but I was a Rida. I knew that these cats would beef but they didn't beef like I beefed. I introduced them to that on sight mentality – meaning wherever I saw you, with whomever you were with, I was getting at your ass in a real way!

I kicked back for one day and prepared myself mentally for this war. The next day I returned to the hood. I got to my favorite corner on 9th and Sumner and posted up. A lot of young cats were approaching me saying that they wanted to be Diamonds, begging me to put them on my hood.

A news crew came through and was doing a story on gangs and asked if they could interview me. I agreed. I did the interview from the corner detailing my plan to take over that hood. After the interview, Andrea came up and told me that her cousin wanted to meet me. She began to tell me that her cousin was from out of state and a college graduate. They called her Natasha.

Le'Taxione (a.k.a. YoYo)

Natasha didn't know that Andrea had already told me that she was interested and tried to feign a lack of interest at the introduction. After she introduced us I asked her a couple of questions. How old was she and where was she from. She was five or six years older than me but I liked the fact that she wasn't from P.O.

After she answered my questions I told her to get at me and walked off the porch back to the corner. I'd never chased a female in my life and I wasn't going to start now. If she wanted to be with a Diamond she was going to have to get past that hard to get bullshit.

Around the same time I met several other females who were very interested in this out of town Crip. I was introduced to Amber, Jenny, Nesha and Shonna. I started a relationship with all of them. Why not? This was my California demonstration and it was imperative that regardless of being in P.O. that I kept it Cali. This is what gave me the edge on these P.O. cats. They were about 10 years behind California and I exploited that fact to my benefit.

Amber was a very light skinned female with long hair and hazel eyes. She was tall and thin but very proportionate. She laughed a lot but I saw the pain beneath her laughter. She had been involved in a very abusive relationship with this cat named Johnny and she truly hadn't gotten past that.

Nesha was short, thick and dark skinned. She was a hustler. She was into the identity theft game and was good at it. She'd go into clothing or sometimes jewelry stores and come out with what people ordered. Then she'd sell it half price. Nesha was very outgoing.

Shonna was a mama's girl. She stayed with her mother but frequented house parties. She was dark and very thin. She was more like a homegirl than a girlfriend.

Jenny was brown skinned with short hair. She was thin

with long legs. Jenny's self esteem was very low. It was obvious that though she was a beautiful girl, she couldn't see her own beauty. In Portland the standard of beauty was light skin with long hair. I'd never seen so many ethnically mixed people in my life. Jenny's hair was very short which you could tell had been the subject of cruel jokes. She was very reserved and quiet but one of the things I truly liked about her was that there was no man alive outside of me for her. She wouldn't unnecessarily speak or talk to other men and though I was not loyal to her, she was very loyal to me. As a matter of fact, she was one of the most loyal females that I'd ever been with.

Amber and I would go out to eat and have sex. Nesha and I would go shopping and have sex. Shonna and I would get high and have sex, but Jenny and I would spend a lot of time talking…then have sex. They all had different positions in my life and as long as everybody played their position it was cool.

I didn't trust Amber, Nesha or Shonna but I did trust Jenny and she never betrayed that trust. This being the case, I spent more time with Jenny than I did with all of the rest put together.

Chapter 43

"You can't bang and have money..."

- YoYo

I continued to man the hood by myself and my California bravado continued to draw enemies.

One day this red rag named El-Dog came through the hood flyin and hit me up. I hit him and his Homies up as they flew past in some type of Regal or Cutlass. Later on that night El-Dog and his homeboys came back and got off on me – boom-boom-boom – pack-pack-pack!

"Inglewood Family nigga" they yelled.

I busted back when I figured they were retreating – buck-buck-buck-buck. "Diamonds mutha fucka!

Words can't explain the feeling that I got inside every time I was involved in a gun fight. The adrenaline mixed with the homicidal mind and suicidal proclivities of a true banger made me unstoppable. I was YoYo the Crip Monster. Can't stop. Won't stop. Don't want to stop! The gun battles magnified that fact.

When Duce heard about what happened he got back active and I was happy about it. Duce was a Crip monster too and he and I went to war with the whole town. I started putting cats on the hood (initiating them into the Diamonds). One of the first cats I put on the hood was a cat I named Lil Black. I would put cats on the hood and give them the homies from Fresno names to identify the fact that I had put them on, legitimizing their membership.

Lil Black was a young Rida. After getting down with me I went with him on a mission to get off on some red rags. This validated the fact that they were too his enemy and he theirs. I would repeat this ritual with all of the new homies that I put on the set.

It was important that I went on the mission with them. You never wanted a soldier to think that you were asking him to do something that you wouldn't do. That way you stayed attached to the soldiers. I didn't believe in that mentality that made it cool for the older homies to send the younger ones to put in work while they sat at home waiting to hear the outcome. Plus I loved that shit.

I planned hits on the red rag's hoods with military precision and began setting up our hood like a military fort with soldiers posted everywhere, that was my strong point. I stayed military minded and taught the young homies the pure philosophy, tactics and techniques that would someday save their lives in battle. I taught them everything from when to get off to how to get off and what to say while they were getting off.

I introduced them to the on sight philosophy and the never leave a homeboy behind doctrine. I taught them about loyalty, honor, respect, integrity and retaliation. I made them Diamonds and they loved me for it.

We began to throw Crip parties which included a lot of

Original Diamond Boy

young females. They were used to seeing the Crips from L.A. come through flawsin' their Chevys, Caddies, and Cutlasses on Roadsters and Daytons (rims) but they weren't used to kicking it with pure bangers. They weren't used to the love that we exhibited towards each other. We jacked, hit jewelry stores and gun shops for our paper and protection and while our L.A. counterparts got money, they weren't as violent. Not that they couldn't have been, but in the dope game you can't bang and have money.

They entered into business endeavors with red rags in order to proliferate drugs in the communities for the more they proliferated the more money they made. I saw this as a weakness and spoke vehemently against it.

Chapter 44

"I'd stand on the corner in order to let cats know that regardless of how many red rags were in the area, that spot was controlled by Crips."

- YoYo

El-Dog went to jail and the Inglewood family became extinct. By this time we were also beefin' with red rags out of L.A.. In '87 we were actively beefin' with the Pirus, Lutus Park, Syndo Mob, Bounty Hunters, Rollin' 20s and a new hood was beginning to form called Woodlawn Park.

I turned over control of the Diamonds to Duce and took a trip back to Fresno to come up on some more heat that was not from the state of Oregon. Once I got there I was riding with my homegirl Lady Tyson and she was shermed out. The police pulled us over and because I had a warrant for not reporting, I was taken to Fresno County Jail. I was given 90 days for parole violation.

Le'Taxione (a.k.a. YoYo)

I talked to Jenny and the Natasha frequently. Jenny kept me posted on the war and Natasha now wanted to be my woman. They both expressed their loyalty and sent money to my books for the 90 days that I was down.

I got out and talked to my homeboy Big Bread (RIP) from 62 East coast. I told him that I was going back to Oregon where I had started the Diamonds and that I had planned to also start the 62 East Coasts there. He gave me his blessings. This showed that our hoods were truly one and it opened the door for the L.A. East Coasts to enter the scene.

I visited the homies and put the heat that I'd purchased in The No in a duffle bag and got on the Greyhound back to P.O. Once I got back to P.O. I told Duce of my plan to start the East Coasts to enhance our territory and create an ally that we could depend on. He understood.

We now had a spot on Grand off of Ainsworth in the vicinity of Woodlawn Park. I called a meeting, distributed the heat and began to designate hit teams that would rotate the obligation to put in work. We were getting at the red rags in shifts and they didn't know how to deal with that.

A week later the movie Colors" hit theatres in P.O. At this time I had only five or six cats on East Coast but that was about to change. The movie served as a major recruiting tool and I was a major recruiter.

I chose not to go to the movie with the homies. I felt like I'd been living Colors all my life. I didn't need to watch the movie but Duce went with the little homies and they tore up the theatre.

By this time my little cousin Jason had just started banging the hood and because he had watched me all his life he was far more advanced than the other little homies. On my name he was accepted in The No as a Diamond though he started in P.O.

Original Diamond Boy

The next day I went by Natasha's house. She stayed on 30th and Killingsworth, a well traveled strip by everyone. We talked for a while and she suggested that I move in with her. I didn't like the idea but I ended up keeping a couple of outfits at the house for when I'd come through and spend the night. Every time I'd spend the night at her house I'd have the little homies, Looney, Lil' Solo, Lil Crazy, Lil Cboy, and Jason come pick me up the next day. I'd stand out on the corner in order to let cats know that regardless of how many red rags were in the area, that spot was controlled by Crips.

A cat walked up to me that day and introduced himself as Popeye from Grape Street. Grape Street was a Crip hood in Los Angeles. He said he had a sister that lived in the neighboring apartments who was interested in meeting me. I told him to go get her. He walked away and came back with this very black female whose body was nice as hell. He said "This is my sister Laila."

They began to explain that they were from L.A. and that she had been watching me and wanted to get at me. I took her number. She told me that she was living with her sister but that she was moving in the next week and to call her before then. I saw the homies pulling up, said "right" and got in the car.

"Who was that, homie?" Looney asked.

I told him. Looney was one of my closest little homies and he ran the car when Duce or myself weren't around. Looney patterned himself after me and was a straight killa.

Chapter 45

"...everytime they would attempt to respond to one shooting, they would get a call to respond to another."

- YoYo

The Diamonds were established and the East Coasts were growing so we had to expand the turf that we controlled and we did – by violence.

My plan to hit red rags in shifts proved to be a very effective tactic. Then I dispensed squads of five to sweat enemy hoods and would have the first squad hit their hood and 15 minutes later have the next squad hit another hood. This threw the police off because every time they would attempt to respond to one shooting they would get a call to respond to another. Then I'd wait until shift change at the Portland Police Department and Duce, Soldier Boy and I would go and put in work.

At headquarters I would have the homeboys patrolling the front and the back and have Lil' Solo up in the tree in

Le'Taxione (a.k.a. YoYo)

front of the house with binoculars. Red rags attempted to creep on us but we saw them while they were two blocks away, positioned our soldiers and lit their asses up when they drove through. These military tactics kept our spot from getting shot up and saved lives. The whole town would talk about how the Diamonds and the East Coasts demonstrated like a military brigade.

Chapter 46

"I woke up one day and decided we were going to take Woodlawn Park."

- YoYo

I woke up one day and decided we were going to take Woodland Park. We lived about four blocks from there. Woodlawn was a red rag hood and in order to protect headquarters I felt it essential that we take the park.

I called the homeboys and the homegirls and told them to get to the spot. I told the homegirls that had children to bring them along with diaper bags and strollers. I called Jenny and told her that I would need her to baby-sit the homegirl's children for an hour at the spot. Once everyone arrived I told them the plan.

The females with strollers and diaper bags would go to the park first. They would put the heatas in the diaper bags, hang the diaper bags on the strollers and walk to the basket ball court in Woodland Park. The Homeboys would come

Le'Taxione (a.k.a. YoYo)

afterwards and take the park.

Jenny finally arrived to watch the children so I sent the homegirls to the park. It was about 1:00 p.m. and we would give them about ten minutes, then we would walk to the park.

We started on our way. Once we got there, there were red rags on the court playing basketball. I walked through their game and said "West Up Cuzz?" They didn't say anything. I grabbed the ball and said "Cuzz, We takin' over this park. From this day on, this is a Crip park."

When I looked up the police pulled up from every direction, pulled their weapons and ordered everyone to the ground. The females simply walked away, heatas and all as planned. All except Baby. Hot mouth stayed there the whole time ridiculing the police and I was happy. They were getting tired of the gang activity in P.O. but it was about to get worse.

Chapter 47

"He had violated the sanctity of the home, making his home or anybody else's home related to him a primary target. That was the rule!"

- YoYo

In '88 the Homeboy Lil Chocolate came to the spot and said that he had located a low income housing complex where a few cats claiming to be Crips hung out. We immediately got in two cars and drove out there. It was called the Columbia Villa Housing complex. Once we arrived I fell in love with it. It was the only place in P.O. that reminded me of the projects.

We got out of the cars and began to walk through the hood. I saw a couple of young cats awkwardly dressed like Rips but no signs of a set. Then I saw Popeye.

"West up Loco?" I said

I was happy to see a familiar face that could give me the grapes (information) on this hood.

Le'Taxione (a.k.a. YoYo)

"What's up?" he asked.

I was used to hearing cats from Grape Street say "Watts up" but he never said that. I made a mental note of it and kept rotating.

"Who hood is this Cuzz?" I asked.

He told me it was nobody's but that there were a few Rips there.

I asked him what he was doing out there and he told me that his sister lived out there on Adriatic street. We went to a small park and it reminded me of the mini park in Fresno and right then I told myself "I'm going to stay out there".

Popeye introduced me to A-Bone and Seven. They were the young wannabees that I'd noticed earlier but they weren't no punks. A cat named Tarrif got off the bus at a stop in front of the mini park. Tarrif was a red rag and everybody knew it but these cats acted like it was a normal occurrence. I tripped.

"What's this slob doing here?" I asked

When nobody answered I opened my Pendleton exposing the sawed off shotgun that I had tied at both ends with a shoestring and hung across my shoulder.

"What the fuck you doin' out here?" I asked him.

He was slow to answer so I took the gauge off of my shoulder and slapped him with it. Then I cocked it. I was going to blast him on the spot but Popeye, A-Bone and Seven told me not to do it right there.

"There's too many people watchin'" they said.

This told me that they weren't ready for this kind of activity.

"Cuzz If I don't kill this nigga now, he'll be back." I told them.

"I'm not coming back." He said crying.

I let him go but I knew that this cat was coming back. If he had enough heart to come to this hood by himself he

Original Diamond Boy

would definitely come back and I was right.

After he left I said "Cuzz, ya'll got to protect your hood. You can't let these Red Rags come through like that".

"His mother lives here." A-Bone said.

"Make her move! Your mother lives her too and it's only a matter of time before his homeboys convince him to give them the best route to creep on you." I told him.

I sent the homeboys back to our spot in case the boy Tarrif told the police about being slapped with a gun and I went to Laila's house with Popeye just in case the homeboys were pulled over. I, being the one who slapped him with the gun wouldn't be in the car, nor would the gun.

I walked into the house and Laila's Face lit up.

"What's up YoYo! What you doin' out here? Why didn't you call?"

"I came over" I answered.

She smiled and I saw a little boy and a little girl and asked her if they were hers. She told me they were and that the girl was named Embaba and the boy's name was Raymond.

I walked around the house and looked in all of the closets. I always did that after those cats jumped out on me in The No. I went to her bathroom. Once I closed the bathroom door I looked in her medicine cabinet to see what kind of medication was being taken. If there was a prescription for penicillin I knew that someone had gonorrhea and not to hit them panties.

I looked under the sink in the cabinet to see if there were feminine hygiene products. If there was none, the female wasn't clean and I would not hit them panties. Everything was on point. I was definitely going to hit them panties.

I came back into the front room after my inspection.

Le'Taxione (a.k.a. YoYo)

We heard gun shots – pow-pow-pow. I ducked, grabbed the children and ran them into the back room. I came back into the front room cradling my sawed off. I burst out of the back door in the direction of the gun shots. I'd always exercised this tactic. It was statistically known that people get blasted more often running away from gunshots than running to them. Of course, this could have been because people with common sense never ran towards gunshots, but I'd been lucky using this tactic.

Once I got outside I crouched down looking for the shooter.

"It was Tarrif. He went that way." a female, who would later find out was named NaeNae said.

He was long gone so I asked Popeye where he stayed. Popeye and I went to his mother's house in the Vill. I walked up on the side of the house and peered through the window. It was dark inside and I couldn't see anything moving. I told Popeye to go knock on the door while I stood on the side of the house next to the window. He knocked and I heard a woman say "Who is it?" I faced the window and blasted into the house twice – boo yaaw-boo yaw! He had violated the sanctity of the home, making his home or anybody else's home related to him a primary target. That was the rules! Do unto others as they do unto you.

When we got back to Laila's house, Popeye told her everything. I sat on the couch and lit up a joint. Popeye had a 40 ounce of 800 (malt liquor) in the ice box. He got it, popped the top and we celebrated. I called the spot and told the homies what happened and they asked if I wanted them to come get me.

"Not tonight. This block is hot...police everywhere. Come get me in the morning." I told them. "Duce love.".

"Duce love." Jason shot back and we hung up.

That night I stretched out on the couch. Laila woke me

up, grabbed my hand and led me to her room. I lay in the bed as the moon shined through the window. I watched her silhouette as she took off her clothes. She had a bangin' little red bone body with grayish eyes and shoulder length curly hair and I looked forward to the experience. She climbed in the bed and laid her head on my chest. I traced her body with my hand. That night I hit them panties.

The next day she asked if I would move in with her. I told her that I'd spend the night from time to time but that I had my own spot.

The homies came at about 10:00 a.m. After they picked me up I had them take me to Natasha's house. I took a shower and changed clothes. Natasha called me to the room and said "Let's have a party tonight."

"Cool." I said. "I'll be back. I got some things to handle".

I had not spent any time with Jenny since the Woodlawn Park takeover and I wanted to kick it with her. I liked talking to Jenny. She was the sweetest, most innocent one of them all. I told her that I wanted to spend some time with her at the tel (motel) that night, she was with that.

That night I got us a room and we spent the night talking and laughing. We didn't have sex but we had fun. I'd given Jason the tel room number in case something happened. They had the party anyway that night. That morning Natasha called the tel screaming.

"Why didn't you come to the party?"

"I had other things to do." I told her.

"You layin' up with some bitch!" she said and hung up the phone.

I immediately got up and took Jenny home and mashed to Natasha's house. *How dare this bitch hang up on me,* was my first thought. Then I asked myself *how in the hell did she get the number.* I pulled over and called

Le'Taxione (a.k.a. YoYo)

her from a phone booth.
"Hello" she belted.
"Let me talk to Jason!" I demanded.
I could hear her scream "Jason, YoYo want you."
"West Up Cuzz?" Jason's voice came over the phone.
I said "Cuzz, who told that bitch that I was at the tel?"
"That nigga Lil Solo told her that." He answered.
"Don't tell him I'm on my way. Duce Law." I instructed him.

I pulled up in front of the spot, jumped out, and bailed up to the door and rung the doorbell. Jason opened the door and I pushed passed him. At a glance I could see beer bottles everywhere and Jason and his girl, May, were sitting on the couch and Lil' Solo was laying on the other couch.

I walked in the room where Natasha was and got my .38 off of the dresser and walked back into the front room with the .38 and my sawed off. By this time Lil' Solo was awake and as I walked into the front room I tossed him the .38. He let the trey eight hit the couch and bounce off onto the floor.

"Pick it up Cuzz." I said.
"What for?" he asked.
I cocked the sawed off and said "Nigga pick it up!"
Jason said, "Don't do this YoYo."
I screamed "Shut up nigga! And told Lil' Solo again to pick it up.

He still wouldn't pick up the trey eight so I said "Nigga, I'm gonna count to ten and if you don't pick it up, I'm gonna blast yo ass anyway!"

Lil' Solo jumped up and ran right through the screen door and down the street in nothing but his boxers.

"Why you do that YoYo?" Jason asked.

I told him that if he'd tell a bitch about something small, he'd tell the police about something big. Those words turned out to be prophetic later on in life - Lil' Solo turned snitch.

I reluctantly spent the night at Natasha's house that night after reiterating the posture that I'd taken at the inception of the relationship.

"Look Cuzz, I told you from the giddy up (beginning) that you were not going to be my only female. That's the demonstration and if you can't come to grips with that, this is where the road turns."

"Diamond Callin'"

I'm wanted dead or alive will I survive to see another day getting' high
2-0-9 avoiding the chalk lines where soldiers lye
I'm losin homies to phonies that don't deserve the glory
And scandalous bitches and snitches is left to tell the story
Chaos is gory and for me up out of my resignation
I'm on a binge for revenge here comes the confrontation
No time for waitin' no patience because revenge is swift
Retaliation no faking when I let the clip spit
Then I trip, what about the promise that I made my lady
As I dip to be a father to my little babies
Am I shady to love the dub like I love my cubs
Hold my mud and ask forgiveness from the God above
Run amuck or you'll get bucked that's how this bangin' goes
You'll get stuck down in the ground if you ain't on your toes
Then your body'll rest in grief with a graveyard wreath
Some may call for peace but they've yet to see
The Diamonds callin' for me.

Chapter 48

> *"Fight Cuzz" I told him as I spread two fingers over his heart... "Don't let go."*
>
> *- YoYo*

There was a murder in the Piedmont apartments and Lil Crazy, Lil C-boy, Curl, and myself were summoned to appear in front of the grand jury on the murder. This was my first time in P.O. being scrutinized for murder, but it wouldn't be my last. We all walked away from the grand jury without an indictment at that time. But little did we know that that grand jury hearing would eventually lead to major contention within the ranks and that contention would spark betrayal.

Duce had moved to Seattle so I groomed Soldier boy to run Diamonds while I ran East coast. I would eventually run both but for then I wanted Soldier to run it. By this time we had other homeboys from Diamond in P.O. but they were doeboys. Cats like Slim, Rico, Bay and others. They

Le'Taxione (a.k.a. YoYo)

would rotate in and out of P.O. for the purpose of getting money.

I'd established Diamond by the gun and this facilitated their endeavor to come behind that and set up shop. That didn't bother me at all. They'd put in work in Cal but now they were on something else. That was the choice they made. But I chose to stay in the trenches with the soldiers.

Jason had entered the dope game and was very successful at it but his bangin' suffered. Don't get me wrong now. He would put in work but not on the strength. He mostly revolved around his dope spot. In this gang shit once you lose the desire to destroy your enemy it's time to retire from the trenches and rotate on the periphery and that's what the doeboys did. But us banga's, we stayed in the thick of it, nose to the grindin' stone and loved every minute of it. We didn't have the cars, jewelry and houses that our homeboys that slung dope had but we had the corners and without the corners the doeboys couldn't get money.

I watched the Columbia Villa Crips emerge under my direct guidance. I taught them everything from the physical to the psychological, to the philosophical aspects of this Crippin'. I even taught them how to throw up their hood. I mentored A-bone and Seven, the original CVCs. We rotated and put in work together on the daily.

Everyday I'd strategically position soldiers around the mini park. One day some Inglewood families tried to ride through and dump on us but because we were strategically positioned we were able to light them up and run them out of the hood.

A couple of months passed by with no more attempts inside the hood to get at us but now we were beefin' with the police. They would come through, make all of us get on our knees and check our pockets, all while using excessive force. They came through so frequently that we would have

Original Diamond Boy

to hide our heat in a tree stump and stay at least ten feet away from the stump. This put our lives in jeopardy and one day we got tired.

We were all on the basketball courts. There were about 20 of us and the police came through talking shit over their squad car intercoms.

"We're tired of you dirt bags always out here. Take your black asses somewhere else." They boomed.

As usual, I spoke up "Fuck you peckawoods!" And the homies joined in. We slung insults back and forth and all of a sudden a bottle came from out of the crowd.

"BaaYaaw! It crashed up against the police car and splattered. We then began throwing rocks and bottles at them. They called for back up and when they arrived they emerged from the cars, guns drawn. I was the only one that got arrested that day. I was booked for inciting a riot and released.

The next day a news crew came to the Vill to cover the incident. They'd heard from some of the residents that the police had started the confrontation and they wanted to interview us. While they were filming, I jumped in the news van and took off. I drove around the Vill in the van and came back and parked it in the same place I got it from. We laughed our asses off about that and it broke up the monotony, at least for a minute.

A week later we were all at A-Bone's house. We started drinking at about 1:00 p.m. that afternoon. We decided to go to the rec department. I told Lil' Black to go up on the roof so that we couldn't get crept on. About an hour later, the Inglewood families tried to come through again and again we let them have it, causing them to wreck their cars. Lil Black opened fire first, letting us know that they were coming. A-Bone, Seven and myself ran out to the street and let off on them. They didn't have a chance.

Le'Taxione (a.k.a. YoYo)

Later on that day, two Mexican females came to the hood. A-Bone was getting at them when I approached. I asked him their names and he told me.

"Cuzz, who know these bitches? I told ya'll you can't let these stray ass bitches just come into the hood like this. You don't know these bitches." I said.

We'd have long meetings about knowing your hood and everybody in it. I spoke many times on how females were used by the enemy to set you up. The homeboy, Solo in Fresno was set up by some Mexican female which resulted in his demise but the homies were young and they'd not experienced this gang shit to that extent and though they listened at the time, this occurrence let me know that they really didn't take it all to heart. I walked over to the mini park by myself and sat on the picnic table bench and watched as the young homies showered the females with attention.

They walked off together. I guess they went to Seven's house. I was sitting on the bench drinking some Wild Irish Rose (wine) when Tanay and Nakesha walked up. Tanay and Nakesha were some of the young homegirls. By this time, night had fallen and I told them to go home in case the red rags came back through on some get back (retaliation). After having to raise my voice at them they left. Lil' Nakesha liked me but she was too young. I could tell that her feelings were hurt but it was for their own safety.

A-Bone walked up with another lil' homeboy that I didn't know by name, but his face was familiar. I told him to take the shotgun over to the adjacent parking lot in case the red rags came through.

"You can hit them from that direction." I told him.

He took the gauge and walked over to the parking lot. At that time, Soldier Boy, Seven and those same Mexican females came from the direction of Seven's house.

Original Diamond Boy

They were about five feet away from me when I heard an engine rev and tires screeching. By the time I turned my head in the direction of the car I heard multiple gunshots and I felt someone or something push me off of the bench to the ground. When I hit the ground I laid as flat as possible on my stomach. I lay so flat that it seemed as though my body had sunk into the earth beneath me.

I looked in the direction of A-bone and I could see that he was returning fire but the cat that was with him wasn't. A-Bone dumped on the car as it road towards him. I looked in the direction of Seven and saw that he was laying flat on his back. I crawled on my stomach to him. When I got to him, his eyes were opened but he wasn't talking. All of this transpired in the midst of gunfire.

I scooped Seven up, placing my body between him and the gunfire. After the gunfire ceased I looked at my homeboy. I noticed a small hole in his forehead.

"Hold on Cuzz." I said.

A bus came and stopped in front of the mini park.

"Tell them to call an ambulance." I told Soldier. I looked back down at the homie and told him to hold on as I cried.

"Fight Cuzz." I told him as I spread two fingers over his heart. "don't let go."

I could feel his body shake and it seemed as if his soul elevated. I knew he was dead but I continued to hold him crying asking God "Why didn't you take me?"

Blood rushed from the back of Seven's head onto my black khakis. A-Bone came from across the way, saw Seven and went crazy. They had grown up together from childhood to adolescence. The sight was too much for him to bare and he was never the same from that day on.

The ambulance and police arrived on the scene but I was gone psychologically. As I sat there cradling Seven, I

Le'Taxione (a.k.a. YoYo)

was already plotting the get back. Somebody had to pay for this life cut down in it's prime. Somebody had to pay for the anguish that I saw on his mother's face, the pain that tore her insides apart!

Somebody had to pay!

Chapter 49

"Rest in Paradise Homie. I'll see you when I get there."
- YoYo

Seven was no longer with us.
The container that held his spirit was empty so I relinquished his body to the ambulance personnel. The police asked me what I'd witnessed.

"Nothing." I answered. "I can describe the sounds but nothing else."

There was no way that I was going to allow the police to save those niggas by arresting them. They had to see me and feel the wrath and if I couldn't catch them, anybody that they loved would suffice.

The next morning they arrested those bustas claimin' Inglewood Family. They weren't even certified members. They were wannabees but that's the reality of this gang lifestyle. Wannabees are the first stage of gonnabees!

The night after the assassination of Seven I organized

Le'Taxione (a.k.a. YoYo)

our get back campaign. Everybody met at Soldier Boy's spot. Cats had gotten drunk and the alcohol gave them a false bravado. I couldn't put in work with anybody that displayed a willingness driven by liquid courage (alcohol) so I got rid of all of the alcohol and waited until everyone sobered up. Just as I thought, courage faded.

"Who ready for the get back campaign?" I asked once everyone was sober. It got so quiet that you could hear a mouse pissin' on cotton. Those who weren't ready, I excused from the details by sending them home. There were only two cats from CVC that put in work and the rest were Diamonds and East Coasts. We hit red rag hoods in shifts all that night.

It was time to prepare for the comrade's funeral. Emotions were running high and Portland police expressed concerns to the media for gang violence during and after the funeral. I orchestrated the Diamonds and East Coasts entry and exit to and from the funeral and though we knew that the Portland Police Department would exhibit a visual presence at the funeral to deter any violence, we would still attend the funeral strapped (with guns).

There was a media frenzy at the funeral. We all attended in blue Khaki suits with blue rags tied on our heads Aunt Jemimah style and the media caught all of that in their attempt to sensationalize the tragedy.

As I walked by the casket with the empty container in it, I placed my two fingers on his chest and said "Rest in Paradise homie. I'll see you when I get there." I didn't think that I would be alive that long and it seemed that death was getting closer and closer to me.

We met back up in the Vill and the 4/3 Gangsta Crips from L.A. came to pay their respects. My Homies J-Bo, Ace and Sherm Dog were a few among the 4/3s that I knew who paid their respects. Also Stax and Spades from IVC paid respects. It was a somber time that exposed the Portland Crips to mortality and the seriousness of the lifestyle we chose to live. Needless to say, a lot of cats reevaluated their decision to Crip. Most fell off but the ones that stayed down became more security conscious.

A newspaper article came out stating that the cats that were arrested for Seven's murder said that they were not trying to kill Seven, they were trying to kill a Crip named YoYo. After the story broke animosity rose between the Diamond, East Coasts, the CVCs and Kerby Block Crips. They felt that since they were trying to kill me, it was my fault that Seven got assassinated. I told them that if they gave a fuck about Seven that they would have put in work.

Chapter 50

"They blamed me and other cats from Cali for their gang problem and they wanted me off of the Portland streets."
- YoYo

One day, Popeye and I were in the Vill. Popeye was slangin' dope and though I was with him I wasn't slangin'. I had a half pint of Nightrain in a paper bag when the police rode up on us. I threw the bag to the curb and Popeye threw his pill bottle full of crack rocks. The police didn't want Popeye, they wanted me. They blamed me and other cats from Cali for their gang problem and wanted me off of the Portland streets. They lied and said that the crack was mine and arrested me for possession of a controlled substance. They put both Popeye and I in the squad car then they let him go. I would find out later in a police report that Popeye had told them that he and I came up from California to sell drugs and that I was a general in the Crip gang. I called Laila and told her what her brother had done and that

Le'Taxione (a.k.a. YoYo)

he needed to come ride his beef (do his time).

I was attending the court dates but Popeye was a no show. Finally they offered me a deal which consisted of me doing nine months in prison after which I would be eligible for parole. I pondered the possibilities. I couldn't tell on Popeye though he had implicated me. I didn't get down like that and if I went to the pen I could get at the Inglewood Families that supposedly tried to kill me. I took the deal and was sentenced to prison.

Chapter 51

"Prison is a microcosm that reflects society at large."
- YoYo

My reputation preceded me as always. Once I hit receiving, there was a Crip porter that came with the welcome of all the Crips on the yard (in the facility). The first thing that I asked was whether the Inglewood's that smoked (killed) Seven were there. He told me that two of them were, and I asked the rhetorical question "Why are they on the line?" The reason they were still on the line was evident. Nobody there really gave a damn about Seven. But when I hit the line all of that was going to change." Duce Law!

Once I got to the clothing room, a cat from Harlem 30s named Pretty Boy was working there. Pretty Boy was a light skinned cat that in my opinion slipped into this Crippin' on a banana peel. He was a doeboy who had been jacked and forced to protect himself and though peer pres-

Le'Taxione (a.k.a. YoYo)

sure was his motivation, he left the cat that jacked him slumped (dead). I could tell that his every move, his every mannerism, his every gesture as far as this Crippin' was concerned was laborious and unnatural. Every word that came out of his mouth was forced. For this reason I didn't trust him.

"West up Cuzz?" I jabbed at him.

"What's up Homie? He shot back.

"What set that is?" I asked him. This is how Cali Crips got at you when we sought identification.

"Huh? He asked confused.

I knew right then that his Crippin' was suspect.

"What hood you from Cuzz?" I asked him.

"It's Harlem 30's." he said.

"Denker Park?" I asked

Denker Park was where Harlem's rotated. That was their turf. He looked puzzled, but I gave him the back door (a way out of the conversation).

"Hook me up with all new state ish (state issued clothes)." I told him. He did and I bounced (left).

"This is O.S.C.I. (Oregon State Correctional Institution) I said to myself as I shook my head in amazement. I was assigned to unit eleven and once I hit the tier cats were in their cells looking out of their windows screaming "YoYo, What's up Cuzz?" I could hear them beating on their doors and screaming "What that Crip Like nigga?"

"Shinin' like a 62 karat Diamond!" I hollered back. They began hitting me with the Crip whistle.

In the chaos I heard a little voice say "Watts up nigga?" I screamed "Who dat?"

"T-Low nigga!" he responded.

T-Low was one of my young homies from Grape Street. He had fell a couple of years prior for a hot one (murder). I remember we used to laugh about how his crime went

Original Diamond Boy

down. Some white boys tried to run him over and T-Low got off a single shot with a .22 and killed the man. I used to say shit like "T-Low and his trusty duce duce".

"West Up Loco!" I said to him.

"Bay is in here" he hollered.

Bay came to the window of his cell and said "West Up Homie?"

Bay was one of the Homies from The No that came to P.O. to sell dope. When we were in the No, he and Soldier Boy used to hustle together. After coming to P.O. Bay literally got rich off of the dope game. I mean he made millions.

They put me in the cell with a pimp cat that I called Portland Slim. Slim was a tall, light skinned cat with long hair. As soon as I came in, he said "Damn man, these niggas act like you a celebrity or something."

"I just got a few Homies." I told him.

He introduced himself and I told him my name. He asked me if I got high.

"Fo sho." I replied.

He pulled out a joint, stood by the door and lit it. There seemed to be more drugs in prison than on the streets and I mean every kind of drug, crack, heroin, weed, pills, you name it and you could get it in prison and the effects were the same.

Prison is a microcosm that reflects society at large so all of the social ills that are prevalent in our society is prevelant in the prisons of our societies. Because the prison environment is a closed society, all of those ills are more intense.

Slim passed the joint to me. I hit it one time and was high. I hadn't smoked anything all the while that I was in the County jail and because of this fact my tolerance level had dropped. As we say in the streets "my lungs were vir-

Le'Taxione (a.k.a. YoYo)

gin". Slim and I began to talk about how the prison operated. He gave me the grapes on the movements and activities that were available during said movements.

We talked for a while. I could relate to Slim's demonstration because I'd been exposed by Rip to the lifestyle that he chose to live but I could tell that he wasn't as polished as Rip so like in most instances that I'd experienced throughout my life, I was intellectually advanced. But in that conversation, I learned a lesson from Slim and that lesson was that intellectual prowess must be tempered lest you cause your counterpart in dialogue to shut down in the midst of conversation. How did I learn that? He told me.

A C.O. (Correctional Officer) came to the cell and said that the Lieutenant wanted to see me. I thought "I'm high as giraffe pussy and now the Lieutenant wants to see me. After giving me directions the C.O. radioed for the cell door to be opened. I walked to the Lieutenant's office. There was an older Mexican sitting behind the desk with a scowl on his face when I got there. I immediately went into "It's Crip, fuck you!" mode. Anytime I felt threatened, disrespected or even apprehensive, instead of becoming an introvert like most people, I'd go into Gangsta mode. So then I was prepared for any bullshit that might fall out of this coward's mouth.

"I'm Mr. Mesina" he stated.

I didn't speak, just nodded my head.

"I know where you're from and your whole criminal history. I even know the crimes that you're suspected of committing.".

"You know this scared straight shit ain't never nothing." I interrupted.

Scared straight was a program that was used in California systems to try to scare children away from a life of crime.

Lieutenant Mesina said 'I'm not trying to scare you, but I promise you that if you start that gang bangin' shit here, you'll do the rest of your time in the hole (solitary confinement)".

"I don't give a fuck about the hole. I came to birth from a single cell and that bullshit you screamin' might affect these mascots (cats that looked and acted like gang bangers but were really cowards), but I'm true to this shit! I didn't get turned out. I got turned on!" I told him.

"As long as we understand each other's position." Messina said. Then he said "I have the people here that killed Seven. Is there going to be a problem?"

"That's street business and I'm going to keep it in the streets." I told him, but in the back of my mind I was saying "I'm gonna hit these cats with a bone crusher (manufactured weapon) as soon as its convenient.

"Alright. Return to your unit." He instructed.

I could already see the difference between this system and the California system and though this system wasn't as violent or as extreme as California, they did get it crackin'.

I returned to my unit and T-Low hollered and asked me where I went. I told him "to see some cat named Mesina."

"He tried to get at you on some bullshit, huh?" T-Low asked.

"Yeah, but I gave it to him raw."

I told T-Low I'd have to holla at him later and he said "Fo sho." Then stated that every body would 'be' at the yard that day. I went back into the cell.

When Rips talked, we'd replace the 'Bs" in our language with "Cs". So instead of saying "because" we'd say "cecause". Or instead of saying "get back at me" we'd say "get cack at me". When we wrote, we'd do the same thing and would never write a word that had a 'ck' in it in its original form because 'ck' meant Crip killa. So we'd

Le'Taxione (a.k.a. YoYo)

change the spelling from a 'ck' to a 'cc'.

Once I got back into the cell, Slim said "Mesina tried to lecture you, huh?" I answered "You know the drill".

"I see it didn't work. Everybody else he calls down there stays for damn near an hour. He must have seen you wasn't the one." He said.

We laughed and he lit up another joint.

After we got smokey (finished the joint), I told him to give me the grapes on how to get shit in. He began to detail the VR (visiting room) for me and I soaked it up like a sponge. I would definitely be going to check some money while I was down and selling weed was the only way that was plausible in a system like that.

They called lunch and upon arriving at the chow hall I could see that it was segregated. I saw the red rags tables, skin head tables, the misfit tables and the Crip tables. I got my tray and hit my designated tables. The Crips that I knew that were present were J-Bo, T-Low, Bay, Alpoe, Pretty Boy, Chocolate, Vamp and Saltine. I was well received by the Crip car (group), but there were some that I didn't really care for as individuals, though I loved them as Crips.

They all shook my hand giving me the universal Crip shake expressing their gratitude in finally meeting me. After exchanging pleasantries, I asked the question "Who's driving the car?" (who's making the decisions for the Crips?). to my surprise, they had no shot caller.

This surprised me because in Cal we stressed structure, organization and discipline. These three principles saved lives, squashed internal squabbles and showed power. Because these principles were not active, I knew that there was chaos in the car but I would have to wait until we got to the yard to truly observe and assess to what extent.

One cat that stood out to me that I didn't know before coming to O.S.C.I. was a cat that called himself D-Loc. D-

Loc was about 19 years old and had been sentenced when he was 16 as an adult. This was a tactic that the courts used disproportionately against black youth in their so called attempt to quail gang violence. I knew that he was a Rida from the introduction and I saw discontent on his face when certain Rips introduced themselves. *"This was the cat I would get to brief me on the circumstances inside the Crip car"* I told myself.

After we finished eating, we all got up and left the chow hall and I saw the curiosity in the eyes of each car including the C.O. car – Yes, the C.O. car. The Corrections Officers were a gang too and when observed, one would find that they too expressed the gang mentality in their daily operations.

When we hit the yard, I told T-Low to gather all of the Rips on the bleachers because I wanted to meet everybody, but my intentions were two fold. I also wanted to introduce structure to the car and would do so after talking to D-Loc one on one.

I watched T-Low go to different pockets of Crips and as he did so I said "D-Loc, West Up Homie?"

"You know, the same ol' shit!" he answered.

I could still see the little boy in his face and eyes, but at the same time I saw strength in his demonstration. He was big as hell from hitting the iron which also meant that he had been experiencing the most pain.

"Come holla at me." I told him and we walked off together.

"What you fall fo Homie?" I asked him.

He told me "attempted murder". I asked him where he was from.

I could tell he wasn't from P.O. His demonstration was different. He was more real than most of the cats from P.O. He told me he was from Arizona.

Le'Taxione (a.k.a. YoYo)

"I'm gonna keep it real as penitentiary steel Cuzz." "I saw this look in yo' face when some of the Rips introduced themselves." I said.

"Cuzz, these niggas is fakes and frauds." He said.

I responded "Fo sho. But fakes and frauds got a role to play in this kind of environment. Peep game homie, I see that the Crip car is raggedy as a bowl of sour crout. Now we can leave it like that and be the laughing stock of the penitentiary or we can pull the true Rips and build a respectable structure."

"There's only a chosen few that I fuck wit." D-Loc stated.

I saw that the Rips were at the bleachers so I told him I understood and that after the meeting we would compare notes on who's who. Duce Law!

We walked back to the group and I began.

"Look Cuzz, I'm YoYo and I don't know how or why the Crip car is as raggedy as it is but this shit gonna change. This ain't how we demonstrate. We gonna exercise some structure, some discipline, and some protocol from this day on. Now you fake ass niggas that ain't with this shit, get the fuck up out of the car."

I knew by couching it the way that I did that no one would leave. Nobody wanted to be deemed a fake in this Crip shit even though there were a lot of them that were fake. I waited for a minute as everybody looked around to see who would walk off. Nobody did. I began to detail my plan for structure and organization. I asked the cats that I knew from the bricks to operate in specific capacities inside the car and when it came to who would drive the car, I left it open to election. The next day we would hit the yard and everyone would let it be known who they thought should run the car.

I got back to the cell and my pimp partner, Slim said "I

see you movin'. What they said about you is true."

"How you hear about me?" I asked pointedly.

"These cats been talkin' about you comin' for the past couple of months." He went on. "they speak of you very highly. I've heard it all from your military tactics to your ability to knock a bitch" These cats need some leadership."

Without going into Crip business I said "Shits gonna change around here Cuzz" and we left that aspect of the rotation alone and started talking about females.

The next day I woke up and went to breakfast. I saw all of the homies and could tell that there was an air of unity. I greeted the homie D-Loc "West Up Homie!"

"Who you riding with on the leadership position?" I asked him.

"I'm wit you Cuzz" he said and I returned the sentiment saying "I'm wit you homie". After breakfast we shook hands and went back to our units.

When I got back to the cell, Slim said "Say man, you know it's a few of these cats that don't like you?"

"A few?" I asked rhetorically. "Cuzz it's a whole bunch of these niggas that don't like me, but fuck'um and feed'um fish. I'm not here to be liked. I'm here to be respected and the first nigga that cross the line is gonna serve as an example for everybody else."

I knew the nigga Moca from Harlem 30's from the bricks. I'd went to put in work with this cat before and I didn't respect how he got down in that instance, but the nigga would fight. He had written to me a couple of times while I was in the County and I wrote him back expressing that though I respected that he was a Crip, I had discontent with him personally and that if he wanted to see me (get down) we could do that upon my arrival. After that letter I didn't her from him again.

I'd heard about his case. He'd been convicted of rape

Le'Taxione (a.k.a. YoYo)

and kidnap and though I didn't believe that he'd actually raped the girl in his case, she was only 14 years old and I had no respect for that. Even in the criminal element, there is supposed to be a "street piety©" which prohibits certain crimes such as rape, child molestation, robbing the elderly, snitching, etc. A violation of this code put you on the outside of the car in Cal and subjected you to vicious assaults which many times resulted in death.

I nurtured and cultivated my California mentality. It is what set me apart from other cats in P.O. and that mentality prohibited me from accepting Moca as a homie even though he was from the house (California). This sparked enmity between us and though it never caused us to clash, it prevented us from uniting. For this reason I knew that this cat didn't like me, and the feeling was mutual.

This fact automatically caused friction between Pretty Boy from Harlem and myself, but this was to be expected. Pretty Boy was a Harlem and he couldn't in his mind betray his hood by forsaking Moca but in all reality, it didn't matter who a cat was or what set he was from in Cali; if you transgressed the bounds, you were green lighted (approved for death.)

I didn't give a damn who didn't like it, I couldn't accept Moca like that and whoever didn't like it "Fuck'um and feed'um fish".

Slim told me some more of his pimp tales as we waited for morning yard. The yard bell rang and the cell doors opened like the gates in the Kentucky Derby and everybody came out just like the horses.

By the time I got to the yard, all of the homies were their waiting for me. D-Loc was the first to greet me.

I turned toward the car and said "Each one of you gonna state one by one who you choose to drive the car. I choose D-Loc." I stated.

"I choose YoYo." D-Loc stated.

After it was all said and done, I was chosen to run the car hands down. Moca, Pretty Boy, Vamp and a few other cats chose not to attend. I took note of who they were and then began to dictate our demonstration as a car. I immediately chose D-Loc as my right hand. He was young, strong and loyal. I also chose J-Bo, T-Low, Bay and Saltine for specific positions in the car.

Bay would be the treasurer, J-Bo was enforcement, TLow intelligence, Saltine made our weapons and D-Loc controlled the soldiers. I contacted Laila after the meeting and told her to come and visit me by herself. She said she would that Saturday.

Chapter 52

"We need to take you to the hole and strip search you."
- YoYo

I told D-Loc and J-Bo that I'd planned to get the car's economic foundation started by slangin' weed, but once we got the money right, those Inglewood families had to get put off the yard in a real way. Duce Law! They agreed.

Laila began visiting and bringing in weed for me. I'd have Bay slang the weed, send Laila ends (money) for herself and the children and keep the rest for the car's hygiene, clothes and food needs met.

In three months I had sent thousands to Laila and the car was financially secure when one day I was coming back from a visit and the C.O.s said "We need to take you to the hole and strip search you". One of those hatin' ass niggas had dropped a dime (told on me.)

My hair was extremely long so I used to swallow about 15 balloons of weed at the visit and put four in my pony tail

Le'Taxione (a.k.a. YoYo)

for immediate access when I got back to the cell.

The C.O.s cuffed me and took me to the hole and began to strip search me. I started from the top down. First I took off my shirt, then my pants, my shoes, and my underwear but when I got to my socks which was all I had left to take off, one of the C.O.s was called out to sign some papers. When I saw this, I said to the remaining C.O., "You mutha fuckas always fuckin' with somebody." As I stated this I took off my socks, one at a time and threw them away from me into a corner and when the C.O. turned to get them, I got the balloons out of my pony tail, put them in my mouth and swallowed them as he went through my clothes one more time.

After he finished going through my clothes the other C.O. came back and ordered me through the body search procedure.

"Take the rubber band out of your hair. Hands up. Let me see your palms. Run your fingers through your hair. Behind your ears. Lift your penis. Your balls. Turn around. Let me see the bottom of your feet. Bend over, spread your cheeks and cough."

I complied.

When nothing was found, he told me to get dressed. They escorted me out of a door and said "Return to your unit". When I got back to the cell, I told Slim about what had transpired. He said "They on you man. If I was you, I'd be cool for a minute". I took his advice and stopped hittin' them for a minute though I continued my visits.

Chapter 53

"You can't just choose me with words. You got to choose me with actions."

- YoYo

A Mexican cat named Pancho hit the line a couple of weeks later. I'd met Pancho on the bricks when he'd had his female Anne gave me a ride after I had shot at some of his Homeboys. Pancho was a red rag but because he was not black, they didn't accept him.

His female Anne was dark skinned with light brown eyes, long hair. She was tall and full figured. As I sat in the backseat I caught her on several occasions looking in the rearview mirror at me and smiling.

In prison he played on the fact that he'd given me a ride that day because the red rags in there didn't accept him. In essence he used me to keep them off of him. I didn't trip because his ex female, Anne would make three way calls for me when he would call her to speak to his two daughters that they had together.

One day I'd gotten on the phone with her and she asked "What do Pancho be saying about me?"

I told her that he'd stated that he loved her and wanted to be a family again. He hadn't told me that but I thought that that was what she wanted to hear so I served it to her.

"He can forget that" she answered.

"Ya'll ain't together?" I asked and she said "Hell naw!"

"Didn't you see me lookin' at you in the rearview?" she asked me.

I told her that I had but that I was on some other shit at that time.

"Who do you fuck wit out here?" she asked me.

I told her it was this female named Laila off and on.

"Is she the one you be havin' me call for you?" she asked and I told her it was.

"But I'm with this Crip shit all the time." I shot at her to let her know that the Crip shit didn't change, regardless.

She told me to take down her number just as Pancho walked up and asked "did you get through?"

"Naw." I answered.

I then told Anne to tell Pancho what she had just told me.

I had to get down like that so that there would be no misunderstanding that could cause me to have to do something to Pancho. I'd seen hoods go to war over a female's desire for a cat from another hood. I gave Pancho the phone. I watched his eyes as they welled up with water. He handed me the phone and walked away.

I got back on the phone and said "West Up?" What did you tell Pancho.

"I told him that I was choosin' you and that him and I couldn't be together."

"You can't just choose me with words. You got to

choose me with actions." I told her.

"Tell me what to do." She answered.

I told her to get on my visiting list and we'd go from there. Then I told the homeboy D-Loc about what happened and he said "Crips up; slobs down!"

Anne got on my visiting list and when she got there I gave her strict instructions on what being with me entailed. She was with it. The next week she came back up, kissed me and pushed 14 balloons into my mouth with her tongue. We were back on with a new source.

Anne was surprised with the money that I would send to her house and after a month I was ready to handle that business with the Inglewood families.

I had both Laila and Anne come up on the same day to visit and had them both bring balloons. When I walked into the visiting room I could see that Laila didn't like the fact that Anne was there to visit me. I came in, kissed Laila first and then kissed Anne. After swallowing all of the balloons I got at both of them.

"This is the drill. I'm with both of ya'll and both of ya'll are doing what is necessary to help me while I'm on my back. Whichever one of ya'll got a problem with this, get up and get on."

Laila got up and left. I focused my attention on Anne.

When I got back to the cell I told Slim about what transpired. He got excited and said "That was pimp shit". I corrected him and told him "that was Gangsta".

I met with Saltine and told him to make me a bone crusher and to bury it under the bleachers. I told D-Loc and T-Low that the next day I was going to hit the Inglewood family boy that smoked Seven. I told them that when they called yard in and everybody was at the entrance waiting to get in the unit, I was going to stab the boy and Saltine would come get the weapon and get rid of it. I then gave D-

Le'Taxione (a.k.a. YoYo)

Loc all of the weed.

D'Loc didn't like the fact that I was going to do it instead of Alpoe, who was from CVC. I told him not to trip.

"This is somethin' that must be done and that coward been here all this time with them slobs and ain't put in no work."

D'Loc replied that after this, Alpoe had to get off the line too. We all agreed. That night I got high as a hippie and kicked it with slim.

The next day at breakfast they came, cuffed me up and took me to the hole. Lieutenant Mesina came to the hole.

"I got the knife and I know what was going to happen but I don't know who was going to make the hit." He said.

"Then why do you have me in the hole? I asked him.

He told me it was because he thought that I had green lighted the hit.

Later on that night D-Loc came to the hole and they put him in my cell. I asked him what they got him for.

"I cussed out the police so I could come see you." He answered. "And I brought some broccoli (weed).

D-Loc got out of the hole in three days but I stayed there for three weeks on administrative segregation before they let me out. When I got out they put me in unit 4 with my old cell partner Slim. He told me that right after they came and got me, they got Saltine and snuck him out of O.S.C.I. Saltine was a snitch

We talked about my parole board hearing which was coming up in about four months and how this situation would affect it. He told me that they liked to see cats with outside support and those that had it almost always got paroled. I immediately launched a plan. I called Laila and explained that if we were to get married that I could get out when I went to the parole board.

"What about when you get out?" she asked me.

I told her that we could get divorced. She agreed and I set it up.

Laila came and when the Chaplain left to go make copies of the marriage certificate I took her into the visiting room restroom and hit them panties and at that moment my daughter "Eusi" was conceived.

Chapter 54

"The reality of it is that I loved my hood more than I loved my own children."

- *YoYo*

I got news from Jason that some slobs had shot up into our G-Mom's house but that he, Soldier, C-Ride and some other homeboys had got back at them. That would be something that I would have to handle when I got out I said to myself.

I went to the parole board and as planned I expressed that I'd just gotten married and had a daughter on the way. They paroled me.

I got back to the unit and sent the news to my homeboy D-Loc. He sent word back that he needed to see me on the next line movement. I shot to the cell and told Slim the good news. Slim was genuinely happy for me.

"Let's get smokey." I suggested and he lit up a joint.

Once we got high the reality of my parole became more

Le'Taxione (a.k.a. YoYo)

evident. Slim broke the silence and said "Man, you shouldn't have got married."

"Why?" I poked.

He paused for a minute and told me as cool and tempered as a pimp could that there would always be a better bitch. I reiterated my position on the marriage which was to appease the parole board and we left that subject alone.

I met with D-Loc on the next line movement.

"West Up homie?" I asked as I shot my hand out to him.

He hugged me hard and long. We had developed a very close relationship. I'd even put him on the hood. This was my comrade and the love between us was evident. When the slob Ty stole on me, D-Loc was the one to rush his ass while I was discombobulated, preventing him from taking advantage and launching an all out assault. The coward, Vamp from neighborhood watched the slob walk up behind me and didn't say shit.

"Homie I'm gonna miss the hell out of you." D-Loc said.

I answered "Cuzz, I'm coming right back."

I couldn't let the red rags that shot up my G-Mom's house walk the streets and the work that was put in by Jason, Soldier and the other homies was cool, but it wasn't to my satisfaction. These niggas needed to be terrorized with the get back and that's what I'd planned on doing as soon as I hit the bricks. Duce Law!

There were some things that were sacred even in this gang bangin'. That code had been transgressed when they shot up my G-Mom's house. Now their whole hood was a target. Duce Law! No one was sacred and I would be the one that made this gang shit real for them.

"I don't want you to come back homie" D-Loc said. "But I know that you got to do what you got to do. Just be careful Cuzz."

Now those on the outside looking in will say "He has a daughter on the way, why would he jeopardize all of that for revenge, even when someone had already exacted retribution for the shooting? Why?

The reality of it is that I loved my hood more than I loved my own children. At first glance this sounds unbelievable, and for years I've struggled with this issue. Yes, there is credence in the point that I had a daughter on the way and that should have and would have been a reasonable man's focus, but there is nothing reasonable about the miscreant aspect of the gang mentality and that mentality makes retaliation mandatory.

My primary activity was gang bangin'. Being a father was nothing more than a secondary response to a circumstance that transpired through the primary activity. This truth is harsh and brutal but it is a truth that is made evident by the gang banga's wanton desire to put in work that could possibly separate him/her from their children.

"Fuck Yo Set"

Pay attention is it my mission to ball or fall
Initiated as a Diamond since I learned to crawl
At age 11 cancelled Heaven came to terms with hell
Never knowing in my future I'd be placed in jail
In a cell will I succeed make my enemies bleed
They say the strong must survive so on the week I feed
The jungle creed makes it mandatory struggle and strife
Is there a heaven for a Diamond am I fucked for life
And to you coward ass niggas talkin behind my back
Let it be known your in danger as I lace this track
Now picture that all my enemies in bullet proof vests
Teflons penetration I'm screamin' 'fuck yo set'
To the West is where I flex witness lyrics explode
Eradicating through my conversation bustas and foes
I'm chose my soul exposed to this evil and shit
I'm hearing voices and my only choice is trust no bitch
As I hit give her a deadly dose of pleasure and pain
Another bitch done fell victim to my venomous game
And to you coward ass niggas contemplatin' my death
Keep you heata when I see you I'm gonna test yo flesh
Fuck yo set.

Chapter 55

"May the Crip God forgive us."

- YoYo

The day that I was being released, the homeboys were yelling out of the cell windows "Stay up Cuzz!" "Keep it Crippin!" and "Stay busta free homie!"

"Till they kill me Cuzz!" I hollered back.

I had already planned my revenge so there was no doubt that I was coming back and the last thing that I hollered to T-Low was "Save a bunk Cuzz. I'll be back."

It was April 27, 1990 when I hit the bricks. I called a meeting at Anne's house and Crips from all hoods showed up except Kerby and CVC. Kerby's numerical representation was 4/7 and CVC's was 3/7. In my absence the word had been spread that in my act of getting off on the Inglewoods, that got at us the night Seven was killed, that I shot Seven, causing his death. This had been said at a Crip party and my homies had went off and tore the party up.

Le'Taxione (a.k.a. YoYo)

The Kerbys and the CVCs made an alliance calling it "a 7 thang" and the 62s and Dead End 60s made an alliance calling it "a 6 thang". Now add the rumor, and you got beef. The homies expressed the fact that they no longer gave a damn about Kerby or CVC and every time they saw them, they got at them.

It came up in the meeting that the Kerbys and the CVCs were having a party in the Vill.

"And we'll be there." I said.

We all left for the party that night. We met up outside of the Vill to make our unified entrance. I'd told everybody that we would leave our heat at home and if there was a problem we'd smash them from the shoulders. My intentions were to squash the beef but it had become too engrained.

We entered the party and I could see the fear on most faces and the disdain on the others. We had not been invited but I didn't care. I'd put in more work for this hood than anyone of those cats claimin' CVC and that was my invitation.

Everything was functional up until the time Lil Chocolate showed up. Lil Chocolate was a shooter and while in most instances the beef with the Kerby's and CVCs was from the shoulder, Lil Chocolate was bustin' on cats on sight. Lil Chocolate was young, skinny as hell and couldn't fight so he employed the heat to create the damage that he couldn't create from the shoulders. That was his demonstration.

When Lil Chocolate came in, cats immediately began to huddle up and whisper. The homies came to me and said "These niggas is about to trip."

"And if they do, we gonna run through they ass like Ex-Lax." I said.

One of the CVCs said something to Lil Chocolate and

Original Diamond Boy

took off on him (socked him). Jason jumped in and it was crackin'. We ran through them in front of their females. In the midst of the melee' gunshots rang out – pow-pow, but they came from outside of the party. The fighting stopped and we went outside to see who was shooting. The police pulled up with a whiteman in the back of the police car, got out and said that they had caught this guy running through the complex with an assault rifle. While we were at each other, this white boy shot into a crowded party indiscriminately.

That situation reminded me of what a Muslim brother named Tweedy had told me while I was at OSCI. I had gone to a Muslim service while serving my sentence and had even read the Koran in my cell at times. Tweedy told me "We strive to kill each other and they strive to kill us all".

"*May the Crip God forgive us.*" I said to myself.

The next day we met again at Anne's house. We talked about what had transpired the night before. I gave Jason his props (proper respect) on how he demonstrated. Now I would use the name that he chose for himself "Bear".

I'd contacted C-Ride the day that I got out and had told him that the next day we were going to put in work on the red rags that had shot up G-Mom's spot. I could hear the fear and cowardice in his voice. He didn't want to put in no work, but because it was me, he acted like he did. C-Ride was a mascot but if he was cornered he'd attack you. That didn't mean shit in this bangin' though because if you push a butterfly into a corner, he'll fly directly at your face to get away. This bangin' took overt aggressive action and C-Ride didn't have that in him.

The day after our skirmish in the Vill, Bear and myself went to C-Ride's apartment where he lived with this female from P.O. named Tammy. Tammy was our homegirl Shay

Le'Taxione (a.k.a. YoYo)

Shay's sister. Shay Shay was from the hood but Tammy messed with the Kerbys at one time. We got there and that coward C-Ride didn't even answer the door. I spoke through the door to him.

"I know you in there Cuzz. From now on keep Diamond out yo' mouth busta and when you get yo' courage up, come get beat off the hood. From this day forward, I don't even know you Cuzz. Die slow."

We got in the car and pulled off. When we got to 15th and Ainsworth we saw a red rag's truck.

"I'm fis'to get off on these slobs cuzz." I said.

"Bust on them niggas." Bear replied.

And that's what I did – buck-buck-buck-buck! I let them have it and Bear drove off. When we got back to headquarters I reloaded and said "Cuzz it's time to get back at them Partridge Family Niggas". (We called Inglewood families Partridge Family out of disrespect). I called Soldier Boy and the homeboy J-Loc from the 357 (Trey Five Seven). We met up at headquarters and planned our campaign of violence.

After the meeting Anne called me to the back room and said "YoYo you just got out and you already doin' shit to go back. Let them other niggas put in work."

"You knew it was Crip on mines when you started fuckin' with me Cuzz." I told her

"I know, but I love you and I don't want you to get locked back up!" she said emotionally.

I told her that she didn't have the right to love me like that because I couldn't return it like that.

"I love the hood baby and getting' locked up is part of this shit." I told her

"And so is getting' killed." She said

I answered "I live to die and I die to live and in between all that I Crip to the fullest."

Original Diamond Boy

I saw her eyes fill with tears but it didn't affect me in the least. My heart had grown cold a long time ago. I was 'street poisoned' and there wasn't a cure in sight.

We left and got in a female's car that I'd met while in traffic and spent an hour with at her spot and went to put in work. We rode on 7 established red rag spots and called it a day.

I went to a club called Cleo's that night with the homies and Anne. This cat that had known Anne from when she was with Pancho said something to her. I don't know what he said but I was full of that Hennessy and had no understanding with a cat approaching my female. I immediately asked him "What you say Cuzz? And before he could reply I took off on him and dropped him on the side of the club.

I told Anne to go home because I anticipated some funk (conflict) and I didn't want her to get caught up in the middle of it. She complied.

I went back into the club and saw baby that I'd met before at the bar drinking a Black Russian. Her name was Phylicia. I would come to find out later that a female named Anisha whom I'd been with in the past was her niece.

"What you doin' here?" she asked.

Strollin' and controllin' I answered. I ordered another Hennessy and watched the room as we talked. My Homies were getting' at females and periodically shooting glances at me to make sure that I was alright. Bear came to the bar and said "YoYo you need to go kick back". I agreed. Phylicia volunteered to take me to her house for the night but Bear didn't dig that and he voiced it.

"Naw, you not takin' my brother to your house. He told her.

I told him it was cool but he said that he was going to follow us to see where she lived. He did and when we got

Le'Taxione (a.k.a. YoYo)

to her apartment Bear rolled down his window and said "If anything happens to my brother, I'm goin' to come here and turn it into a graveyard." Then he pulled off.

It was my intention to hit the panties that night but when we got into the house it began to get dark. The Hennessy was taking it's toll on my clean system. I told her to let me take a shower. I'd hoped that the shower would revive me, that was the last thing I remembered. I blacked out.

I woke up the next morning looking around the room thinking "What the hell?" Phylicia came into the room wearing nothing but her bra and panties.

"You're finally up, huh?" she asked sarcastically

I lifted the covers realizing that I was naked. I immediately panned the room for my boxers. At that moment Phylicia's little daughter ran into the room with my boxers on her head laughing. She must have been about three or four years old.

"Give me them girl." Phylicia said as she snatched them off of her daughter's head. She handed them to me then she pulled the covers back and got in the bed and snuggled up against me.

"You passed out on me last night." She said and ran her hand between my legs.

She found what she was looking for and stroked it. I immediately became erect but then there was a knock at the door.

"Damn!" she exclaimed. "Who is it?"

"Bear." Came the response.

She put on her housecoat and went into the living room to open the door. I counted the money that I had in my pocket - $700. That was about right so I got dressed. She came back into the room and said "Your brother wants you." I told her to let me get her car again for a couple of hours. She gave me the keys off of the nightstand and asked "When we gonna finish what we started last night?"

"Tonight." I said as she walked up, we hugged then I boned out (left).

When we got outside, Bear and I decided that we would drop off his car and go put in some more work. When we got back to Anne's house, Laila had called and wanted us to pick her and my daughter up. She had seen a car that she wanted and since she now had my daughter, I wanted to make sure that she had a car to transport all three of her children. Because I ended up doing more time at O.S.C.I. than I was supposed to, my daughter, Eusi was born right before I got out.

Anne said that she had told Laila that she would make sure that I picked them up. That's how Anne was. She understood that I was going to have other females and never sweated me about it. I would find out later in the game that Anne had been messin' with the homeboy Bay on the say low (secretly) while we were together. I didn't trip though – turn about is fair play.

I was taking a shower when Anne came into the bathroom. She stayed in there talking to me all of the while I was showering. She complained that I hadn't had sex with her.

"Cuzz, I haven't had sex with nobody." I told her as I got out of the shower and began to dry off.

She got on her knees in front of me and asked "Can I give you some head?"

Before I could answer, she placed me in her mouth. I entertained it for a minute but not to the point of completion. I pulled back and said "I got business to take care of."

I was fixated on this get back and until that was exacted, everything else would have to wait including any sexual desires.

Le'Taxione (a.k.a. YoYo)

I got dressed and Bear and I got into Phylicia's car and boned. As Bear drove, I told him that we needed to pick up Laila and Eusi first and take them to get a car; then we'd pick up Soldier and J-Loc. We did and although I had pictures of my daughter, this would be my first time seeing her in person and she was so beautiful!

Laila got in the backseat with my daughter, gave us directions and we started off to get the car. As we were riding I saw a group of red rags standing on the corner and hit them up as we passed.

"Hit the block and go back. I'm gonna bust on these slobs." I told Bear.

By the time we got back, they were gathered in front of someone's house. Bear stopped in front of the house and I jumped out and said "What that Crip like fool and started bustin'. I got back in the car and told Bear "Drive.

This was my daughter's first time witnessing me bust on an enemy but it wouldn't be the last.

We got to the house of the lady that was selling the car. Laila bought it and drove back to her G-Mom's house. We went and picked up Soldier and then went to Natasha's house to see the little girl that she said was my daughter.

We pulled up, got out of the car and walked up to the house. I knocked on the door and heard Natasha yell "Who is it?"

"Who you want it to be?" I hollered back.

The door flew open and she stood there holding my daughter Aajabu.

"What's up Cuzz? I asked as she turned to the side inviting me in.

We walked into the house and she closed the door. I walked around the house and checked all of the closets. Once I was sure that the house was clear, I came back into the living room and asked "Is this Aajabu?" She answered

"Sure is." As she handed her to me. I played with my baby for a minute and then told her that I had some business to take care of, but that I'd be back to see her.

"When is a good time to come back?" I asked.

As she smiled she said "tonight". I caught the message but acted like I didn't.

As we came out of the house, some red rags rode by and hit us up. As I hit them back up I yelled "Fuck yo dead homies!"

We jumped back into the car and gave chase. As we caught up to them J-Loc and I leaned out of the window on opposite sides of the car, aimed at there car in front of us, and lit them up. We turned off the street and went back to headquarters.

Chapter 56

"I have to go back and get my hat! To leave your hat, regardless, was philosophically the mark of a coward."

- YoYo

The news was ablaze with televised reports of the work that we'd been putting in. Word got back to us that red rags were telling the gang task force that the Duces were the ones getting at them. The community was up in arms because these shootings were happening in broad daylight.

That night I'd decided to go out with Phylicia. She recommended that we go to an after hours club called Batman's on Williams Street. I agreed. Batman's was an after hours club that doubled as a gambling shack. Before I fell, a cat from Santana Block Crips named "Anything" frequented Batman's so I was under the impression that it was a Crip spot.

Once we arrived at the club, we had to go through a

Le'Taxione (a.k.a. YoYo)

door that led to a stair case in order to enter the upstairs establishment. As we began walking up the stairs we found that the stairwell was littered with red rags.
As we walked up the stairs, one red rag got at me "What's up Blood?"
"West Up Cuzz!" I shot back.
Upon entering we walked by a gambling table and I quickly noticed that it was all red rags gambling. As I passed, one got at me again "What's up Blood?"
"West Up Cuzz! I again shot back and continued to escort Phylicia around the corner to the bar.
Once we got to the bar a pimp cat named Diamond Dee greeted me. Diamond Dee was a pimp from the No that used to be a Godfather and though he was a former enemy I was happy as hell to see him.
We began to drink and I noticed that the after hours club was slowly emptying. People were leaving in anticipation of a confrontation between me and the red rags and why wouldn't they? I was the only Crip in the club making it mandatory for them to try and make an example out of me.
Something inside of my head was screaming "get the hell out of here before these niggas kill you" and though my pride wouldn't let me show fear, I was scared as hell.
"These cats are going to try to kill you YoYo." Diamond Dee said and then asked me if I had some heat.
"Naw Cuzz, I'm naked as a porn star." I replied. He pushed me a .25 semi automatic handgun and said "It ain't much but you can have it". Now the playing field was level. It would all boil down to heart and accuracy and when it came to that I'd place myself against anybody.
I grabbed Phylicia by the hand and began to leave the club. She'd brought me there placing me in the line of fire and now I'd use her as a human shield to effectuate my get away.

Original Diamond Boy

We descended the stairwell and once we reached the street I put the heat in my right hand, and placed my right arm around her neck, putting her between myself and the red rags who were standing across the street. I whispered to her "when we reach the corner, run.". I knew that they wouldn't shoot while she was with me because she was from P.O., and the red rags weren't gangsta like that.

As we reached the corner, she ran. I sprinted towards the enemy and began bustin' – pop – pop – pop! They busted back - buck – buck – buck – buck! It was obvious that I was out gunned and they had superior fire power so I took cover behind a car. I rose and busted again pop – pop! And they busted back. I could hear the shots hitting the car. I waited until they stopped firing and made a break for it.

I barely escaped with my life making it to a convenience store. I realized that I had lost my hat in the gun battle. I told myself "I have to go back and get my hat!" To leave your hat, regardless, was philosophically the mark of a coward.

I got a ride back to headquarters, got my sawed off and a couple of homeboys and went back for my hat.

When we got back there I found my hat next to the car that I'd taken cover behind. After retrieving my hat I became infuriated. While the other homies waited in the car, Meaty and I went back to the club. We opened the door to the stairwell and found it again littered with red rags. I let off, boo yaw – boo yaw! "It's Diamond nigga!" I screamed.

After that particular incident, Batman's was closed down. It had already been under scrutiny and that was the last straw.

The next day we were riding and I was drinking a tall can of Olde English 800 malt liquor. It seemed as if the whole Portland Police Department convened on us. We were ordered out of the car at gun point and the vehicle was

Le'Taxione (a.k.a. YoYo)

checked for weapons. At that time we had no weapons. I had decided to just get lit that day and that's all we were doing.

Bear, Soldier Boy and myself were taken to the Justice Center and booked on various attempted murder charges. It had been three days since I'd been released and I was locked up again.

Soldier Boy was released but Bear and I sat waiting to see if the grand jury was going to indict us. Bear bailed out but I had a parole hold. A few days later I was released and an article on gang violence came out naming me as a factor in the rise in gang violence.

When I went to report to my parole officer I was re-arrested. The grand jury had indicted us on numerous counts of attempted murder.

The Oregonian reported "The level of violence also depends on which gang members are on the streets. For example, police said, a 25 year old Crip from California named YoYo was released from state prison April 27, 1990 and arrested as a suspect in an April 30, 1990 drive by."

Chapter 57

"After it was all said and done and the gavel cracked, I'd been sentenced to five years."

- YoYo

I met a cat named Mississippi who was fighting a murder charge. We became good friends and were celled next door to each other. There was a female named Simone who worked at the jail as a food manager. She actually liked Mississippi, but she was very dark and he didn't like dark females so I had to do all of the talking.

I got at her through the window where she set up our food to be served to us. I had her flashing us her breast for about a week then I mashed on her.

"Say Cuzz, bring us some weed up in here." I told her. She nodded in agreement.

The next day she raised the blinds, motioned me to the window, pulled the weed out of her bra and pushed it through the food slot, then she closed the blinds. All of this

Le'Taxione (a.k.a. YoYo)

transpired in a matter of seconds while Mississippi kept the guard's attention off of me. That night we got high and kicked it all night. Simone repeated this for about a month; then she quit her job.

While I was fighting this beef it came out that Lil'Crazy, Curl and Lil C-boy snitched on Looney about the murder in the Piedmont Apartments. I couldn't believe that shit. The cold part about it was they didn't even have to snitch. They volunteered the information. These cats would have to be dealt with severely and I would be the one to do it.

At trial, several Inglewood Familys came to testify against me. One was in a wheelchair with red rags hanging off to it. All of them were in gang attire with red rags in their pockets. I thought to myself *"What part of the game is this? These cowards started this beef and now here they are in this courtroom testifying because the beef got stuck between their teeth."*

The jury found me guilty and the judge asked "Do you have anything to say?" I stood up.

"You mutha fuckas found me guilty based on the testimony of other gang members and just gave me a case because I'm YoYo! I don't give a fuck how much time you give me. I'm going to do it standing on my head!" I said.

I exhibited this bravado and defiance out of the hurt and shame that I felt for not knowing what they were talking about during my trial. The legal jargon was a whole different language in and of itself. I would later discover that the language that was used in the court is based for the most part on Latin. How could I receive a fair trial when they were using a language that I didn't understand? Was the question that I asked myself. But it wasn't the first time and it wouldn't be the last.

After it was all said and done and the gavel had cracked, I'd been sentenced to five years. I smiled to myself. Five years didn't feel like shit and yes, I planned to do that wino time standing on my head so to speak.

Chapter 58

"I fought the demon off by saying over and over in my mind Jehovah, Jehovah, Jehovah."

- YoYo

As I slept that night I found myself in a very real struggle. It seemed as though I was dreaming but I was wide awake. I lay flat on my back paralyzed as this foul looking and smelling demon straddles me and attempted to wiggle itself down into my body.

This had been a regular occurrence in my life. When I was young and we lived in the projects, there was a little aberration that we children would see and sometimes interact with. My mother called him Mr. Farkwire and though he wasn't the same as the demons that came later in my life, he was just as real.

In my adult life, my experiences with these demons came in various ways. Either the demon would try to infuse itself with me, have sex with me, or just watch me from a distance. I'd found out that the demon that would try to have sex with me, in my state of what I described as a subconscious consciousness was called succubus. Still the other demon that would try to infuse itself with me was far more evil and insidious.

As the demon continued to try to merge itself into me, I tried to speak but couldn't. I tried to move, but couldn't. I tried to yell, but couldn't. I fought the demon off by saying over and over in my mind *Jehovah, Jehovah, Jehovah*. When it fled I jumped up sweating and tired. I would have this experience for the most part of my life and the intensity would elevate each time.

Chapter 59

"All of the females that were interested in me while I was on the bricks fell off."

- YoYo

The next week we were shackled, placed on the grey goose (prison transport bus) and transferred to prison. I could see O.S.C.I. off in the distance and I smiled. Bear had had a separate trial and a paid for attorney. Though he did none of the shooting in the violent crime spree, he actually ended up doing more time because while I was going to court from jail, he was out on bond and I got credit for time served. He was already at O.S.C.I. when I arrived.

When I got there and they had a care package ready for me when I hit the line. It included hygiene articles, food, and brand new state clothing. I was treated like royalty. My Homies were happy to see me and my enemies were nervous. I had a reputation for beefin' out of the blue and going to the extreme when I beefed and this fact had them all leery.

We had at least seven or eight Duces on the line when I got there so I decided to sew up the weed market so that none of the homeboys would have to want for anything.

I moved into the cell with my homeboy Doom. Doom was short, heavy set cat that drank a lot on the bricks but he had major squabs (fought very well). He was a real cat that exercised to the fullest the code of ethics that I taught the homies. He was one of my truest homeboys.

The next day we all met on the yard and I briefed the homies on my intentions. They were with it.

All of the females that were interested in me while I was on the bricks fell off. The only one that stayed down (at least financially) was Laila. There was no doubt that she was letting other cats hit her panties but she made sure that I kept my finances straight by bringing me weed.

I had her visit every weekend and it was always business. I didn't like the fact that she was letting those suckas out on the bricks get at her but it was unreasonable for me to expect her not to. I'd never had a female while I was locked down who kept it a hundred (100%). Not one of them stayed down for me in all aspects. Every one of them laid down with other cats. That was the reality of incarceration and I accepted it, although reluctantly.

Deception

What a tangled web we weave when we plot to deceive
Nobody grieves for these G's in these penitentiaries
So nigga please get up off yo knees don't beg for tomorrow
When all you seein' in these cells is the pain and sorrow
Our lives are borrowed who will I follow this world is corrupt
Who'll give a fuck when I'm laying stuck and turn my ashes to dust
So I run amuk I'm Diamond tough a protégé' of the system
The choices given got me trippin but this Diamond keeps glistenin'
And plus the tensions escalated and it's turned into trauma
And everyday I walk the earth can't escape the pain and the drama
That's on my Momma I need a blessin my protection expand
But it's no longer in her hands her roughest pup is a man.

Chapter 60

"As long as you don't stop the clock I don't give a damn where you send me."

- YoYo

The beef between us and the CVCs had subsided a little, but we still didn't interact with each other so I made it Duce Law that their money wasn't any good. This fueled the beef but I didn't care. I felt like the Duces had held down the Vill when them niggas was just puppies and now they had the nerve to attempt to beef with us over some bullshit...fuck 'em and feed 'em fish. And if they didn't like it we'd make it real for they ass!"

Laila stayed down and handled business exactly as I'd asked. I never questioned her about who or if she was laying down with anybody. Even if I did, she'd lie. Laila was a liar, period-point blank. She could look right in your eyes and lie. But she would handle business.

We got money at O.S.C.I. for about four months before

Le'Taxione (a.k.a. YoYo)

they transferred me out to Eastern Oregon Correctional Institution (E.O.C.I.). Lieutenant Mesina didn't want me at O.S.C.I. I was called into his office.

"I know that you are introducing marijuana into the institution." He said.

"If that's so, why am I not in segregation?" I asked him.

He told me that I had too many homeboys there that would gladly ride the beef (say it was theirs) for me. I smiled

"So I'm sending you out." He said.

"As long as you don't stop the clock, I don't give a damn where you send me." I answered.

The next day I was on the grey goose. E.O.C.I. was way out in the boondocks where it snowed all winter and stayed as hot as hell all summer. Upon arrival they put me in the cell with this coward named Mike. Mike was a light skinned wannabee who didn't have a set. He was like a groupie. He hung around Crips but nobody would put him on their set. Mike was a busta but he was alright so I made him my house mouse (a cell partner that keeps the cell clean).

All of my homeboys were on the other side of the yard. I was the only Duce on the east side yard with all the CVCs. Lil' Solo, J-Boy, Lil' Bo, Hoax, Lil Black and Lil Chocolate were all on the west side yard. About a week later Bear touched down there and they put him on the west side yard. They were trying to keep me isolated from the homeboys because they knew that I was about organization and discipline. The only way that I could get to the west side yard was to get into it with the C.O.s and that's what I set out to do.

The night after Bear got there I packed my property and told myself that first thing in the morning I was going to get at one of the police. Breakfast was called and as soon as I

Original Diamond Boy

came out of the cell I started.

"What the fuck you lookin' at Cuzz?" I said.

The C.O. looked around as if I was talking to someone else.

"I'm talking to you." I said and walked towards him. I wasn't going to assault him but I knew that if I walked towards him, it would cause him to push his panic button. He did and eight C.O.s came running. I simply turned around and placed my hands behind my back. They cuffed me and escorted me to segregation.

When they let me out 20 days later, they put me on the West side yard with the homeboys. Though I knew J-Boy, Lil Black, Lil Chocolate, Lil' Solo and Lil' Bo, I didn't know this cat named "Hoax". The only ones who had the authority to put him on the hood were Duce, Soldier and me. He'd claimed that Duce put him on the hood, but Duce was in Seattle and I didn't have a hook up on him so I couldn't check into it.

We all hit the yard after lunch. I immediately made it mandatory that we'd all work out together as a unit in order to show strength. Everyone agreed. C.O.s were really paying attention to the things we did and said so instead of us saying "Duce love" or "Diamonds Forever" when we parted I began saying "Two of um". That phrase encompassed 62 Diamond and 62 East Coast.

Everything was cool for a while but apparently the coward Mike had told the CVCs that I'd disrespected their hood while we were in the same cell on the East Side. If I had, I wouldn't have given a damn about him telling them that. But the fact was that I hadn't disrespected them in the least.

When we went to chow, we could see the cats on the East side though we had no physical contact with them. When we saw the CVCs they were shooting stone faces

Le'Taxione (a.k.a. YoYo)

(giving disrespectful looks) at us. I turned to J-Boy and said "you see these bustas?"

"Fuck them niggas Cuzz!" He said.

I hollered "Moe, You niggas got beef or something?"

Moe was some off brand cat that had joined CVC late and called himself calling shots for their car.

"Fuck you Six Duckies!" He answered.

I responded "Fuck you C.V. Sissies" and told him "Nigga if you got beef, bring it to the Islamic services!" Though we were on different sides, we could all attend Islamic services together.

I got back to the cell block and told everybody to be at the Islamic service on that Friday. Friday came and they let half of us out, but delayed the other half. I was in the first half and I mashed to the services. Lil Chocolate and Lil' Bo caught up to me. Once we got there, we finished prayer and though we were outnumbered, I still got at them.

"What you niggas want?" I challenged.

Moe started plea bargaining.

"Cuzz, Mike told me that when ya'll was in the cell, you disrespected CVC."

I walked up to Mike, spit in his face and said "If you take that and won't fight, you'll suck a dick and won't bite."

The coward wouldn't get down. I turned to Moe and told him "Cuzz, you out of pocket taking a civilian's word over another Rip and for that Cuzz, you got to see me."

"Fuck that nigga up YoYo!" Lil Chocolate chimed in.

The police came in running and screaming "Break it up! Break it up!"

Lil' Bo and I were cuffed up and taken to segregation. Seven days later Lil' Bo got out of segregation but I was placed in administrative segregation which meant that I could be held there almost indefinitely.

Original Diamond Boy

When I had my hearing, I found out that the CVCs in general had made statements against me. In particular Moe and this transformer (one that changes hood alliances), Lil' A-Bone had made statements related to the fact that I was attempting to move against the CVCs and that I wanted them all off of the line – statements that I unequivocally denied.

Chapter 61

"I asked him could he fish and he answered "I'm a deep sea fisherman."

- YoYo

After two weeks they let me out of segregation and as soon as I got out I had Laila come to visit and bring me weed. She drove all the way to Eastern Oregon to visit.

Once she got there, we kissed and she pushed the balloons into my mouth. We sat and talked for a while and I began to swallow the balloons. When I got to the last one, it got caught in my throat and I began to choke. I started coughing and Laila hit me on the back and when she did, I coughed up the balloon onto the floor. I immediately covered it with my foot. The visiting room officer came over to my table and asked "Are you alright?" I told him that I was and that the soda had gone down the wrong pipe. When he walked away, I picked up the balloon from the floor, put it back in my mouth, took a drink of soda and swallowed it.

Le'Taxione (a.k.a. YoYo)

The visit came to a close and I told Laila how much I respected the fact that she'd driven that far to handle business for me. I slapped her on her ass as she left. After all the other visitors left, the visiting room officer walked up to me and told me that the Superintendent wanted to see me. This was not a natural occurrence so I became anxious. A Lieutenant or a captain, yes – but the Superintendent?

I was escorted to his office and when I entered he smiled and said "This is the notorious Mr. YoYo?"

"The one and only." I answered.

He told me to have a seat and as I sat he started.

"I've been getting a lot of kites (inmate communications) on you. This prison has been on pins and needles since you've been here and now I have people identifying you as the problem." He explained.

I sat silently and he went on.

"I can't allow you to disrupt this prison." He said. Then he turned to the officers and said "Take him to the hole."

Though I was on my way to the hole, I wasn't mad. I knew that once I got there I was going to get as high as giraffe pussy.

They stripped me out, did a body search and assigned me a cell.

"Who in here?" I asked the tier after I made my bed. "A whole bunch of nobody." Was the answer.

"Who dat?" I asked.

His name was Travon and he told me he wasn't gang affiliated.

"You got a red headed stepchild?" I asked him. This was convict terminology used to ask a guy if he had a match.

"I got a few red head stepchildren and they live on the strip." He answered. In other words he was telling me he had matches and a striker.

Original Diamond Boy

I asked him if he could fish and he answered "I'm a deep sea fisherman". Fishing was done by taking string from a blanket, sheet, socks or underwear and tying it together, adding a comb, a segregation bar of soap or something else with weight and shooting it out under your door. The person that you were fishing with either connected with your line and you pulled it into your cell or hooked something to his line so that he could pull it back into his own cell. Travon saying that he was a deep sea fisherman meant that he fished very well.

I rolled up a couple of joints using some bible paper and after retrieving the striker and matches, I hooked a joint to Travon's line and he pulled it back in. It just so happened that Travon was from Richmond California, the same place my father lived after being adopted. We got lit and talked all night. We repeated this for two weeks before we ran out of weed.

I had another Administrative Segregation hearing and was told that because of my influence at EOCI, I was being transferred to Oregon State Penitentiary (OSP).

"The Unforgiven"

Now can your mind picture the bible scriptures being took and hidden
Not to mention being tainted by the unforgiven
My position is that religion being fabricated
And sold to the people by the church the truth's been decimated
Eradicating mental patients is the nation's rule
And adolescents shoot their pistols in the classroom
Are we doomed? Cause' as a nation we don't love our children
Child molesters stalk them or the parents be the ones who kill them
I can feel them they packin heatas for their preservation
And Crips and Bloods go to war without provocation
Peeling caps is the reason youngstas carry straps
And 9 times out of 10 in the end the shootin victims black
Now picture that cause as a nation we're reduced to sinners
Come feel the wrath in the path of the unforgiven

Chapter 62

"Religion as a whole has been used as a tool to relieve people of their responsibilities as vessels of God that must in their human development strive to become a reflection of Him."

- YoYo

I got to OSP and was placed on Ad-Seg with the homeboy Baby-Loc and a Muslim brother out of New York named Alamin. Alamin was an older brother. He was about 65 years old but had the appearance of a brother in his early 40's. He had been transferred from New York after the Muslims rioted at one of the facilities. He was deemed a leader and for that reason they sent him out of state.

Baby-Loc was a Crip from 357 (Trey Five Seven). He'd been locked up in Oregon for about seven years, five of which had been spent in Ad-Seg. Baby-Loc had shot a cat's arm off at a party with a 12-guage shotgun and while in prison he had led a riot between California and Oregon cats which landed him in Ad-Seg.

Le'Taxione (a.k.a. YoYo)

I became close with both Alamin and Baby-Loc almost immediately. Though Baby-Loc and I were still active Crips, Alamin would counsel us on issues of life and Allah. Aalamin had a wealth of knowledge and I wanted it all.

Under the toutelage of Alamin I began studying everything under the sun. I studied the Hegelian principle, mathematics, philosophy, biology, theology, physiology, psychology, anthropology, sociology, political science, African culture and history, etc. Then I studied the sun. I had an insatiable appetite for knowledge and found myself ordering books in my quest for growth.

In 1991 I decided to get my G.E.D. The instructor came through with the practice tests and I scored so high on his pretest that he gave me the actual test. I passed on the first attempt.

I began to learn things about black people that were never taught to me in school. I found that we had a glorious past. We were not found in the jungles of Africa, naked, with bones through our noses as they'd implied in school. We were the mothers and fathers of civilization and all of the sciences. These facts instilled a sense of pride, honor and self worth in me that I'd never experienced at such a magnitude before.

Because it was a Muslim brother that I studied under, I began to really study Islam, but not what is erroneously called Orthodox Islam. I studied Islamic history as a whole and being a black man in Amerika I was attracted to Islam as taught by the Most Honorable Elijah Muhammad.

I saw in what is erroneously called Orthodox Islam a veiled racism that required that its adherents adopt an Arab culture rather than adopting the principles of Islam. I, being viewed in Amerika as a second class believer in Christianity, refused to accept being treated as a second class believer in Islam, so I rejected religion and clung only to its principles.

Religion as a whole has been used as a tool to relieve people of their responsibilities as vessels of God that must in their human development strive to become a reflection of Him/Her so I thought. Given this, I had an aversion to religion and even in the teachings of the Most Honorable Elijah Muhammad, in my aversion to religion I saw inconsistencies; not in what he taught, but in those who claimed to be believers in what he taught.

Chapter 63

"Over the years of gang bangin', I'd developed an aversion to the color red..."

- YoYo

When the new Intensive Management Unit (IMU) opened at O.S.P., Baby-Loc, Alamin and I were slotted to be the first of it's occupants. Then after serving my time in solitary confinement, I was finally released to the general population where I was again well received.

I had been taking college correspondent courses while in solitary, earning credits in sociology, anthropology, African culture and political science so it was natural for me to enroll in the college courses that were made available through the prison.

I also started attending Nation of Islam services. The minister at that time was a red rag from Swans named Damu. Damu had allegedly killed a couple of people. The Lieutenant from the Nation at that time was another red rag

Le'Taxione (a.k.a. YoYo)

named Ecundu. Ecundu was Damus's crime partner and as they'd entered crime together, the also entered the Nation together.

Though I was studying the teachings of the Most Honorable Elijah Muhammad, I still felt a twinge when I'd see red. Over the years of gang bangin', I'd developed an aversion to the color red and though it was my intention at that particular time to change my life, that aversion was still real and present.

One night, while I was asleep I had a vision. There was a black man standing on the steps of the Sphinx speaking to masses of black people. Though I could hear the man's voice, I could not see him so I made my way through the crowd to try to see this man. As I got closer, I could see his figure, but could not see his face. I continued to get closer and closer. I finally got close enough to see this man but he was facing away from me so I couldn't see his face. Then he turned to me and I saw him. The man was me.

I awakened with a new found love for black people and a desire to correct the wrong that I'd caused amongst them. My thought was not to the exclusion of other ethnicities; but to the inclusion of my own.

I decided to do something to effect gang violence prevention and intervention and though I still suffered from the miscreant aspects of the gang mentality, I wanted to be essential in the fight to stop black on black crime.

Chapter 64

"I could see the disbelief in Chaos' face but the reality was that he'd just killed a man."

- YoYo

I continued to study and grow and near the end of my prison sentence, I was transferred to Columbia River Correctional Institution (C.R.C.I.). C.R.C.I. was a co-ed facility which had a work release program. Upon my arrival, I was accosted by females. They'd all heard about my reputation as a gang leader and still saw me in that light.

I began teaching Islam as taught by the Most Honorable Elijah Muhammad and what was so ironic was that there were two red rags that I'd both shot at and shot while on the bricks that attended the services. I was far from holier than thou and though I believed in what Elijah taught, the Crip in me was alive, although inactive.

As throughout my entire prison sentence, Laila would bring me weed through our visits and as through my entire

Le'Taxione (a.k.a. YoYo)

prison sentence, I continued to sell and smoke weed.

I had two females at the facility that claimed me as their man. These two could not have been more different. Cherry was a young gang affiliated female and Myisha was an older prostitute. We were allowed to interact during chow, recreation and facility events such as church and holiday celebrations. We were not allowed to be intimate with each other, at least that was the rule.

Like any rule, this one was made to be broken. I'd had sex with Myisha at a church function when the outside volunteer had not shown up and we were left in a room for approximately an hour together with no supervision. I'd slipped into the recreation equipment room during rec time with Cherry and hit her panties.

Though I'd been locked up for close to three years with no intimate contact, I had sex with these females once; and even then only out of a need for conquest rather than due to any emotional attachment. I still had not been emotionally available for any woman and though they both professed their love for me, I was unwilling to allow myself to love them. This was about companionship, not relationship and I kept it like that.

I'd become eligible for work release and was afforded the opportunity to work for a non-profit gang peace program. I jumped at the chance. My job consisted of going to schools and counseling students who were at risk in predominantly black communities although we did gang counseling with students of all ethnicities.

Due to my own gang experience and notoriety, I became the premier gang counselor and was allowed flexible hours by the institution. I'd go out to work at 10:00a.m. and wouldn't return sometimes until 2:00 a.m.

The day came for Myisha to be released. We spent that whole morning together and when it came time for her to go I could see her hesitance. This perplexed me. She'd been incarcerated for approximately 18 months, yet when it was time for her release she was hesitant. She had grown attached to me and the inspiration that I'd given her through our verbal and spiritual interactions. Now, one might say that at that time, I was not spiritually mature and that would be correct; but even in my spiritual infancy, God was making the gifts that he'd given me evident by showing me the effect that I could have in the lives of others.

I'd done my gang counseling work for approximately seven months and had secured a job doing the same work with the same employer once I was released. While I was leaving the institution to work, I'd had sex with Laila and she'd gotten pregnant again, but we weren't together. I'd started divorce proceedings before I was released. We had gotten married only to influence the parole board's decision to release me from an previous prison sentence and I had no desire to remain married to her.

I'd found out that Laila had been sexually active with one of my enemies and though I'd never invested in who she'd allowed to play in her panties, that was different. I was furious. I had been betrayed. She'd invited an enemy into her bed in the presence of our children. An enemy that had actively advocated not only my transfer to another facility but one who actively advocated for my demise. This I could never forgive and she would bear the brunt of my venomous indifference.

During my going in and coming out of prison on work release, I'd established a mirroring circle called the M-1s. I financed a weed operation that would be manned by a few of the young homeboys. In my miscreance I justified the weed trade by telling myself that weed grew from the earth naturally and did not impact people's lives as crack did.

I'd met a soldier named Chaos and though he was a live

Le'Taxione (a.k.a. YoYo)

wire, he would listen and respect my instructions as the O.G. (Original Gangsta) when he was in my presence. I say 'when he was in my presence' because if he didn't have me there to instruct him, he was left to his own devices and would react instantaneously without thinking.

One day, right before I was released from prison I was in the community slated to be at a high school on Killingsworth called Whitaker for a presentation on gangs, but before my presentation I went to Hoax's house to check on our weed operation. Chaos, Hoax, a cat from Neighborhood Crips and I were present. Hoax was counting some money when I asked "Where's the money from the East Cost homeboys?"

"It's not in yet." Hoax stated.

I turned to Chaos and the cat from Neighborhood and said "Go get that end (money) from the Coast Homies."

Chaos and the Neighborhood cat immediately shot downstairs, got into the car and pulled off bumpin' rap artist Cellie Cell. As they pulled off I said to myself *"I hope Chaos don't trip."* I regretted not going with them, but it was too late. They had pulled off. After reassuring myself that everything would be alright, I turned my attention to Hoax counting the money.

The phone rang and I answered "Diamonds are us!" It was Chaos telling me that he had picked up the money and was on his way back to the spot.

"Come straight back homie. I got to leave in a minute. Two of um."

His voice came back "Two of um'." And we hung up.

It seemed as though everything was going cool until I heard a car come screeching to a halt outside of the apartment. I looked out of the window and saw Chaos and the Neighborhood cat jump out of the car and head towards the door. They burst through and I could see that some-

Original Diamond Boy

thing was wrong.

"West Up Cuzz?" I asked

"I had to pop one of them slobs!" He answered.

"What? Cuzz, I told you to come straight here!"

He went on to tell me that they were at the stop light on Alberta and 15th and...

Before he could finish I knew that it was all bad. Alberta and 15th was where the red rags hung out, at this house on the corner.

"These niggas started trippin' Cuzz. They was hittin us up and shit!" Chaos went on to explain. "When they started comin' off the porch towards us I got off!".

I immediately turned on the T.V. and there it was. "Man killed in gang shooting". I could see the disbelief in Chaos's face but the reality was he'd just killed a man.

I sent Chaos to a motel and told him to not even look out of the window and went to deliver my presentation at the high school. I returned to the facility and thought about the events of the day as I lay in the stillness of silence. I replayed the whole day and its conversations.

Chaos was my homeboy and this Crip code made it obligatory that I look out for him but he'd taken a life, whether out of fear or necessity; a life had been taken. A life that deserved to thrive. A life that was precious in God's eyes.

The next day I called my comrade Big Bread (Rip) in Los Angeles and told him to expect Chaos. Once his departure was facilitated, Chaos left P.O. for L.A.

I shut down the operation. Because we were all hood, we'd be under the microscope. My release was imminent I had to preserve that and I did.

Chapter 65

"I'm going to do that which I must do to remain breathing and above ground."

- YoYo

My release date came and Laila came to pick me up in the Lincoln that I'd bought while I was on work release. I didn't like driving then and to this day I'm still not enthused about it. There were too many risks involved with driving if you were gang bangin'. It was impossible to stay up on your surroundings while trying to navigate traffic. Not to mention the gang banger's traffic laws that were in themselves separate from civilian traffic laws. Like never being caught at a stop light and always drive in the right hand lane to ensure you could always turn if the light was red. This practice was imperative for if an enemy ever caught you either in the left lane or stuck in traffic at a red light, your car would become your casket. I chose to remain acutely aware of my surroundings so that I could thwart any attempt on my

Le'Taxione (a.k.a. YoYo)

life and for this reason I didn't like driving.

After Laila picked me up, we first went to the Parole Office. I wanted to do that so that I would not have to worry about reporting again for the rest of the month. My parole officer was a tall Caucasian lady named Vikki. Vikki was used to dealing with mascots. This was evident by the way that she began our conversation.

"I've read your file YoYo and I'm not going to tolerate your violent gang behavior." Vikki said.

I cut her off.

"First of all my work is gang peace and that will be my demonstration unless someone transgresses that endeavor."

I continued "There's no need to try those scared straight tactics on me. I'm a seasoned veteran of these streets and regardless of what you say; I'm going to do that which I must do to remain breathing and above ground."

The texture of the conversation immediately changed and Vikki became more understanding of who I was and what she was dealing with.

"I'm proud of your gang peace work and I want the best for you." She said. It's my job to assist you in your endeavor to be a productive member of society."

I told her that I respected that and gave her a urine analysis and left.

I'd already made up in my mind that I would not report to Vikki again. As always, I'd paroled to my mother's address though I didn't stay with her. After my meeting with Vikki I went to Laila's house to be with my children. We played, talked and became reacquainted with one another.

Embaba, one of the children, told me about Laila's sexual escapades with my enemy. Embaba was a very unique child. She was extremely intelligent though she stuttered when she spoke. I remember when she was very young and I was potty training her. She was so stubborn. I'd put her on the pot and tell her that she could not get off until she'd used it. Then I'd leave the restroom and close the door behind me. She would sit on that pot and sing her name "Em ba ba, Em ba ba..." If that didn't get her the attention that she wanted, she would get off the pot, lay down at the bottom of the door and sing her name through the space between the bottom of the restroom door and the floor. When I'd come to the door to check on her, she'd run back to the pot, sit on it, and would be smiling up at me when I opened the door. She turned it into a little game and would cry if I didn't play.

Embaba expressed her discontent with seeing a man walk around the house in his boxers, especially since I didn't do it. I sat Eusi, Embaba and Raymond down and explained to them.

"That's how the game goes." I said. I told them that Laila and I were not together and that she had the right to seek comfort outside of me. I'd been such an absentee father and considering my gang activity I didn't want them to think wrongly of their mother. I found myself protecting her honor with the children, not because her actions were honorable, but because though I'd taught the children math, cooked their meals, washed their clothes and provided for them financially, the fact that I wasn't there for them or anybody outside of my hood emotionally, my own actions were not honorable.

I continued to do my gang counseling work and any interviews requested by the media. I also began attending Nation of Islam meetings.

There was a function being held at the House of Emoja on Alberta Street that would host the Nation of Islam spokesman at that time, Khalid Muhammad (RIP). I attended as a gang counselor along with a couple of brothers who were also gang counselors. There were two sisters at

Le'Taxione (a.k.a. YoYo)

the function with Minister Khalid Muhammad, one of which was a light skinned sister named Deon. Sister Deon had freckles, long hair and was very pretty. She was doing what the Nation of Islam (NOI) called 'holding post' (providing security) for Khalid Muhammad. Not that he needed any security, but this was procedure in the NOI.

I was the last speaker and after I'd spoken on gang violence, the meeting was adjourned Minister Khalid congratulated me on my work with the gangs and I thanked him for his work with Black people. Before everyone left, the sister that was with Sister Deon told me that sister Deon wanted to meet me and I agreed.

We were introduced and exchanged telephone numbers. They were staying in Seattle and we vowed to stay in touch. I'd given sister Deon the number to Laila's house because at that time that was the most likely place to find me. I'd gotten an apartment, but didn't have a phone, nor did I have any furniture. As a matter of fact, all I did have was clothes, shoes, a radio, a bed, a plate, fork and spoon. But it was all mine.

Though Laila and I were not intimate, I'd stay at the house most of the time. I truly wanted to be a good father, but I did not want to be a husband and I anxiously awaited the divorce to be finalized. One day while I was at Laila's house, papers related to the final stages of the divorce arrived in the mail. All she had to do was to sign the documents and return them and she assured me that she would.

A couple of days later, I went back to Laila's house and she informed me that Sister Deon had called and asked if she would have me call her as soon as possible. I asked Laila if she'd sent the divorce papers back and she told me that she'd sent them the next day.

"We are no longer married." She said with a sigh of relief. She could have not been as relieved as I was.

Chapter 66

"It was a superficial attempt for those in positions of authority to gain notoriety at the expense of the gangs."

- YoYo

I got a message from my parole officer who had scheduled a basketball game between the Crips, Bloods and the police department saying that she wanted me to participate. I called her back and as she began to explain her position I told her that I would not play in a game with the same people that not only falsified a criminal charge against me, but were presently harassing and using excessive force against my comrades in the streets.

"If you don't participate, I'm going to issue a warrant for your arrest for violating the conditions of your parole." She said.

I said "I'm the gingerbread man, catch me if you can.".

Now because I refused to participate in a symbolic game, I was forced to go on the run. Some may say, "all

Le'Taxione (a.k.a. YoYo)

you had to do was to participate in the game, but my 'street piety©' wouldn't allow me to participate in a game that looked real for the camera, but wasn't real at all. The game wouldn't address the enmity between hoods and it wouldn't address the enmity between hoods and the police. It was a superficial attempt for those in positions of authority to gain notoriety at the expense of the gangs. It was a form of recreational escapism that might have addressed behavior for a couple of hours, but it would not address the gang mentality and that's where our problem lied.

The homeboy Hoax was doing very well in the dope game. He and I had grown close, so close that he'd pick my children up sometimes and take them to fast food restaurants. One day he'd come up short on his re-up money and though he had the money at home to purchase what he needed, he was in traffic and stopped by my spot and got the money from me to prevent driving all the way back home. I thought nothing of it because Hoax and I rotated like that. If I needed something and he had it, I could get it from him and vice versa.

One day about three weeks later, we were all in front of Laila's house. Some of the homeboys were on the corner gambling and Hoax was winning. I walked up on the game and playfully said "Let me get that end since you're winning." He acted like he didn't hear me and continued counting his money.

I became furious. Who did he think he was that he could just simply disregard anything that I said to him. Now I demanded.

"Cuzz, Kick my mutha fuckin' ends in!"

"Just a minute homie. Let me finish this game." He said.

I felt slighted and disrespected. I went into Laila's house and got a bat. I came back outside and began bustin'

Original Diamond Boy

out the windows of his car all the while demanding "Cuzz Kick it in!" He immediately came towards me with my money in his hand.

"Here Cuzz." He said cautiously extending my money to me.

"Can I get my car Cuzz?" he asked me. I didn't say anything. I just stepped to the side giving him access to his car. He got in and pulled away. Then I saw the brake lights come on. He jumped out of the car and went to his trunk. As I watched, he opened his trunk, pulled out his heat and started talkin' shit.

"Cuzz you disrespected me!" he said.

"Nigga you better use that mutha fucka cause if you don't kill me now, I'll kill you when I catch you." I told him. I didn't have my heat with me at Laila's house. My children watched as I stepped into the street. If Hoax wanted to bust on me, I didn't want to jeopardize my children.

He turned and jumped back in his get away and skirted off, wheels screeching. I told myself I'd have to kill this fake ass cubic zirconia since he had the nerve to pull a pistol on a true Diamond and then didn't bust.

Though I was attending N.O.I. services, I would still wear a blue bandana in my suit jacket breast pocket. I sold Final Call newspapers on the corner of MLK and Killingsworth and even did security for the minister on occasions, but it was still Crip with me. I had not yet eradicated the miscreant aspects of the gang mentality and an evening that involved my homeboy Lil Chocolate would hurl me back into the gang scene.

Chapter 67

"...I got some old Khakis, rubbed them around in the dirt, put them on, put on a wig and made my way to Unthank Park."
- YoYo

One day as I sat at the house I got a call from a cat named Shysty. Shysty had been put on the hood a year earlier and though he was from my hood, he was more of my brother Duce's homeboy than mine. Shysty said "Homie, they caught Lil Chocolate at the liquor store and busted on him."

"Where was he hit and who did it?" I asked.

"He was hit in the head by the Unthanks." He answered.

We'd beefed with the Unthank Park Hustlers before. They were a new hood that was a mixture of Crips and Bloods and they were trying to make a name for themselves.

I immediately went into war mode.

Le'Taxione (a.k.a. YoYo)

"How many of them have you put in work on?" I asked Shysty.

"It just happened." He answered.

So I asked him what the fuck he was doing on the phone with me. You should be puttin' in work.

That same night I got some old Khakis, rubbed them around in the dirt, put them on, put on a wig and made my way to Unthank Park. I parked the car five blocks away and got a shopping cart from the store parking lot and pushed it to Unthank park. Once I got in the park, I sat down by the shopping cart and waited for one of those Unthanks to come through.

About two hours later, they did and I opened fire on them with a Mac 11 semi automatic assault rifle. I shed the disguise, got back to the car and drove to Laila's house where I spent the night.

The next day the Minister came to Laila's house to speak to me about the gang violence. He read the story of Cain and Able from the Koran and drew parallels between the Crips and Bloods but I wasn't trying to hear him. The Unthanks had shot my homie and they had to pay.

Chapter 68

"...I thought we was homeboys..."

- YoYo

There came a point when there was a funeral for some red rag and I decided to attend it with blue rags in every pocket. I wanted to disrespect them and incite the beef at the funeral but they didn't bite. The news spread of the appearance at the funeral this let everyone know that I was bangin' again.

I stopped attending the mosque and started full fledge bangin' again. In the midst of that war there was a Crip party that was thrown by the 60s for themselves, 62 Diamonds and 62 East Coasts in honor of the homeboy D-Loc being released. I knew that Hoax would be there but only if he thought that I wouldn't. I spread the word that I had to go back to Fresno for a while and that I'd throw another party for D-Loc when I returned.

I waited until everybody that was going to show up at

Le'Taxione (a.k.a. YoYo)

the party would be there. It was about 12:00 a.m. when I arrived unexpected.

I walked through the door and every head turned. I quickly scanned the room to locate Hoax. He was sitting by himself in a green leather recliner. I knew that he would be heated. He always was, so I'd have to get the drop on him. All I had was a .38 revolver and I knew he'd have an 18 shot 9mm.

I walked over to D-Loc and as I hugged him I whispered in his ear "Get Ronnie and Donnie upstairs so I can holla at ya'll". Ronnie and Donnie were the shot callers for the Portland Dead End 60s. Once I saw them go upstairs I followed them.

After walking into the room I closed the door behind me.

"How you feel about me poppin' this boy?" I asked the homies.

"Cuzz that's Six Duce business." They replied.

D-Loc said "Pop him Cuzz."

I told them to go downstairs and start sending people up. I told D-Lock to tell Sheryl Dog to get all of the females upstairs. We went downstairs and as we did that Gangsta two step to the music we whispered in cat's ears "go upstairs." As they did so the front room became empty leaving Hoax and myself.

As the last people were going upstairs I pulled out my heat and walked up to Hoax. He was still sitting in the chair.

"West Up Cuzz?" I said and popped him once – pow!

He began screaming – "AAHHHH! YoYo please Cuzz!

"Remember what I told you Cuzz?" I asked him

"I thought we was Homeboys." He said.

"We was until you pulled yo heat on me and didn't bust." I went on and reminded him "Cuzz I told you not to ever pull yo' heat on nobody and then don't bust."

I remember Rip telling me that "If a nigga ever pulls his pistol on you and don't shoot you, he's a bitch."

"Drop yo heat nigga." I ordered Hoax.

He hesitated and I popped him again – pow! He screamed again.

He dropped it and I picked it up and left.

Once I got back to the spot I looked at the heata I'd taken from him. It was a Taurus 9mm and I said to myself *"This nigga's a bitch. He should have lit my ass up"*. Then I mused, *the heat won't shoot by itself. Somebody has to pull the trigger.*

The next day I heard that my homeboy J-bo from 4/3 had taken Hoax to Emmanuel hospital, kicked him out and told him that if he snitched we'd kill him..

I left for Fresno the next day just in case Hoax told so I would be out of reach. One thing about Hoax; he didn't snitch…that time.

Chapter 69

"This is the Original Diamond, Mr. YoYo. He helped start this shit!"

- Big Ran

When I arrived in Fresno, Rip met me at the airport. It was good to see Pops. We talked and laughed about the Hoax thing all the way back to the West Side. Once we got to his house I called my Cousin Snip Snap from Modoc Diamonds. A lot had changed in The No. Red rags were extinct and now the Diamonds were split up into clicks like Modoc, U-Boys, C-Street, the Pound, Finkwhite, Garret Street, Lee Street, VPs the A Street Mob, etc.

Snap came to Pops house on Amador in Fink White hood. I couldn't believe how big he'd gotten. I remembered when I'd got into the shootout with Boney Face and my gauge jammed. He was just a little boy, about seven or eight years old. He'd watched the shoot out and after my heat had jammed I had to pick him up to get him out of the line of fire.

Le'Taxione (a.k.a. YoYo)

We went to Joe's liquor store, got something to drink and returned to Pop's house. Snap started giving me the grapes on how the Diamond had split up into clicks and how some of the older cats had chose to become leaders in these clicks.

"Where's Big Ran?" I asked him.

Big Ran was the young homie that we'd forced to stay in school. He was from the hood but we needed him to be legitimate so we kept him in school. This had paid off. Big Ran had gotten certified in computer graphics among other things and designed gear for the homies. Snap told me that Big Ran (or Big Blue as we frequently called him) had a shop right next to Wayne's liquor store. I had to make an appearance at that shop. I knew that all of the homies would be coming through there at various times and I wanted to address this click scenario.

We decided to go to the shop the next morning and that we'd stay all day.

"But for right now nigga, let's get keyed." Snap said. And we did.

The next morning we got up, got dressed and walked to Big Ran's shop. When we got there the shop was smokey as hell. Big Ran's shop was where the homies not only made clothing orders but also smoked their weed. When I entered the shop Big Ran said "West Up Cuzz?". He was happy as hell to see me. He ran to me and hugged me hard. I hugged him back just as hard. Big Ran had become diamond headquarters and all of the homies corresponded through his business.

After we hugged, Big Ran turned to the young Homies in the shop and said "Ya'll know who this is? This is the original Diamond, Mr. YoYo. He helped start this shit!" Then he pointed to the wall where an obituary of Big Oso was hanging.

Original Diamond Boy

Pointing to it he said "That's the only nigga that's above this nigga in this Diamond shit Cuzz!" The young homies said that they had heard about me and they all walked up and hugged me.

I sat down at one of Big Ran's tables where he worked on designs for clothing and began to speak.

"Cuzz I heard about how the Diamond has been divided into clicks."

I turned to the young homies and said "Cuzz we controlled this whole West Side. The Diamond was solid and worthy of fear but this division is making us weak and vulnerable to any outside influence that can make an organized advancement against us." Then I ask them "Why claim a piece of the Diamond when you can claim the whole thing? Separated we are Diamond chips, but together we are Diamond karats."

The young homies nodded in agreement but the division had become too engrained. Too much blood had been spilled and the pain was too deep. The beef was too thick.

I told Big Ran that we needed to organize the initiation of Six Duce Day (S.D. Day). S.D. Day was the second day of the sixth month. It was the day that I wanted to bring the Diamonds together to talk to them.

I traveled the West Side and spoke to the heads of all the clicks expressing my intentions to call for a function that all Diamonds would attend in peace. After I'd been given their word that there would be no beef Ran and I started putting up flyers announcing S.D. Day at Fink White Park.

We did a couple of interviews for the Fresno Bee describing what needed to be done in our communities to ensure a lasting peace among its occupants. The condition of my set reignited my desire to work in our communities as a voice for the hood; a voice for those whom many organiza-

Le'Taxione (a.k.a. YoYo)

tions received funding to help, but never did; a voice for those who's activity was being exploited by so called black leaders who would line their pockets by using descriptive rhetoric to articulate the problem, but never the solution; a voice that had been a participant in the very activity that we sought to eradicate; a credible voice; a voice that wasn't for sale.

Chapter 70

"I'll never denounce the hood..."

- YoYo

S.D. Day happened at Fink White Park and it gave us a glimpse of what we could accomplish. The power there was electric and the attitude, jovial. There were a couple of Hoover Crips that attended and my homeboy C-dog didn't like that, but I told him that they were there at my request. He accepted that.

A couple of years prior, my Homeboy T-Dog had been brutally murdered by some cats out of L.A. From what I heard he was shot to death and as he lay in the streets, these cats got in his car and ran over him. C-Dog had not gotten past the way his brother had been murdered and this, I'm sure, played a role in his dislike for those outside of this Diamond. The homie wasn't the same after that incident. I wish that I could have been there to help the Homie T-Dog but I got the news while I was in prison in Oregon. I cried

Le'Taxione (a.k.a. YoYo)

that night for the homie and based on how the story was told to me I penned this verse for him.

"O.G. Stat"

They smoked my nigga T tell me who's concerned with this fuckin homicide
Took him off took his ride and even took his fuckin life
It's time for funkin' I'm all in bring the fuckin' dumpin' no time for thumpin'
Run to the stolen pop the trunk and
Let's make em feel it! They sealed it when they took my soldier
Past the dozier before they two seconds older
Cause that nigga that they took wasn't no hook in this shit
I watched him come up from a pup before he was claimin my set
And it's a fact that the niggas was wit him didn't cover his back
They was on relax with O.G. stat and didn't crack-at-the-gat
You niggas is bustas under cover bitches claimin' this shit
That's on the real ya'll probably squealed while they was splittin' his wig
Lets have a meetin' meet for what my nigga just got bucked
No time for waitin suspended animation is where T-Dog is stuck
He'll go insane rest in pain until we handle this beef
Jump in the stolen and let's get rollin' so he can rest in peace

O.G. stat and didn't even crack-at-the-gat
Where were you at, you could have went crack-at-the-gat
This is a fact I would have went crack-at-the-gat
You niggas got O.G. stat and didn't even crack-at-the-gat.

The Lee Street cats showed up late. They rode in in a line of about six Cadillacs headed by Insane (RIP). I didn't respect Insane's decision to head one of the Diamond clicks. I saw it as him perpetuating our division. Lee Street was beefin' with Modoc at that time. Though I had little homeboys from the Doc, I didn't choose sides. I had family that represented the U-Boys, Modoc, V.P., the Pound and Fink White. I couldn't choose one side over the other if I

Original Diamond Boy

had wanted to.

Surprisingly there were no fights, no mad doggin', no stone facin'. It was all love and respect. At least on the surface. We'd set up a stage and a microphone for the cats who rapped. Earlier that day the Homies Big Ran, J-Bone and I went to the meat market on Pottle and purchased the meat and accessories. Wolf did all of the barbecuing. Big Ran started the function off by thanking all of the homies that came and giving a brief history of the Diamond Boys. He thanked me for organizing it and said to the crowd "Nobody but YoYo could have made this call!" He then asked those who wanted to rap to line up and told them that they would take turns at the mic. I moved through the crowd meeting the new homies and getting a perspective on the widespread beef.

I had invited a homegirl named Twila to S.D. Day. Twila was one of the Homegirls that really represented this Diamond. She was Mexican and Black with long hair and a squeaky voice. I'd been kickin' it with her ever since I'd gotten back to The No. She was a real cool female. She and I talked extensively at S.D. Day and I was surprised to find that a lot of cats didn't know the history behind this Diamond. It had been lost in the beefs.

After S.D. Day, Big Ran and I began planning a talent competition that would be held at the Hinton Center with the same goals of promoting peace in our communities. We organized the Hinton Center event by going to all the hoods, even those across town and inviting them to attend and perform. We coordinated with the House of Hope, another violence prevention organization, sought a permit with the Fresno Police Department and employed the Nation of Islam's Fruit of Islam to provide the security. The Fresno P.D. didn't think that we could have this event without any violence considering the beef between hoods,

Le'Taxione (a.k.a. YoYo)

but we did it again.

The Homeboy Stone won the rap contest with Young Drunk in a close second place. I was proud of my homeboys. It was also sobering to know that I had the respect in the hood necessary to call for this event and that clashing clicks attended without incident.

"*I'll never denounce the hood*" I thought out loud.

After the Hinton Center event, I scheduled a flight back to P.O. One day before I could get on that flight Insane (RIP) was lit up supposedly by a rival click. He was out in front of Wayne's Liquor Store and some cats crept up and got off with an AK-47. Though he had been hit, he wasn't dead. I went to Community Hospital to speak with him before I left Fresno. I walked into his hospital room, and although he was lying in a hospital bead, I could see that he was going to be alright. I sat down in the chair and said "West Up Cuzzin?" "What's Up YoYo?" he answered softly I gave it to him raw.

"Look Cuzz. You're out of pocket for perpetuating this division among Diamonds. You're going against the grain and these are the repercussions. If you keep on getting down like this, one of these young cats gon' smoke you Cuzz."

He looked up at me and said "Cuzz, It's Lee Street." Once again my words would prove to be prophetic.

That night as I sat on the porch with my homegirl in the King of Kings housing complex she began to recount the story about one of my homeboys that I'd asked her about. She said that one day he was coming over the Jensen overpass, lost control of his vehicle and plummeted to his death. I found this very disheartening for at the time of his death his female was carrying his child. The Homegirl stated that at the moment he'd plummeted to his death, his female had gone into labor and eventually gave birth to his child. After hearing the story I merely stated 'life is death and death is life…the two are inextricably bound and co-dependent.' At that moment, I thought of a song to commemorate the homeboys that rest in silence and called it "Nobody Cries".

"Nobody Cries"

To live and die in The No where everyday we try to fly like a rocket
Keep it real and keep a gang of skrill deep in our pockets
And every night it's like a war zone constantly bangin
Niggas lay between the chalk lines others keep slangin
And those that's hangin' got to choose a set
You disrespect with your life, you got to pay the debt
A cold bet, and you can see the pain in our eyes
Mixed with the drama and the hate burning deep inside
Nobody cries
The jungle creed makes it mandatory
The strong must feed on any pray it's self explanatory
Chaos is gory there's no glory in our mothers eyes
All we receive is cold stares when we pass by
But still we ride
A baby cries in the morning light
But just before that homie died in the still of night
Is this my plight to live strife on these Fresno streets
These memories makin it hard to stay on my feet
Peep nobody cries

Nobody cries where we dwell
Some strive for heaven but we trapped in Hell
Niggas scared but they rushin' cars to make the sell
Preoccupied by that paper chase laced with venom
There's two children at the house to feed father forgive them
The choices given got us packin heat
Khaki's creased Chuck Taylors on a nigga's feet at night we creep
Dressed in black on a forever hustle reach for the sky
We leavin puddles after every scuffle somebody dies
And as a mother's tears hit the earth

Le'Taxione (a.k.a. YoYo)

On the West an adolescent girl is giving birth
The babies cursed cause his father's just been laid to rest
Picture a thug screaming Diamonds with his final breath
Death
Nobody cries.

Nobody cries for the widow and every day her pillow case stays wet
By the disdain that causes emptiness deep in her chest
Shortness of breath as she contemplates life and death
Another test that's bestowed upon humanly flesh
Just take my hand and I'll guide you through this stress filled life
I'll be your Diamond in the rough through the struggle and strife to be
concise I will hold you when you feel insecure
And kiss away your salty tears cause this Diamond is pure
I can ensure burning passion everlasting is trust
Eternal lust and compassion explode when we touch
Heavenly Father why bother resurrect us tonight
Show us the light and set us free from this stress filled life tonight
It would be nice if nobody cried.

We'd sat on the porch until about 3:00 a.m. smoking weed and reminiscing about how the hood used to be. Our feelings of nostalgia were cut short when rapid gun fire erupted. Soon thereafter, we'd watched a cat run up the sidewalk in front of us. He got approximately two doors down and began beating on a door.

"Grandma, let me in." he said faintly, and then fell to the ground.

As he lay on his grandmothers front porch, from where we were it seemed as though he was just exhausted.

We went into her apartment. Soon after we heard sirens and the closeness of the sound brought us back out onto the porch. The ambulance had stopped at the apartment two doors down and the EMTs were performing CPR on the cat as his body lay lifeless. He'd been shot and as they transported him into the ambulance, now armed with that information, I knew that he wasn't going to make it. The next

Original Diamond Boy

day, we learned that he'd died. I'd only been back in Fresno for a week and had already witnessed a death. This was the reality in the No. This was how cruel the West Side could be, yet I loved it. That day I got on the plane and flew back to P.O.

Chapter 71

"Why would I kill the cat that was financing my studio time?"
- YoYo

Once I got back to P.O. I was asked by the A.M.E. church to attend a gang peace summit in Kansas City as a representative of my hood. I found the opportunity interesting and agreed.

The gang peace summit in and of itself was a very enlightening experience. I met gang leaders from all over the United States and the message that I heard was very similar. The gang's ideology had been twisted and was now out of hand. We all wanted an end to the senseless violence in our communities and we all noticed that the arrival of crack cocaine caused the disintegration of the morals and principles we once had. We all wanted peace but were not optimistic about peace. That same year, peace treatises were entered into by rival gangs across America.

Upon my return I'd contacted Big Bread from 62 East

Le'Taxione (a.k.a. YoYo)

Coast (Rip) who was also at the Summit in Kansas and he informed me that Chaos had been arrested and that he was being extradited back to P.O. for homicide. Apparently Chaos had been given a place to stay and a sack to supplement his income but he'd placed himself on front street by being out in the hood putting in work.

D-Loc contacted me and told me about a lick (robbery) that he had planned in Milwaukee. It was supposed to have been a $50,000 lick and at that time my pockets were leakin' (I was broke) and I needed that change so I went with him. We hit the lick without incident and flew back to Seattle where Anne now lived and posted up there.

I'd gotten word from Soldier Boy that a few of the homeboys had turned snitch. I took this very personal because these same cats used to be around me and I'd always expressed disdain for snitches. On several occasions I'd told them that if I ever was informed that any of them were snitches, I'd get at them in a real way.

Armed with this news I told Soldier Boy to keep the cats close to him and that I didn't want any of the homeboys in P.O. to do anything to them.

"Make them think that it's cool Cuzz and I'll get at them." I said and then hung up the phone.

I told D-Loc that a few homeboys had transgressed bounds and needed to be dealt with. Since it was I that had put them on the hood, it was I that had to deal with them. I booked a flight to P.O. without anyone knowing. When I got there I caught a cab to Laila's house where I kept a .45 semi automatic.

"When did you get down here?" Laila asked.

"It makes no difference" I told her.

She knew from experience that when I didn't let her in on things, it was for her own protection.

She asked me how long I would be there and I informed

Original Diamond Boy

her that I would be leaving the next night.

That night I went to a Crip party, but I sat across the street for what seemed to be two hours. I was in the bushes waiting to see T-Boy. He finally came out of the party drunk and talking loud as usual. T-Boy was a rida at one time and was known for blastin' cats. I could tell that he was heated but that wouldn't save him tonight. He'd snitched on a cat and got him 12 years. He would have to pay for that. I raised up out of the bushes, leveled my heat at him and let off – buck-buck-buck. I made my exit.

The next night I rode the bus back to Seattle. I did this two more times before my name began to circulate as the shooter but I always traveled under fake names so I wasn't worried.

One morning I got a call at about 6:30 or 7:00 a.m.. I picked up the phone "West up?" I said.

"YoYo?"

It was my mother on the other end.

"You been there all night?" Moms asked.

"Yeah. West up? I know that you didn't call me this early to ask if I been here all night."

Mom's said "You know Kuan got killed last night?" The first thing that I thought was that Laila was dead. Laila was also known as Kuan so I asked Mom's "My children's mother Kuan?"

"No." she said. "Baby's husband Kuan."

Baby had married this big dope dealer named Kuan. Kuan and I were cool. As a matter of fact I used to spend the night at their house and Kuan and I would go to clubs together.

Moms went on to say that whoever killed him kicked their door in to rob him and even pistol whooped Baby. When he didn't give them any money, the guy shot him in the face and pushed him out of his two story apartment

Le'Taxione (a.k.a. YoYo)

window. Then Mom's dropped the bomb.
"Baby said that it was you that done it." "Why she think it was me?" I asked.
"She said that although they had on ski masks she heard your voice."
"I've been here all night. Ask Anne." I reiterated as I handed Anne the phone.
Anne got on the phone and said "He's been here writin' raps all night and Two stayed up with him."
Two was Anne's daughter. She would sit on my lap while I wrote rap lyrics and regardless of how long it took, she would stay right there with me and say the lyrics back to me as I would go over the song.
Mom's was satisfied. I got back on the phone and said "I'm on my way down there."
When I got to P.O. I went straight to Mom's house, Baby was there. I said "Cuzz, why you tellin' people that I killed Kuan?"
"All I can remember is your voice." She said.
"That's because I was talking to you and Kuan that night on the phone." I reminded her. "Why would I kill the cat that was financing my studio time? I asked her.
Mom's interjected that she was pistol whooped and that the last voice she heard was mine.
"That's the voice that stuck in her head." Mom's concluded.
Baby started crying so I put brakes on the conversation.
Rumor had it that this guy named Cat was behind Kuan's murder. I'd hooked up with some of Kuan's people and orchestrated a plan to put in work but the day that we were supposed to do it, they didn't show up. If his own family didn't want to put in work, neither would I so I shot back to Seattle.

Chapter 72

"One of my closest young homies was Killa from the Doc."
- YoYo

I decided to go back to Fresno for a while, but the homeboy D-Loc had another lick in Boston that he wanted to hit. I'd been in Boston before and even had a couple of cats down there claimin' my hood at one time so I went. After we hit that lick I flew straight to Fresno and D-Loc flew in the other direction.

Once I got to Fresno I hooked back up with Karen. She lived across town so though I would spend the night at her house, I would always go back to the West Side by 10:00 a.m.

I spent a lot of time with the young Modoc Homeboys. One of my closest young Homies was Killa from the Doc. Killa was just that, a killer, but he was very attentive when I would talk to the young Homies. The beef between the Diamond clicks was still rampant.

Le'Taxione (a.k.a. YoYo)

I remember when I took my Cousin Oneshot, who was at that time claimin' the Doc, over to my son's house who was now bangin V.P. My son gave him a look that I'll never forget. I told my son (Askari) "That's your family". He said "I don't care." In retrospect I should have heeded my son's discontent because Oneshot ended up crossing the Diamond while we were doing time in the Washington State Penitentiary.

Chapter 73

"...I'm going to make this gang shit real..."

- YoYo

Laila had moved to Tacoma, Washington in late '94. I went to Tacoma to see my children early the next year. Once I'd gotten there Embaba told me that Laila had been sleeping with the cat that lived next door and that the cat was disrespectful to them when he'd come over. I immediately confronted Laila with this information and like always she lied.

"I ain't been messin' with nobody. Embaba is lying." Laila said.

I grabbed Laila by the hand and walked her next door to the cat's house.

"We're going to find out who's lying.." I told her.

I knocked on the cat's door and when he looked out of the window he saw us standing on his porch. At first he would not open the door, but I was persistent and kept

Le'Taxione (a.k.a. YoYo)

knocking. He finally answered.

"Look Cuzz, I ain't got no beef with you. I just want to know if you've been sleeping with this female." I told him.

"Yes." He said.

Then I got at him about my children.

"Nigga, my daughter said that you'd been disrespecting my children."

"Naw man. I swear. I wouldn't do that." He said.

I told him "If I find out that you did Cuzz, I'm gonna kick your door in and kill you and your bitch. Duce Law!" we walked back to Laila's apartment.

Two days later I saw the cat moving out of his house and laughed.

"This is the type of niggas you layin' down with." I asked to Laila rhetorically

I went to the store not knowing that Laila lived in a red rag neighborhood. I had on an all blue Khaki suit with a blue devil jacket. Once I got to the store I noticed that I was in a red rag hood because they were all standing in front of the store. I couldn't turn around. There was no cowardice in my demonstration so I held my head high and walked past them into the store and bought some Newports and a 40 ounce.

On the way out I had to initiate interaction and I did.

"West up Cuzz?" They didn't say anything so I kept it pushing. I was heated and any time I had my heat I felt that my chances were 50/50 regardless of my opposition's numbers.

I got back to Laila's apartment and told her what had happened. I told the children to go into the room and lay down for awhile just in case these cats wanted to trip.

About 30 minutes later a knock came at the door.

"Who is it?" I asked as I clutched my heat and swiftly moved to the side of the door.

Original Diamond Boy

"Bobby" a voice replied.

I yanked the door open with my heat pointed at the knocker.

"West up Cuzz?" I asked.

"Don't shoot me man." Bobby said.

Bobby was a white cat and the interesting thing about that was that when I processed that, I lowered my heat and placed it behind my back as if because he was white he meant me no harm. My enemies were red rags but this cat was white.

"You smoke weed?" Bobby asked.

"Hell yeah!" I replied.

He pulled out a fat sack and I stepped out on to the porch with him and closed the door. He pulled out a weed pipe and I said "I'm from Cal Cuzz, we use Zig Zags." Bobby didn't have any Zags so I went into the apartment to get some. When I came back out bobby's back was turned towards me and I could see he had a red rag in his pocket. I asked him "You a slob Cuzz?" He said "Yeah, but I ain't trippin."

"They got white slobs down here?" I asked.

"Yeah." He replied.

I busted out laughing. This shit is crazy, but in all reality it was no crazier than me thinking that because this cat was white, he posed no threat.

I rolled up a joint and as we smoked he gave me the grapes on the state of Washington. He also mentioned that he too was a jacker and that he knew some licks that we could hit. Bobby had to cut out, but told me that he would come back by the next day at about 12:00 p.m. He reached in his weed sack and pulled out a chunk and handed it to me. I went back into Laila's apartment and got higher than giraffe pussy.

The next day Bobby came by and I asked about those

Le'Taxione (a.k.a. YoYo)

licks. He said that he was setting them up. This time I brought him into the apartment. He pulled out his SKS semi-automatic and handed it to me saying "I want to show you that I'm not shady." I took his gun, looked at it, handed it back and said "Cuzz we both heated. I ain't trippin'."

The next day Laila and I walked to the store. Before we got there a red rag hollered "What's up blood". I got right back at him "West Up Cuzz!" Then we walked into the store. I didn't have my heat with me because I'd been in their hood for a few weeks with no problems.

As I walked out of the store with my 22 ounce of 800 malt liquor, the cat was standing out in front of the store barkin' (talking shit). I let him talk until I got close enough to touch him and as soon as I did, I busted him in the head with my 22 ounce. The bottle shattered. Blood streamed from his head and he started hollering like a bitch – AAHHH! AAHHH!

"Ain't no use in you hollerin'. I'm gonna give you one of those California ass whoopins." and proceeded to beat him. He turned to run into the store and when he did I tried to kick a field goal in his ass. When my foot met his behind he hollered again and clinched his cheeks so tight that he took the shoe right off my foot.

When we got back to the apartment, Laila and I laughed our asses off. Bobby came by and told me to lay low for a minute because the tribal police were out. Apparently Laila's apartment was located on Indian land and instead of the City Police coming out, the tribal police had jurisdiction.

After Bobby and I hit a lick for a pound of weed, I shot to P.O. for a minute. While I was down there Laila moved to the Hilltop of Tacoma.

When I got back to Washington, the Los Angeles Crips had been beefin' real heavy with the Tacoma Crips. I was pursuing my music so I really didn't get involved.

One day a female from Tacoma gave me a ride to the Fred Meyers store in order to purchase a pair of 501 jeans. As we were riding, another car pulled up beside us and the cats in the car yelled "Fuck California!"

I gestured to the cats and hollered back "Pull over mutha fucka!" We pulled over into a gas station and I jumped out of the car.

"Nigga is it a problem? Fuck Washington nigga!" I said.

The driver said "Cuzz, we thought that you was one of the niggas that killed our homeboy!"

I told him "Nigga, I'm from Fresno, but it's all Cali. If you got a problem with L.A. keep it between ya'll nigga and leave Cali out of it."

It seemed as though we'd come to an understanding until the next day when there was a funeral for their homeboy. I was at Laila's house in the front yard with my son, Ndege. I was watering the grass when a car full of Tacoma Crips drove by and yelled "Fuck California!" out of the car.

"Fuck Washingtell!" I yelled back as I hit them up with the Diamond. I'd began to refer to Washington as Washingtell because of the inordinate amount of snitching that the cats that called themselves gang members were doing.

Laila came out of the house and asked what was up. I told her "These cats keep disrespecting out of speeding cars."

"You know this is their hood." Laila said.

"I don't give a fuck!" I told her. "I'm not selling dope or fuckin' none of their bitches. These niggas come by here one more time, I'm going to make this gang shit real for them."

Laila told me she was going to the store "please don't do nothin' crazy." She pleaded.

Le'Taxione (a.k.a. YoYo)

"If these niggas leave me alone, everything will be cool." I replied.

Laila walked to the store and I continued watering the lawn. Eusi, Raymond and Embaba were in the house and Ndege was outside with me. The same cats came back by about an hour later, parked and jumped out of their car with pistols in hand. As they came towards my son and I, I told myself *if they crossed the half way point I was going to let off on their asses.*

As they came towards me I watched their mouth's moving but couldn't hear what they were saying. I had gone into kill'em all mode and didn't give a fuck about what they were saying. Everything was moving in slow motion. As they passed the half way mark I leveled my 18 shot 9mm at the one that I could see was leading the assault and busted on his ass – pow pow! I heard him scream and knew that the bullet had found its mark. I turned to the next couple of them busting twice at each of them.

I watched the bullets as they left the barrel and though I was aiming at their heads I watched the bullets drop in slow motion but I kept bustin'. The first guy that I'd hit dropped his heat and retreated jumping into the car. One of the other cats, though he clutched his heat did not bust back and that told me that these cats were bitches.

I turned my attention for a split second to the car and busted up in it. I pierced the car from the front end to the back. I saw their driver trying to start the car so I shot out the tires. I hit three of the four tires and flattened them. Then I turned back to the two cats outside the car who were now running and screaming. I busted at them again.

I grabbed my son and went into the house to reload. I got my box of shells and began pushing them down into the clip saying out loud "These niggas want beef? I'm gonna give it to them!" It was my intention to get every one of them. *How dare they get at a G in the presence of my son. They didn't take my son's life into account and now they had to pay.* Laila walked into the house while I was loading the clip and screamed "YoYo! Don't do this!" I snapped back when I heard her scream at me.

"We got to get you cleaned up" she said as she grabbed me by the hand and led me to the kitchen sink.

She grabbed the bleach from under the kitchen sink and began to wash my hands with it. We then went into the room and I changed clothes. While I was in the house, these bustas got into the car and drove it on three flat tires to the hospital.

A moment later the Tacoma police arrived guns drawn. They had the first guy that I shot in the back of their squad car and when he saw me, he began pointing. I was immediately arrested. When I arrived at the police station, they attempted to question me. They asked "Why did you shoot at those guys?" I said "No mouth." They asked me "What did you say?" I repeated "No mouth."

They did a test on my hands and clothing that was supposed to tell them if I had fired a gun. The test came back negative for gun powder residue. I was booked into the Pierce County jail for attempted murder. The next day the Tacoma News Tribune reported the shooting.

I fought the attempted murder charge for approximately five months. During that time, I'd gotten into two physical altercations with the County jail C.O.s. One day I was in my room when one of the guys that I'd shot was brought into the pod. I could see that it was him through the window on my cell door. As soon as he put his mattress down I called him to my door.

"Say Cuzz, come up here." I shouted. He came to my cell and tried to act like he didn't know who I was.

I said "Peep game Cuzz, you cowards jumped out of the

Le'Taxione (a.k.a. YoYo)

car on me with pistols and after I let you have it you suckas told the police on me. Cuzz, I'm facing a gang of time and if I'm going to do all of this time, I might as well throw yo' ass off of the tier when they open these doors."

"Cuzz, I didn't tell on you." He said.

I saw the fear in his face so I gave him the back door.

"Cuzz if you didn't tell, you contact that district Attorney tomorrow." He agreed.

The next day he contact the D.A. and all charges were dropped, but I had a fugitive warrant that subjected me to extradition. I chose not to fight the extradition so that I could be returned first to Oregon and then to California.

Chapter 74

"I was still jackin' to supplement my income…"
- YoYo

After serving my parole violation I was discharged from all supervision from California and Oregon. I'd been rapping since '85, but I'd begun to take it seriously. Outside of bangin', it was the only thing that brought me any solace. I decided to go back to Washington and try to create an opportunity for myself through rapping. Once again, a blue khaki suit, a few thousand dollars and my heat was my traveling kit.

Baby and Bear were already out there. They'd moved to Washingtell after I'd blasted those cats up on the Hilltop. It seemed as though that was the routine. Every state that I'd go to and put in work, either the family or the homies would appear in afterwards and ride off of the work that I'd put in. I didn't trip though. It was all hood.

I thought that I would immediately have to put in work

Le'Taxione (a.k.a. YoYo)

again. While previously in Washington, I'd jacked cats and made them run down the street naked. One time I made two dope dealers get naked, face each other and I duck taped them together. It was my tactic when I jacked, to either shoot a cat upon entry or to humiliate them by making them get naked.

Once I got to Tacoma, I found a motel on South Tacoma Way and paid for a room for the month. I met a cat named Isaiah who would take me to clubs that held rap contests. One night, we went to a club and I performed after my performance, a cat named Superb approached me and told me that he was in the music business and that he wanted to work with me.

Opportunities began to present themselves to me from the rap game, but I still had daily expenses that had to be met so I was still jackin' and bangin' every time I got a chance. A week after speaking to Superb he came by my motel room to pick me up and take me to the studio to record some tracks. The studio atmosphere was very professional. The only place I loved outside of the hood was the studio. I was good at my craft and that fact gave me a perceived avenue to financial stability. I was touted by those that heard me as a cross between Scarface and 2-Pac but in all reality I'd been exhibiting this raw Gangsta style before either one of them exploited the style. When cats would draw those parallels between 2-Pac, Scarface and me, I'd tell them that my lifestyle was what Scarface and 2-Pac rapped about.

That day we recorded various songs of mine such as Evil Seed, Destination Hell, I'm exposed, I Control California, Diamonds Callin' Me, Fuck Yo Set, Diamonds Forever, When Slugs Fly, The Unforgiven, 209 In, Where They At, What's the Score, No Remorse, Can you Care for a G, I'm From that Wicked West and a song that I wrote for my dead homies called Nobody Cries.

Superb was amazed because I'd go through a whole song without any mistakes and then come back and lay the hook.

"Damn Homie. I'm gonna actually save some studio money fuckin' wit you!" he exclaimed.

I decided to record a track I had written in '94 called "I Got My Own Back". The hook (chorus) was "This is a fact, I got my own mutha fuckin' back. When they attack I shuts 'um down like a steel trap. You come to bust, It's guaranteed that I'm gone bust back. This is a fact. I got my own Mutha Fuckin back."

I decided to record this track for two reasons. First of all, I wrote it while I was in Kansas City after an incident where it was perceived by the untrained eye that I was an easy target for gang violence and I turned the tables on my would be assailants so this song was adding insult to injury. Secondly, I wanted Superb and everybody else in that studio to know that I knew that I was in a state by myself, but I was well prepared to handle any situation that presented itself.

After we laid the tracks I had Superb take me back to the motel. Isaiah came by anxious to hear the tracks that I'd laid at the studio. After hearing them he wanted to go to a club and get the D.J. to play them. I disagreed, but I did want to go to a club to celebrate my work and so we did. That night I was approached by several females that offered themselves to me but because I had shot several cats up on the Hilltop, I didn't trust their proposals and I went back to the tel (the motel) alone.

Things were going well but my money was still short. Laila had contacted Baby and told her to tell me that she was moving back to Tacoma and left a number where I could reach her. I called to verify the facts. Baby had told

Le'Taxione (a.k.a. YoYo)

Laila in their conversation that though I was pursuing my music, I was still bangin'. Laila suggested that I take custody of my son Ndege in hopes of slowing me down. I agreed.

Laila arrived the next week and provided me with the documents to secure custody of my son. I did so and received assistance in obtaining an apartment for Ndege and myself, but instead of relieving any pressure, it added a responsibility that would prove compelling. I was still jackin' to supplement my income and was soon arrested for robbery.

Ndege was at Laila's house when I was arrested. As I sat in the cell, I replayed my life. The lifestyle that I'd chosen had brought me all the way to this point. This was my lowest point in life for though at that point, I'd lost my freedom, until that point, I'd never lost custody of one of my children. And as if that wasn't enough, I'd been notified that I was a candidate for the "three strikes you're out" law, meaning that if I lost this case, I would spend the rest of my unnatural life behind the steel curtains of the prison industrial complex.

I studied my case intensely, knowing that whatever public pretender that the courts had assigned to me, his job would be to feign interest to the point where I would become comfortable and then abandon me in trial. Why would he truly fight for my life? When it all boiled down, he was paid by the very same system that sought to give me life. A sentence that would net the system close to $40,000 a year for my incarceration.

I'd fired an attorney for his blatant disregard for my instructions concerning my case and was attempting to fire another. Though the second public pretender had refused to speak with me regularly and when we did speak, he knew nothing of my case, the judge refused to allow me to fire

Original Diamond Boy

him. Can you imagine that? A system that says that justice is blind and that every person deserves to be properly represented in the court of law; and a system that then turns on a dime and says that a defendant can't fire his attorney even though his life is on the line? This made evident the fact that if one truly seeks justice, he must not only pay for it, but he must pay dearly for it. But what about the overwhelmingly vast majority who cannot afford to pay dearly for justice? They become inmates in the revolving door empire.

Chapter 75

"I don't believe in religion homie. I've watched too many people use religion to exploit the masses."

- YoYo

I'd began to read the Bible and the Koran a lot more and this fact kept me out of the fights that I'd been initiating in the module. Though I'd been reading scripture more, I wasn't receiving any peace. On the contrary, it seemed as though the more that I read, the greater the internal conflict became.

The Cain of self had murdered the Able of self a long time ago, but now the Able of self fought to live again and this rekindled a light in me. A light that had been extinguished for years, a light that was not bright, never the less, it was there in the darkness.

Laila was about to give birth to my daughter. I'd told her over the phone to name her Special Divine Faith because that's what I had in God. On February 8, 1998 Special was born. She was alive for twenty minutes, then she died.

"How could this happen God? I named her in your honor? Why would you take her from me?" These were the things that I cried out in silence.

At night I would hear Special calling for me and crying. This became so disturbing that I would dread going to sleep, but that only turned the voices into visions. I' became so depressed that I was prescribed anti-depressant medication but though they allowed me to sleep, they did not erase the deep sorrow that I experienced daily due to my daughter's death.

As I sat in the courtroom during the trial, I listened as everyone who played a role in my trial spoke over my head and my pride prohibited me from saying "Wait a minute...what do you mean by that?" This fact assisted in the court's endeavor to convict me and sentence me to life in prison without the possibility of parole under the three strikes law.

When I returned to my assigned cell in the Pierce County jail assaultive module, I went directly to God:

"God, I named my daughter in your honor and you took her from me and now you've allowed these racists to take my life from me. I know that you are a just God and it was your will that I not be left dead in a puddle of my own blood in the streets. Whatever your will is for my life, let it be done, for I can't exist like this any longer."

I knew that once I got to prison, there would be beef surrounding not only the incident where I shot those cats on the Hilltop, but also all of the cats that I'd jacked and humiliated. I'd already been working out vigorously in preparation for the beef. The fact of the matter was, I'd done all of this dirt in their state and I had to serve time in their backyard.

Original Diamond Boy

We were loaded onto the blue bird, a variation of California's grey goose, which was a transit bus that transferred convicts to prison and as I sat, I planned on making a bone crusher (shank) as soon as I was housed at the prison and stabbing the first cat that disrespected me.

Upon arrival, I was taken to see Captains and Lieutenants who told me that they'd read my file from Cali and Oregon and that they would not tolerate the gang behavior documented in my files. I smiled and asked "where's my cell?" Though they wanted to impress upon me that they were tough, I could see fear in their eyes. They weren't like the California system C.O.'s. They were weak and so was their prison system. You can always tell a prison system by the county jail. If the County jail was weak, the prison was weak. Don't get me wrong. There were times when the prison reminded me of the California system, but not on a continuum.

I was assigned to a cell with a cat named TooLow from Raymond, a Crip out of Cali. He gave me the grapes on what the yard was like. He'd heard rumors about me and the work that I'd put in across the map and recounted some of these rumors. He then told me that one of the cats that I'd shot lived down the tier. I asked him if he had a bone crusher and he said he didn't. I began to make one by first rolling some toilet paper and making a donut (rolled up toilet paper that when ignited directs the flame upward). Then I asked TooLow for an empty stick deodorant encasing. I held the deodorant casing over the flame until it began to melt. Once it started to melt, I rolled it between my palms until it came together. I dipped it into the toilet water to cool it off and solidify it, then I stuck it back into the flames and repeated the process until I got a solid cylindrical mass of plastic. Then I sharpened its tip on the cell floor until it was pointed enough to penetrate flesh.

Le'Taxione (a.k.a. YoYo)

"Cuzz, as soon as this cat comes through, I'm gonna hit him." I said.

Three days later, the cat's cellie came to our cell and said "Cuzz asked me to come down here and tell you that he don't have no beef with you about what happened and he told me to ask you is it cool?"

"I shot him! If he ain't trippin', I ain't trippin." I said.

I was approached by the Cali Crips and asked to drive the Cali car. I told them that I would establish the car, but since my daughter's death, I'd decided to become inactive.

"You ain't crippin' no more? A cat named Lil Spook asked.

"It's Crip till I die homie, but I'm not active. I'm studying the teachings of the most Honorable Elijah Muhammad." I answered.

"So you Muslim?" he asked.

"Not in the conventional sense." I stated. I went on "I don't believe in religion homie. I've watched too many people use religion to exploit the masses. I believe in the principles of Islam, Christianity and Judaism as they apply to man's obligation to God."

I began attending the Nation of Islam (NOI) services and due to my attendance, most of the cats from Cali also attended. I started studying every doctrine that I could get my hands on. While other cats spent their money on other things, I spent mine on books.

Chapter 76

"I began writing a curriculum that would combat the miscreant aspect of the gang mentality targeting the psychological conditioning that perpetuated gang violence."
- YoYo

After I'd reached prison, most everybody that I knew turned their backs on me. Laila continued to support me and my efforts to win my liberation, but by becoming conscious, I had made yet another enemy, the prison administration.

I spoke out against injustices within the penal system and how these injustices procured a systemic racism that was perpetuated by those in positions of authority. This would bring me in direct opposition to the peneological interest. Contrary to popular belief, it is not in the peneological interest to reform or rehabilitate the convict, for it is the convict that is the prison's commodity. I realized that prison labor was the epidemy of capitalism for capitalist

Le'Taxione (a.k.a. YoYo)

have always invested in procuring the most financial gains from the cheapest labor and where can one find cheaper labor than the docile subjugated prisoner?

I'd begun speaking on these issues at NOI services and quickly became the subject of a plot to silence the only voice on the compound that was not afraid to elaborate on said issues. I began to see that the price for speaking truth was isolation.

One day I gave a lecture on self determination through self realization. After the lecture, fifteen officers came to my assigned cell and escorted me to the segregation housing unity (solitary confinement). Little did I know that would be the first of many attempts to silence me by taking me out of the general population.

While in solitary, I decided that I would use the time to further elevate my consciousness for the sole reason of exposing the atrocities that Caucasians committed against black people. I'd hated them for my ignorance. I'd hated them for talking over my head in the courtroom and unjustly giving me life in prison. I'd hated them for my impoverished communities and the general condition of black people across Amerika and in my infant understanding of Elijah Muhammad; I thought that he too hated Caucasians thus giving me a vehicle to perpetuate this hatred.

I taught against the evil of the Caucasian with zeal and passion earning myself the title "The Minister."

I taught against blanket concepts of Christianity, Islam, Judaism, politics and ideologies that we as Black people would espouse without fully understanding, including gang ideology. I began writing a curriculum that would combat the miscreant aspect of the gang mentality, targeting the psychological conditioning that perpetuated gang violence.

Chapter 77

"...there was almost a blood bath in that cell."

- YoYo

In 1999, I was moved to another segregation unit at the Monroe Correctional Complex. I stayed in segregation for approximately one year that time. I was released into the general population where I immediately began speaking at the NOI services and all other black prisoner functions. I stayed in general population for about 40-60 days before the administration fabricated an accusation that I was engaged in paramilitary activities. I didn't receive an infraction for this supposed activity yet the administration decided that I was not suitable for the facility. I found this ironic because this facility was closed custody.

As I sat in segregation waiting to be transferred back to the Washington State Penitentiary (WSP), I realized that as long as I spoke out against injustices, I would be subjected to segregation and intensive management units that were designed not for behavior modification, but rather for psychological subjugation. You can't place a human being in a 9' by 5' cell, deprive him/her of human contact, subject them to sensory deprivation for 23 hours out of each and every day and expect that human being to not experience the throngs of dehumanization.

The dynamics of solitary confinement for extended periods of time wears on the strongest individuals creating in the human anti-social traits that are nurtured even in the presence of other human beings.

Intensive Management Unit:
Behavior Modification or Psychological Subjugation

From inside of this beast called the Prison Industrial Complex, I find that the agenda upon which its foundation was laid is being fulfilled to our detriment. I find that Black men are not only being physically arrested, but they are also being developmentally arrested, their psychological, spiritual, political and cultural development confined and suppressed to the point of retardation. But what transpires behind these steel curtains is only a replica of what transpires out there in so-called free society on a smaller scale.

Prisons were constructed from the recesses of man's mind yet man's mind has become subject to prison cells, the very atrocity born of his incomplete thought. I've watched prison cells cause man's mind to regress to the point where he become primitive in his application of thought to this reality.

I've witnessed confinement to a cell for 23 hours a day in Intensive Management Units (IMU). Sensory deprivation, and the deprivation of human contact cause my brothers to become so consumed by emotions that it distorts their ability to conceive reality. At this stage they lose the faculty of progressive thought and this causes them to become perceptual beings instead of conceptual beings, making it hard for them to grasp concepts that transcend their confinement.

This causes them to fall down on all fours psychologically in regressing, designating for themselves a cave of ignorance as a domicile where ambition is imprisoned. They're cast out to the peripherals of reality and are held hostage there, never pondering the full extent of their inherent potential, therefore never becoming cognizant of the duality in man's nature. Man can exhibit the highest manifestation of life on earth, or he can exhibit the manifestation of an animal in human form, yet it is not a cell that keeps man confined or imprisons ambition.

Physical freedom is concomitant with, and a product of, psychological liberation. These two elements, physical freedom and psychological liberation are procured through abstract intellectual concepts, not physical precepts. The ability to grasp abstract intellectual concepts and apply them to one's plight frees the prisoner; and the lack of ability to grasp abstract intellectual concepts and apply them to one's plight imprisons the free man.

In light of this reality, sensory deprivation becomes self-realization, for it alleviates sounds, smells and circumstances that redirect man's attention from self, causing estrangement between the physical and the intellectual and the deprivation of human contact becomes the introduction to self because it forces man to contemplate self.

It is time that our brothers and sisters overstand that in order to transcend our perceptual confinement, we must elevate our conceptual consciousness. Then and only then will we take psychological liberation and embrace physical freedom.

- Le'Taxione

Le'Taxione (a.k.a. YoYo)

After my first extended stay in segregation, I experienced a culture shock upon my arrival back into general population. Loud noises disturbed me and the mere task of walking to and from the chow hall in the midst of many people agitated me to the point of anger and because in segregation and IMU the light in the cell stayed on 24/7, I now slept with the lights on, subjecting those in the cell with me to the very same control tools that were used against me in the IMU.

While in segregation, I continued to study and long for my liberation. In my studies, I was becoming spiritually cognizant, for while in solitary all I had was God and myself. I read to stay sane. I watched the sensory deprivation and the lack of human contact force men down, psychologically on all fours, to the point where they began to act like animals. They played in their own excrement, attempted suicide and used medications as a way to cope with the concentrated oppression of their spirit and intellect.

I realized that justice was not free. Justice had to be paid for by any avenue open to me, so I made a plan that I would execute as soon as I got back to general population and that plan was to introduce contraband into the institution for a price.

You might ask, "how can one who is conscious and spiritually cognizant resort to violating policies when violating those policies contradicts his moral, spiritual and political stance?." Once again, I justified my actions through the 'moral criminality©' ideology.

I was still in my infant stages of reform and as soon as I was returned to WSP, I put my plan into action. I contacted Laila, who I spoke to in Swahili, making her aware that the courts had denied my appeal and that now it was incumbent that I position myself to pay for the justice denied to me by the courts. She agreed to facilitate my endeavor.

Original Diamond Boy

I didn't trust cats who were from Washington. Though there were some that were solid, for the most part, they were snitches so I created a California cell and surrounded myself with those from the house, as we called it, and began the introduction.

WSP had four man cells and I manned mine with my cousin, Oneshot who used to be from my hood, Ant from 4/3, Shitty from Watergate and myself. I was told by the whole California car to not bring Shitty into my assigned cell, but he was from Cali and had nowhere else to cell, so I brought him in.

The homeboy Ant proved to be one of the most solid cats that I'd ever met. He was a revolutionary Gangsta who had grown immensely since his incarceration and reminded me of my homeboy Lil' Roscoe from Kitchen Crip. Oneshot was family, so I thought, but he ended up turning on me after he joined what is erroneously called orthodox Islam. Shitty too turned out to be a snake.

Ant moved out of the cell because he couldn't take the light being on all day and night but we remained comrades. After Ant moved out, my comrade Slim from 4/3 moved in. Slim was originally from Belize but had spent a great part of his life in Los Angeles and had done 17 years in the California system. Next to go was Oneshot. After he moved out of the cell I thought that I'd gotten rid of the only snake in my midst, but I was wrong.

Now the cell consisted of Slim, Shitty and me. One night we were discussing a situation that had transpired where Shitty thought that Oneshot and Slim had planned on killing him in the cell. He then had one of the young homeboys from Hilltop Crip drop off two shanks at the cell. Oneshot was in the cell when the shanks were delivered and intercepted them. I'd come back to the cell early from recreation and Oneshot made me aware of Shitty's plan.

Le'Taxione (a.k.a. YoYo)

"When Shitty get back to the cell, I'm going to stab him with the shank that he had delivered to stab me." He stated.

In retrospect we all laughed about the scenario, but the reality was that there was almost a blood bath in that cell. After the discussion, I introduced my plan to get the finances needed to pay for an attorney and secure my liberation. All of us were in agreement and the next week I started.

Chapter 78

"...envy gave birth to hatred."

- YoYo

For the next 18 months we made money hand over fist. I'd made enough money to give a lawyer $12,000 to fight my case and I took care of my family, all from behind steel curtains.

One day I was talking to Shitty who too had irregularities in his conviction.

"Say homie, I'm going to facilitate the introduction of contraband for you so that you can retain a lawyer to work on your case." I said.

"Bring in some sherm (PCP)." Shitty said.

Shitty had been addicted to sherm on the streets and it was obvious by his request that he was more interested in getting high than in securing his freedom, but that was only my perception so I dug deeper to see if I had perceived correctly.

"There's no market for sherm in here." I said.

Le'Taxione (a.k.a. YoYo)

"It's for me." Shitty replied

I was livid. "I'm willing to help you get an attorney and all you want to do is get high?" I asked him.

I told him he had to move out of the cell. He did.

I thought that by moving Shitty out of the cell that I'd eradicated the problem but envy had sat in on his heart. That envy gave birth to hatred. In my getting rid of one problem, I inadvertently created another that I would eventually have to deal with.

Slim and I moved a brother named Killa into the cell. Killa was a Gangster Disciple from Arkansas. He was a young, wild brother who I took a liking to and would come to our assigned cell almost daily to drink coffee, eat and play dominoes with Slim. Every time he came to the cell, I'd be studying. One day he asked "What are you reading?"

"The true history of Master Fard Muhammad." I answered.

"Who is Master Fard Muhammad?" he asked.

I answered "Master Fard Muhammad is the great Mahdi destined to come and raise one who would start the reformation of the black man and woman her in the wilderness of North America."

"Who did he raise?" he asked

"He raised the most Honorable Elijah Muhammad." I replied.

Chapter 79

"If Black men are to be reformed, they must know their history for if one does not know himself historically there is no litmus test by which he can gauge his present behavior."
- YoYo

After Killa moved into the cell I could see that he was uncomfortable with the fact that he had no income. He tried very hard to get employment, but because he didn't have a G.E.D. he couldn't secure work that would at least allow him to purchase the everyday hygiene articles that he needed.

After a couple of weeks, I had waited until he and I were in the cell by ourselves so that I could speak candidly to him without placing his manhood into question.

"Brother, I know that it's hard when you are so far away from home as we are and I know you are experiencing feelings of inadequacy due to your inability to purchase your basic hygiene needs, but it is self defeatist to seek employment before you have a basic education.

Le'Taxione (a.k.a. YoYo)

"Man I got to help contribute." He said in his country drawl. "And I feel bad because I can't".

"Go back to school and get your G.E.D. and I'll take care of everything else Brother." I told him.

"It's more important to me that you know how to read, write and calculate than how much commissary you bought this week because without a basic education you can never conceive an advanced education."

He agreed and I supported him not only with food and clothing, but also in his developmental journey from male hood to manhood and though it took him a while, he finally got his G.E.D.

I was as proud of him as I would have been of my own son. Though I never requested that Killa (Mwanzoni) study the teachings of the Honorable Elijah Muhammad, one day out of the blue he said "I want to be in the Nation." I asked him if he was sure and he said "yes" so I immediately set up a study regiment for him and on specific days we'd listen to tapes and study together.

We first studied history. If Black men are to be reformed, they must know their history for if one does not know himself historically there is no litmus test by which he can gauge his present behavior.

Next we studied the dynamics surrounding family and social order, taking an in depth look at slavery and it's ramifications, all the while we were working on language mechanics and enhancing our vocabulary. I stressed to him that an effective articulation is conducive to the conveying of ideas, thoughts and feelings.

I watched him grow. He was one of my greatest students because he applied everything that he learned and benefited from it. I used to tell him "Knowledge is not made manifest in your knowing. It is made manifest in the application of what you know."

Chapter 80

"I'd shunned the so-called Crip car, not because I had denounced the Crips but because I didn't recognize them as Crips."

- YoYo

Though I'd already retained a lawyer, I continued to make money inside the prison. I loved being able to supply my children's needs and wants. It gave me a false feeling of fatherhood that was fueled by being able to give them things.

The Native American car owed me $3,000. It had been brought to my attention that Shitty had went to them and told them that they didn't have to pay me and that the Crips would not get involved. I'd shunned the so called Crip car, not because I had denounced the Crips but because I didn't recognize them as Crips. The day I was given the news about what Shitty had said, the few Cali Crips that I did rotate with, the FOI and I got strapped (with shanks) and

Le'Taxione (a.k.a. YoYo)

went to the yard to confront the Natives.

While everyone else stayed strategically positioned, Slim and I approached the car.

"Say Brother, I heard about what that coward Shitty said to you, but if you think that you are not going to pay me, you're mistaken." I said.

Their head replied "Yeah, that was said, but we don't do business like that."

We ended the conversation and returned to the unit.

Once we got back to our assigned cell I told Slim "When you go to breakfast, tell Shitty to come to the cell. I want to speak to him."

It was incumbent upon me that I personally got down with Shitty to deter any future business problems with other ethnicities and when he got inside the cell I did just that. He was defenseless and quickly succumbed to my rage.

Chapter 81

"The Transformation…"

- YoYo

Not long after that incident, my comrade Slim made a business transaction with a snitch who claimed to be from Santana Bloc Crips and I ended up in segregation, fighting allegations of introducing a controlled substance into the prison.

While I was in segregation, the snitch was stabbed in the neck out in general population. He immediately told the authorities that I had ordered the hit from segregation and I was given two years in the intensive management unit.

For that two years, I studied avidly and looked deeper within myself, identifying the 'moral criminality'© that I used to justify participating in unrighteousness under the premise that it would procure a righteous result. I vowed that I would dismantle the 'moral criminality'© within self and in doing so I effectuated a higher level of consciousness.

Le'Taxione (a.k.a. YoYo)

I resumed work on my gang violence prevention and intervention curriculum, changing it's name from "Diamonds in the rough" to "The Nine Steps to Empowerment Process (N'STEP™), which I completed in 2002. I'd been working on this curriculum since 1999 and though I would spend two of the loneliest years of my life (2002-2004) in IMU, these were two very productive years, for I not only completed the curriculum, but I'd truly become a man mentally, spiritually and morally.

I'd been resurrected from a death of ignorance to a life of knowledge. I'd been teaching Islam to several females through the mail during this two year period, but I'd outgrown dogmatic Islam and invested only in it's principles.

Chapter 82

"WSP Administrative Memo: Subject inmate is attempting to unify all Black inmates into one unified group"
- YoYo

In early 2004, I was rudely awakened to the fact that the lawyer that I'd retained while at WSP had basically took my $12,000 and absconded. He misrepresented me, mishandled my case and did not even notify me that my Habeas Corpus petition had been dismissed. I filed a complaint against him with the bar association and though he had done this to two other clients, they only issued him an admonishment.

At that moment, life in prison without the possibility of parole became very real to me. Again, I'd lost my daughter in '98, my auntie Lou in 2001, my sister Ben in 2002 and in 2004 I found myself again fighting for my own life.

I knew why I'd been the victim of a crooked lawyer and I said it out loud to God. I accepted my responsibility in

Le'Taxione (a.k.a. YoYo)

hindering my own fight to be free by using an unrighteous method in an attempt to achieve a righteous result. This was deeper than the lawyer. This was a spiritual exorcism that had to take place in order to baptize my spirit so that I would, from that day forth strive to be worthy of the blessings of God. I came to grips with that fact after going to God in prayer and making a covenant with Him that His will be done in my life, not mine.

I was released back into the general population at WSP in June or July of 2004. I stayed at WSP for a year, becoming close friends with a Gangsta Disciple named Askari. Our camaraderie lead to a unification of Black men at WSP; a unification that did not escape the eyes of the administration.

In 2005 tensions between a prison gang called the Sureneos and Blacks was exacerbated by an arbitrary assault by the Sureneos against a brother. Askari and I met with the Sureneos shot callers and I initiated the dialogue.

"You don't have the right to green light (give permission to assault) any brother on this compound." I said.

Askari quickly interjected "And because you did so one of yours must get down with one of ours everyday until we are satisfied."

The tone was set, the demand made and the gladiator matches began in earnest that night.

A week later it was common knowledge that the Sureneos were upset about the losses that they were taking at the hands of the brothers and a riot was instigated in the chow hall where they took a major loss as a group.

Several days later we were all returning from Islamic services in lock step and once we were in our assigned cell C.O.s appeared at the door telling me that I had to cuff up and be escorted to segregation. Earlier that month they'd tried to transfer me to the Washing state Reformatory (WSR), but I refused because I wanted to stay at WSP with my brothers and had even had an officer write a disciplinary report against me to do so.

Now I was back in segregation along with my comrades Kisasi, Kimya and Talim. One year out of IMU and now they were trying to send me back.

Two weeks later, they released the comrades and held me. The reason that they used was that I was attempting to unify the Blacks into one unified group.

I knew that the group erroneously called Sunni Muslims had a lot to do with the administrations intelligence. They were friendly with the administration and received favors from them. I also knew that the administration saw the influence that Askari and I had over the Black population and though it was kept on a righteous level, they saw us as a threat and no longer wanted me there.

My comrade Kiababa (Pint) from Hoover verified my assessment when one day we were working out.

"I've never seen them treat anybody as they treat you. They're scared of you and that scares me because I know what they are cable of." He said.

Kiababa was one of the true Cali soldiers that had fell in the Washington system. He was known for stabbing cats but he was in search of something righteous. We walked and talked everyday on various subjects ranging from politics to family values. He was my comrade and had become one of the most sincere students that God used me to teach.

In August of 2005, I lost my father Rip and I was devastated. During that time, I leaned on Kiababa a lot and like a true comrade, he was there for me. Later on that month I was transferred to WSR.

Though I felt the effects of Rips demise, it didn't hit me fully until I was being transferred. As I sat on the blue bird chained up, I broke down and truly cried from the inside out. I'd lost everything. I had nobody and I was far away from home.

Chapter 83

*"It was easier for black men to call me militant,
...than to call me a man."*

- YoYo

I arrived at WSR in August of 2005 and Hurricane Katrina was the topic of every news cast. I'd met one of my son's friends during my transfer who had too been unjustly convicted in Washington. His name was Illegal.

Illegal was a tall youngster from Fresno Playboy Mafia, a red rag set that he'd help create. Once we went through the receiving process we talked about celling up (moving into the same cell) together. He'd been to the pen in Cali, so he knew what to expect from me. Throughout my experience doing time, I'd always been very regimented. Some called me militant when describing me.

I'd been the main perpetuator of the N.O.I. doctrine in the Washington State Department of Correction since '98 and just as people stereotypically used the descriptive term

Le'Taxione (a.k.a. YoYo)

'militant' to describe the Fruit of Islam, they began erroneously using that term to describe me. It was easier for black men to call me militant, to justify why they weren't on the same level, than to call me a man which left no justification for their stagnation.

I did not want to be at that facility. I knew that it was viewed by the administration and the inmates as the best facility to do time in and this led to the inmates doing anything to stay there, including snitching and/or lying on those that the administration didn't want there to justify there transfer out. I knew that it was only a matter of time before they'd concoct a plan to transfer me out. They'd done it before and it was evident that that was still the prevailing mentality.

Illegal and I moved into the same cell and I started him on my regiment. I gave him the Swahili name Haramu and began teaching him Swahili. Haramu became well versed in theology in a very short period of time. The attendance at the NOI services grew as they always did. It was obvious that the administration had become averse to the unity among the black men at WSR.

Then in late 2005, my G-Moms dies. Once again, I had lost someone dear to me and once again I reaffirmed my covenant with God.

"Not my will Lord, but yours be done."

Chapter 84

"I saw Jesus in another light. He was no longer this being way out in space that I could not access."

- YoYo

Soon after the loss of my G-Moms we were having Islamic services and a C.O. came to the window of the chapel and yelled racial expletives through the window. I thought *"this is the 21st century, yet we must still deal with the systemic racism that is prevalent not only in this state but among those who've been entrusted with the authority that demands that they be impartial while dispensing justice".*

I'd began going to a black prisoner's group that at first glance seemed to sincerely be concerned about the injustices suffered by black inmates at that facility, but it would prove to be the most effective tool used by the administration to identify black leadership and get rid of it.

Some outside sponsors of this black prisoners group

Le'Taxione (a.k.a. YoYo)

had developed stagnant relationships with the group's leadership that I felt was manufactured by the administration for the group and their relationships exuded a favoritism that was detrimental to the group as a whole, for it rewarded inactivity and shunned progressive and innovative thought that came from other than the manufactured leadership.

I quickly diagnosed the cancer and it's hosts and withdrew from being active in such an environment of toxicity, but the envy had already entered into the hearts of some, including one of the sponsors.

Right before a major event in February, Haramu and I were accosted and taken to segregation. I'd been attempting to exhaust my remedies against the racist officer that had yelled the racial slurs during our services, so I knew that whatever reason they used to place us in segregation, the real reason was to quail my efforts to exhaust my remedies and this was made evident when the fact that once I got to segregation the internal investigations unit confiscated all of my legal property.

I sat in segregation for 40 days with no infraction, but in that time frame I had another spiritual awakening. I'd began a fast in which I ate nothing but drank plenty of fluids. While I fasted, I read the Bible fervrently and Jesus became real to me. I'd always believed in Him but that belief was multiplied and transformed into faith in Him.

I saw Jesus in a different light. He was no longer this being way out in space that I could not access. He was a real man that not only made God manifest, but who also reconciled man to God. I realized that this is what He meant when He said "I am the door."

I began to attribute aspects of His life to the condition that humanity was in as a whole. I began to see how important it was for Satan to fool people as to their belief of and

Original Diamond Boy

in Jesus, for Jesus was the only one of God's men that would get victory over Satan. It is Jesus that is the most important man in scripture and I realized that it behooves us all to take another look at His life and apply what He taught historically to our present reality.

I was finally released from segregation after I filed a complaint against internal investigations for violating policy that governed personal legal work and I emerged with a reinvigorated sense of purpose and duty.

I pursued the initiation of N'STEP™ behind the steel curtains and though I met opposition, a man named Smitty, who was a sponsor of the black prisoner group championed the push to initiate N'STEP™, and we began a pilot program.

I also began attending a non-denominational religious service where I met the most intelligent, most intriguing, most attractive, spiritual woman that I'd ever met in my life. Her name was Ajali which is Swahili for destiny. She was a short, light skinned sister with green eyes and long dread locks. The spirit of God was strong and radiated off of her like the rays of the sun and though my attraction to her was of a higher nature, she was appealing to the eye.

Our interaction was as electric as scriptural interactions could be. The spirit of God was quickened in every exchange and I left every exchange with her enlightened. This woman inspired me to poetry and I'd never experienced that from a woman because the lifestyle in which I'd chosen to live, in the past, prohibited such emotional intimacy.

We interacted and on this level for a time and then one day I had a dream about the sister and felt it incumbent to let her know of this development. The next day she came into the institution to interact with the group spiritually and I walked straight up to her and said "Sister, I had a dream about you." She looked at me and simply asked "Brother,

Le'Taxione (a.k.a. YoYo)

did it help?" What else could she say? She wasn't there to entertain an inmate relationship. She was there only to facilitate a spiritual enlightenment, but this attraction was bigger than her plan or mine and because of that fact I pursued it.

It was clear that I would have to speak candidly with this sister. I would have to confess what I felt, lest my actions become impure. *"The next time I see her, I'm going to make her aware of that which grows inside of me for her"* I thought.

Our dialogue grew after that, always keeping God and Jesus as the core of our interaction we grew closer. I invited Ajali to our N'STEP™ class and even suggested that she consider becoming an advocate for N'STEP™. Being an intelligent woman, she attended the class to examine it's relevance before agreeing to be associated with it. After she'd deemed N'STEP™ expressive as well as pragmatic and relevant, she began not only advocating it, but she also participated in the class giving presentations and turning in her homework assignments.

There were many students affected by the N'STEP™ curriculum. All of those who studied and applied it's principles began conducting themselves in a more enlightened manor but there were those that Ajali and I noticed excelled in the class. Among them was a cat named Tatum from 8/3 Gangsta and Cash from Gangsta Disciple, but the most improved cats were Tenspot from Hoover, Tubbs from Santana and Haramu from Playboy Mafia.

I watched cats come into the class unsure, but once they finished the process, they spoke like scholars. N'STEP™ identified and gave them the clinical and scientific terms to articulate their violent, traumatic gang experience and they wielded these terms masterfully.

In October of 2006 the black prisoner's group held their

annual summit and because N'STEP™ was garnering so much interest, I was asked to give a presentation on the curriculum. After doing so, the envy of some of the sponsors once again prevailed and my presentation was left on the cutting room floor as they attempted to propagate the presentations of their favorites, but I took the negative and turned it into a positive. I took my presentation from the cutting room floor, sent it to my homeboy Big Ran from Diamonds, and he turned it into a DVD that would eventually compliment the N'STEP™ manual.

It befuddled me that the sponsors of an organization who professed the uplifting of the black communities would discard the only tangible movement at their disposal but that's what envy does. It clouds one's judgment, sometimes to the detriment of organization, and always to the detriment of the individual who harbors it, but rarely to the detriment of its target.

In September, the connection between Ajali and I had grew and became very intense. So intense that we had to decide whether she would continue in her role as a volunteer or resign. She decided that the Christian thing to do would be to resign if we were to pursue this ever growing business connection between us and that couldn't happen while she was in the role of volunteer. On September 9, 2006, she resigned.

I began communicating with her over the phone after her resignation and we began to cultivate a relationship, both professionally and personally. We rose in love with each other.

I'd studied the violent, miscreant aspects of the gang mentality from a psychological, psychiatric, neurological, biological and physiological perspective for nine years and the culmination of said studies was the science I created and called the "Post Traumatic Gang Syndrome" (PTGS)©

Le'Taxione (a.k.a. YoYo)

and with the help of Ajali, in late November of 2006 she resubmitted N'STEP™ for copyright, created N'STEP™ stationary, business cards, e-mail, got a P.O. Box, activated the N'STEP™ telephone line and Ajali became the N'STEP™ CEO.

In December of 2006 there was a conference held in Louisiana and Ajali and I decided that she should attend the conference and in doing so she presented its keynote speaker, Angela Davis with the N'STEP™ Executive Summary. She also made other contacts with black organizations.

This trip was the first time that Ajali and I had been apart and I felt so alone that I ached for her. We had become bound to one another; an integral part of each other's lives. So much so that we were deeply affected by the distance that the trip put between us.

Though I spoke to her everyday over the phone while she was in Louisiana, I couldn't wait for her to get back so that I could once again be the recipient of her sweet lips, her hugs and her enticing glances. When she returned, she was full of optimism and a sense of accomplishment and though I shared her sense of accomplishment, I wasn't very optimistic about the organizational contact that she'd made. Historically, there is an envy that exists, particularly among black organizations. This rampant disease of envy has prohibited us from exercising operational unity for the betterment of our communities. This envy drives its host and when its host is in an organization, it becomes malignant, destroying the organization from within.

This being the fact, it did not deter us one iota. We knew that the work we were trying to do would not be easy and that there would be obstacles, but we vowed to remain in perpetual resistance and we did. This struggle, this perpetual resistance was no stranger to me. In fact it had been the subject of a piece I had authored years earlier in 2005.

Perpetual Resistance – 21st Century Struggle

"Struggle is made manifest on different planes of existence and different levels of consciousness but it is never a single effort put forth against injustice, rather it is a perpetual assault against injustice, making it an action, rather than a reaction!

Everyone who dares to struggle struggles in their own capacity, applying different ideologies and methodologies. Some aid in the struggle through political and/or grassroots activism and others adopt the ideology and/or philosophy of revolution, but regardless of the ideology, philosophy or methodology, struggle must be a perpetual assault against injustice lest activism becomes re-activism and revolution becomes a mere theory of evolution unsubstantiated!

"The essence of struggle is resistance!" I heard one proclaim; but in the 21st century the essence of struggle must be "perpetual resistance"! Perpetual resistance denotes movement, making it incumbent upon those who dare to struggle to launch a perpetual assault against injustice. There are far too many reactionary individuals hiding in the midst of the struggle who offer lackluster remedies to injustices and make concessions to the hegemonious structures which we struggle against!

Struggle is pain and has been ordained for every living organism that seeks liberation from the constraints which surround its existence. Pain and struggle are concomitant and are the constant companions of those who seek freedom, justice, equality and liberation. Those of us who dare to struggle experience pain when we perceive defeat in the

Le'Taxione (a.k.a. YoYo)

embryonic stages of our struggle; sometimes the pain is so intense that it procures discouragement in those who merely call for resistance.

Those of us who dare to struggle, employing perpetual resistance, are cognizant of the fact that perceived defeats in the embryonic stages of the struggle are customary and must be turned into fuel of encouragement that becomes the lubricant for our next assault on injustice!

Those of us who dare to struggle cannot allow our desire to be extinguished by a perceived defeat in the embryonic stages of our struggle. We must remain in a state of perpetual resistance, aggressively assaulting injustice in our advancement.

Mere resistance makes one an advocate of the struggle, perpetual resistance compels one to struggle!"

In late December of 2006 Ajali filed for N'STEP™'s business license and the first official date of business was January 1, 2007. On January 13, 2007, N'STEP™ had its first graduation and a member of the County Council sent a letter of congratulations, as did the Superintendent of the facility, which was read to the graduating class of twelve.

There had been no other class mandated by the department of corrections that graduated in masse as the volunteer N'STEP™ class had. We'd conducted a pilot class for seven months for prisoners by prisoners with no assistance from the Department of Corrections. All materials were supplied by the N'STEP™ class facilitators. I was proud of the students who graduated for they made a conscious decision to go through the process and where other mandated programs could not hold their attention for four weeks, N'STEP™ held their attention and enthusiasm for seven months. This was a major achievement, both for the students, and for the N'STEP™ curriculum.

I had set upon my endeavor to make right the wrong that I perpetuated in communities from Fresno to Boston. This was my redemption and I was far from finished.

We were preparing to start the next N'STEP™ class when I received a letter from the head of prisons in Washington. In order to continue the work, the Department of Corrections would have to have control over N'STEP™; a control that would compromise the integrity of the curriculum. I was told to cease teaching the N'STEP™ class until further notice. I complied.

I called Ajali and gave her the news. She, as I, was very disappointed in the stance that the department had taken. She too had seen the transforming principles of N'STEP™ work in the youth that completed the process and could not imagine why the department would attempt to deter one from engaging in a process that addressed an area where they were experiencing so many problems – gang violence within the prison system.

I told her that it was not in the department's interest to quail gang violence and in many instances; I felt that they encouraged it to justify the funding for intensive management units. On the surface, this seems ludicrous, but I've witnessed the embellishment, by the institution, of statistical data on gang violence in order to receive funding to build IMUs and once they were built, they remained empty for at least another year. Only after the public and high ranking officials questioned the appropriation of funding rendered, did the administration begin to conduct capricious investigations of inmates while holding them in these empty structures for 60-90 days at a time.

Just as it became evident that gladiator matches were being engineered by placing rival gang members in the same recreation yard in a prison in Corcoran California, I'd witnessed gang violence facilitated in prisons in Washing-

Le'Taxione (a.k.a. YoYo)

ton. The prison officials would regularly conduct two separate line movements; keeping rival gangs separated, but then would conduct the movements simultaneously putting the rival Norteneos and Sureneos in the same place at the same time, thereby facilitating gang fights.

Ajali couldn't believe that fact. She'd always thought that those who were in prison committed crimes and those prisons were places for rehabilitation and reformation. Although that may have been the original intent, at this stage in time, prison is the most lucrative businesses in America; so lucrative that it has lobbyist on Capital Hill and many are now investing in the private prison industry; which is why it is now called the Prison Industrial Complex.

'Industrial' means 'of, related to, or used in industry' and is characterized by highly developed industries, so why is the word used in conjunction with prisons? It is the descriptive language used to define the prison's purpose.

If it is an industry, what is its commodity? There is no other country in the world that has as many prisoners as America. There are an estimated 2.2 million people incarcerated in America so its commodity has to be its population. This fact cannot escape those that are conscious and so it did not escape me. As Rip used to say "I can look through muddy water and see dry land."

We could not let the Department of Correction's stance deter us in the work that N'STEP™ was designed to do. It was incumbent upon us that we kept pushing the concept and principles of the curriculum by making it available to the world and to do this, N'STEP™ had to be published. This was the first literary that I'd ever published so we would have to do it ourselves. Ajali and I had coined the motivational phrase "We all we got", meaning that we would have to do this work together for we had no one else that believed in it as we did and that's exactly what we did.

Original Diamond Boy

The N'STEP™ curriculum was already copy written so all we had to do was to find the information needed for self publishing. After we did that, we started the long process of self publishing.

Chapter 85

"The baptism had become my focal point and I studied it from the Koran and the Bible."

- YoYo

February 2007 was a very important month for me for it was February 9, 1998 when my daughter Special Diving Faith died. Ajali and I had begun conducting Bible studies over the phone. We studied both the Koran and the Bible, not in an attempt to sway one another in our belief, but rather to gain maximum overstanding and blessing that can only be accessed through the word of God. We found it ironic that though she was a Christian lady and I a man who believed in the principles of Islam, there was a common thread through both beliefs and it was only the dogma that separated them.

I'd again began to study Jesus intensely. The baptism had become my focal point and I studied it from the Koran and the Bible, but it was not until one day that I was talking

Le'Taxione (a.k.a. YoYo)

to Ajali on the phone that I truly began to contemplate the need to be baptized.

It had been raining hard that day and the list of inmates who wanted to use the phone was very long. I immediately got to the phones and called Ajali. As we were talking on the second call that I made to her, I was asked by the C.O. to relinquish the phone so that someone else could have the opportunity to use it. I was agitated for we were involved in a deeply spiritual conversation that I wanted to continue. If I get off of the phone, I won't get a chance to get back on tonight" I told myself.

I noticed that there was a phone not in use because it was located in a place where the roof was leaking and water was dropping down on it.

"Let me use the phone that no one wants to use." I asked the CO in my desire to continue speaking with Ajali.

The C.O. agreed and I quickly hung up and went to the undesirable phone. I called Ajali and continued our conversation. As we spoke, water leaked down from the roof onto my head.

"Water is running onto my head as if I were being baptized." I said to Ajali offhandedly.

Though she acknowledged what I had said, she continued to speak.

"I want to be baptized." I said to her.

"What?" she asked.

I repeated with clarity "I want to get baptized."

Ajali went through a myriad of emotions, including screaming outrageously.

"Are you sure?" she asked me.

"Yes. I am." I replied and she began to praise God and thank Jesus through tears for this blessing.

After I hung up the phone that night, I prayed fervrently and consulted the Koran again on the baptism.

Original Diamond Boy

The first chapter of the Koran that I began to read for clarification was Chapter two. Verse 136 of that chapter said: "We believe in Allah and (in) that which has been revealed to us, and (in) that which was revealed to Abraham and Ishmael and Isaac and Jacob and the tribes and (in) that which was given to Moses and Jesus and that which was given to the prophets from their Lord, we do not make any distinction between any of them and to Him do we submit." (Maulana Muhammad Ali translation).

"What was it that was given to Jesus?" I asked myself.

I then read chapter 2, verse 285 which stated in pertinent part that the Messenger believes in what has been revealed to him from his Lord and (so do) the believers. They all believe in Allah and his angels and his books and his messengers.

I asked myself *what books was the Koran referring to?*

I went to Chapter 3, verse 3 which said, in pertinent part, "He has revealed to thee the book with truth, verifying that which is before it and he revealed the Torah and the Gospel aforetime, guidance for the people."

So I asked *"What was the guidance?"*

I then stumbled upon Chapter 2, verse 138. I'd read it before, but this time I read it with clarity. It stated that, "We take Allah's color and who is better than Allah at coloring and we are his worshippers."

The word color in Arabic, which is the language of the Koran, is 'Sabgh' which means dyeing or coloring and also dipping or immersing in water, hence Sibghah indicates baptism.

I then looked at the language "to take". The American Heritage dictionary defines 'take' to mean 'to assume upon oneself, follow, e.g. a suggestion, to make or perform'. As a phrasal verb, it is 'to follow as an example'.

Jesus was given the Gospel and Muslims are exhorted

Le'Taxione (a.k.a. YoYo)

to believe in all of God's messengers and to make no distinctions between them. The guidance is the life of Jesus and the gospel and the Koran is meant to verify that, not to abrogate it. In the verse that said "We take Allah's color", some see a suggestion, but I saw a command. This set me outside of the pale of conventional Islam to those who have an infantile understanding of scripture, but my duty is to God and if Jesus underwent the baptism and commanded us to be baptized, I too would be baptized in my quest to please God by picking up my cross and following Him who came not to condemn flesh, but to condemn sin in flesh.

I did not arrive at this decision to be baptized fortuitously. Man in his immature spiritual state asks God for miracles, but because he is spiritually immature, he thinks that miracles are mystical, magical occurrences that are marked by things floating in thin air, when in all reality God performs miracles in our lives daily. If we act upon these miracles, we are led closer to Him. The water dripping down on my head that sparked the thought of being baptized was one of those miracles.

I immediately put in a request to the facility chaplain to be baptized. A few days later he wrote back stating that it was against his doctrinal beliefs to baptize me because I was a Muslim.

The institutional racism and bigotry I had found inherent in many Department of Corrections employees was made evident to me, not only in his refusal to baptize me, but also in the other assigned Christian ministerial volunteer's refusal to do so. But I could not allow him to use the teachings of Jesus to mask his racism so I went to the Bible (King James version) in an attempt to use scripture to purify his heart. I read Ephesians 4:5 where it stated "One Lord, one faith, one baptism."

Galatians 3:26-28 said "For ye are all the children of

God by faith in Christ Jesus. For as many of you as have been baptized into Christ have put on Christ. There is neither Jew, nor Greek, there is neither bond nor free, there is neither male nor female. For ye are all one in Christ Jesus.

I Corinthians 12:13-14 taught that "For by one spirit are we all baptized into one body, whether we are Jews or Gentiles, whether we be bond or free and have been all made to drink into one spirit. For the body is not one member, but many.

John 10:16 said "And other sheep I have, which are not of this fold. Them also I must bring and they shall hear my voice and there shall be one fold and one Shepard."

Finally, the Prophet Muhammad said that in the day of resurrection Jesus would be at the head of the temple.

Armed with this information I met with the facility Chaplain and after taking him through scripture, I told him that the doctrinal belief that prohibited him or any of the Christian volunteers from baptizing me was not grounded in the Bible.

I had my Fiancé' contact Smitty and ask that he perform my baptism and he agreed to do it.

The first scheduled date of my baptism was cancelled, and that plus the chaplain's concern that I was attempting to join two groups, I believe were an attempt to discourage me.

I simply rescheduled and anxiously awaited my baptism, all the while I taught the brothers on the significance of Jesus, the gospel and the application of the principles He taught to one's life in order to experience the power of God.

The day of my baptism came and it was anything but normal. I was told that it had been cancelled again, but while on the rec yard, I saw Smitty who informed me that he was there to perform my baptism. I returned to the unit,

Le'Taxione (a.k.a. YoYo)

got a change of clothes and headed to the Chapel. When I got there, Smitty was standing in the chapel, looking into the tub in which I was to be baptized. He turned to me with a big smile and ask "are you ready?"

"Yes." I said.

As I went up the stairs to be immersed into the tub of water, I began to pray that this baptism not be as those I'd seen and that it be accepted by God effectuating a true transformation. This act was more to me than simply a symbolic expression of faith. This was real and I wanted to experience the cleansing of God while meeting my obligation to follow His perfect example on earth, His son, Jesus Christ.

I got into the tub of water and sat straight up erect with anticipation and fear. As I sat, Smitty began to pray, but I was so deep in prayer myself, I didn't hear all that he said.

All at once, I got a heavy feeling of sorrow, grief, and guilt. My self accusing spirit was bearing witness against me for all of the violence that I'd perpetuated while I served the miscreant aspect of the gang mentality. Violent events flashed through my mind like an evanescent documentary, yet I saw victims and circumstances clearly.

The sorrow, grief and guilt was so deep, so heavy, that I could feel the weight of it on my soul and I began to cry. Smitty then leaned my upper torso backwards and as I anticipated being fully immersed in the water I asked that God forgive me for all that I'd done against self, family, community and humanity.

After being fully immersed, I opened my eyes. It felt as though I was in a watery grave and I thought this must be what the dead feel. It seemed as though I was immersed for minutes, but in all reality, it was seconds. Smitty brought me up from the water and when I was again sitting erect, I pondered what had just transpired for a few minutes before

I got out of the tub.

I felt fully cleansed. My body felt light. There was no more guilt, sorrow or grief. This was the meaning of being born again in Christ. I thanked God for accepting my baptism as more than a symbolic gesture and truly cleansing me.

I got back to the cell block and called Ajali and when I told her I had been baptized she again began screaming uncontrollably. She had to pull over to the side of the road and she got out of the car.

"Thank you Lord, Thank you dear Jesus!" she said over and over again.

I told her all about the experience, detail by detail. She began to cry. She knew of all the resistance that I was experiencing in order to be baptized and that made it just that much more special.

I was blessed to experience the true cleansing of the baptism and to have someone that I loved truly and purely to share it with. As I lay down to rest in the silence of that night, I reflected upon my whole fight to be baptized and again thanked God for not only that blessing, but for the many blessings that he'd been bestowing upon me throughout my life and throughout my incarceration.

Chapter 86

"The year of 2007 would be the year of perfecting one's goals, ambitions and service to God."

- YoYo

In April of 2007 Ajali and I retained an attorney to undo what my previous attorney had done. The trial court in Washington had erroneously given me the three strikes sentence using a class C felony out of California to do so. Many people don't understand the three strikes law. They are under the impression that people who receive three strikes sentences are receiving it due to three violent crimes, but that's not always the case.

Three strikes was geared to incarcerate felons who had committed three violent crimes, but it was doing the opposite. There were cases where people were being sentenced to three strikes for stealing bubble gum, donuts and candy bars. There was a brother in Washington that was sentenced to three strikes for picking a man's pocket and stealing his wallet. I'd talked to this brother extensively. He wasn't a bad brother but he'd been sentenced to life without the possibility of parole under the three strikes law.

Also, data had been gathered that showed that black men disproportionately received the three strikes sentence.

My attorney was referred to me by a brother who he had helped get his three strikes overturned. My attorney looked at my case and saw the injustice that I'd been subjected to in the judicial system and abhorred it. He too knew that I should not have received the three strikes sentence and vowed to do all in his power to get it overturned.

I'd already done major research on my case throughout the previous years. I'd told myself that the next time that I retained an attorney, he would not speak over my head and I would not stand idly by while he worked on my case independently, without my input. I'd be pro active in my fight for my liberation and I was.

I sent the attorney all of the research that I'd done and he would use every bit of it in his filings to the courts. Because he was tied up in a federal trial, I had to wait before he could file my petition so in the mean time, Ajali and I got busy on the publication of the N'STEP™ curriculum. This would prove to be a long and extensive process.

I continued to teach every Friday on the importance of Jesus and to my surprise four brothers out of the Nation of Islam got baptized and all of them recounted the cleansing that they felt afterward. It was a beautiful thing.

Ajali had been receiving letters from other institutions in Washington, written by brothers who wanted to thank me for teaching them and others in the Washington Department of Corrections. These letters of thanks were very humbling and inspirational, fueling my desire to continue to teach and counsel the fallen of humanity behind the steel curtains.

Original Diamond Boy

One day, while talking to Ajali about Jesus and the scriptures, I brought up the fact that though God had been blessing me previously, his blessing, following my baptism had become more frequent and intense. I then recounted a conversation that we'd had in 2006 where I'd told her that 2007 would be a very important year due to its mathematical relevance. I had explained to her that numerically '9' is the number of perfections. This is arrived at because a perfect circle is 360 degrees and 3+6+0=9.

Just as there are nine planets in our solar system, 9 holes in the human body, 9 months in the conception and birthing process, 9 steps in the N'STEP™ process, Ajali's birthday is on the 9th day of the month; and the year 2007 (2+0+0+7=9) equaled 9. The year 2007 would be the year of perfecting one's goals, ambitions and service to God. I believed that if one could do that in 2007, all he or she had worked for would bear fruit in 2008.

Though Ajali overstood what I was saying, I didn't know if she truly gave it the consideration it required. She is a very spiritual and prayerful woman who believes that through that agency, we receive our blessings and she is right; but I also believe that revelation is something that is also veiled and that since mathematics is the highest and most ancient form of language, revelation can be deciphered numerically. This is just one of the many differences between Ajali and myself and though on the surface, these differences would seem to separate us, it is on these many differences that we built on.

Chapter 87

Letter to my Son...

- YoYo

On August 29, 2007, the N'STEP™ manual was published and once again, Ajali screamed uncontrollably. I too was very happy and immediately called my mother to tell her of my accomplishment. When I told my mother, I could hear the genuine happiness for me in the texture of her voice. Mzazi had always wanted better for me and though our relationship was strained for the most part of my life, I could always call her if I needed her.

After speaking to Ajali and my Mother, I was on an emotional high, but once I returned to my assigned cell, I began thinking of those who did not get to see me make this miraculous transformation. I'd lost my daughter, Special, my Auntie Lou, my sister Ben, my father, Rip and my G-Mom, Mama, all before I'd completed the N'STEP™ process that I'd personally went through. This fact sad-

Le'Taxione (a.k.a. YoYo)

dened me. I could hear some of these beloved ones last conversations with me in the silence of my assigned cell. I could hear Ben when she said "YoYo, your are very intelligent and you're going to be a great leader.", but most of all I heard Rip saying in our last telephone conversation after he told me he had six months to live "YoYo, I don't want to hear none of that sentimental shit. I'm tired man. I'm ready to go."

After prostrating and praying that they'd all be accepted into heaven I wrote to my son was doing time in a California prison for representing this Diamond gang...

Salutations comrade,

Your latest communiqué' was just received. It is obvious that our discourse is being dusted for fingerprints. A word to the wise should be sufficient. I am impressed by your growth mentally, physically and spiritually, but disheartened that your intellectual growth has yet to mirror said growth. First and foremost, intellect is the result of deep, solution oriented thought. It is not a result of mental growth when one says "I am not looking to make new enemies, but if I run into my enemy, it's on sight." But it is a result of intellectual growth when one says "my enemy has the right to breathe as long as he does not transgress my right to breathe.

The lifestyle that we chose produced enemies for ourselves and that on sight mentality creates more enemies for ourselves. I overstand your desire. I keep it gangsta because I too choose to cultivate and nurture that part of me, but it is imperative that we not conduct ourselves as thugs under the auspices of keeping it gangsta. We both have comrades that have relinquished their lives representing this Diamond. This is the reality of the lifestyle that we chose in our ignorance, but to honor their lives with death

Original Diamond Boy

is to perpetuate a cycle of death, or even worse, incarceration; leaving our children to be raised by substitute parents that no matter how they try, can never do the job of biological parents from whence they came.

You stated that one can either focus on the bars or on the space between the bars. I say that it is not the bars that keep one imprisoned, but it is the space between the bars, for the space between the bars, if not seen in the proper perspective becomes a limitation far more tangible and formidable than the bars themselves. This is what happens when we look through the space between the bars with an underdeveloped intellect, a new perception feeding from an old mentality. The Koran says violence is prescribed for you and in another place it states there is life in retaliation, but it states to never be the aggressor, for The God loves not the aggressor.

Mentalities are marked by emotions, but intellects are marked by knowledge. A thug's actions are emotion driven, while a gangsta's actions are deliberate and based on a complete knowledge. There are millions of thugs, but very few gangstas.

We are in prison because we failed. We failed because we had a distorted view of reality. It is my desire that you continue on the path that you are on, but transcend your pain and allow your intellect to flourish. Self development outgrows confinement.

You must become more selfish with your life by protecting it with your life.

I love you with all that is me.
Mr. YoYo (Blue diamond)
Le'Taxione (Pops)

I longed to feed him truth and wisdom just as I had fed him this Diamond, and because of our separate incarceration, again I wrote…

Le'Taxione (a.k.a. YoYo)

> Dedication: These are the words to my first born
> (2Pac)

Eusi Almasi,

I am in receipt of your scribe and as before, I'm proud of the growth of my son, but disheartened by your stagnation and seemingly wanton state of reluctance to transcend the artificial paradigm that keeps us in a state of arrested development.

How can one come to realize and acknowledge the truth, yet not apply its context to his demonstration? Because realizing and acknowledging does not compel one to act, so it is the obligation of those who seek change to actualize truth, because actualization compels application of that which is actualized.

I applaud your efforts to "be closer to your natural state" which I take to mean your "quintessential self", but one only comes into the knowledge of his quintessential self or natural state through self examination and correction.

I too have unabated venom for my enemies. That is itself a quintessential characteristic, for everything that The God has created. He has created an enemy for it because it's the opposition of the enemy that brings out of creation that which The God has placed in it. This is a part of a struggle ordained by The God for His creation. The bird starts off in the darkness of its shell and he struggles to free itself from the shell. A rose starts off from the darkness of the earth and it struggles to free itself in order to be kissed by the sun. Man starts from the darkness of his mother's womb and he struggles to be born. Struggle is ordained for every living organism but if you look deeper, the struggle is to come from darkness in to light; from ignorance into knowledge, from the grave to the resurrection.

There are stages in this struggle, and man is created

Original Diamond Boy

with the inherent desire to evolve through these stages in order to become just that; a man! A male grows into a boy and a boy grows into a man, but when we refuse to evolve, we become stagnate in our boyhood stage of development where we feign manhood, but we are just boys playing. So the bible says "When I was a child, I spake as a child, but when I became a man, I put away childish things." It is childish to take a life when your life is not threatened for children have no respect for the value of life.

You stated "How could I or why should I feel that they have a right to breathe when they feel that I don't?" First and foremost, Son, a man is 99% logic and 1% emotion and a woman is 99% emotion and 1% logic. If a man allows his 1% emotion to rule his 99% logic, he is acting other than himself. You say "Why should I feel...?" The fact of the matter is, you should not "feel". To act off of what you "feel" is to act off of emotion.

Don't feel! Think!

Emotion has the tendency to distort one's ability to perceive reality clearly. One must begin to use emotions so that it calls reason into service, instead of allowing emotions to blind one's reasoning. Don't feel! Think!

Every soul must taste death. Every living organism must die, whether it be our loved ones or a plant. Yes, the cycle of death is the cycle of life, but it is a cycle that is to be governed by The God, not man in his immature overstanding of this cycle. Yes, God knows your heart and soul, but it's your actions that are judged by The God so he says every deed that a man does is written down. Why? For it is from man's heart that the real issues of life are formed and pour forth, so if a man's words are magnificent, but his actions are not congruent with his words, you can tell more of the state of his heart by the deeds he makes manifest.

Le'Taxione (a.k.a. YoYo)

So our hearts must be cleansed, not that we become fools and allow our enemies to cause our demise, but cleansed to the point that we only take a life in self defense, or in defense of our loved ones. The Koran says that man will ask why a calamity befalls him; "From whence did this come?" and The God says that "It comes from your own hands." The Koran says that when the decree of death has been ordained, there is none who can hasten it or prolong it. Our comrades and loved ones taste death when it is ordained, not a moment sooner.

Loyalty, honor and respect are characteristics and qualities that are no longer prevalent in the streets. Because the streets breed jealousy, dishonor and envy. Those of us who's foundation is built on loyalty, honor and respect have become anomalies in this rotation called life and we suffer because we thirst and yearn for the days when we were the norm, but no matter how nostalgic we become at the reminiscence of those times, they will never be again for the street demonstration has run it's course and it is time we evolve.

Your street experience was mandated to prepare you for a greater work. I overstand your decision to patiently grow into what The God has ordained you to be, but patience to the extreme becomes procrastination and procrastination denies one the actualization of his/her destiny. Remember this:

Male = mind in matter
Boy = mind playing with matter
Man = mind over matter

Find yourself in this biological equation and strive for excellence. You are very sharp; now strive to be very intelligent. Enclosed is a photo that I took with you on your 5$_{th}$ birthday on Calwa at my Grandmother's house around the corner from your Grandmother's house in The Pound.

Original Diamond Boy

I love you son, with all that is me and I appreciate your decision to engage me in intellectual discourse and building our relationship as father and son; though in my ignorance I walked away from that, I never stopped loving you.

*Love, loyalty, honor and respect,
Samawali Almasi
Blue Diamond (Pops)*

Chapter 88

*"Justice has never been free.
There is always a price to pay."*

- YoYo

In September of 2007, during the Muslim Holy month of Ramadan, I was again taken to segregation for an alleged group demonstration and though a group demonstration as defined by DOC is four or more people engaged in activity that violates DOC policy, I was the only one found guilty. For the first time, Ajali would be exposed to the wiles of a racist and bigoted administration that used retaliation as a tactic to deter one from exercising the lawful grievance process designed for redress for wrongs done to him. It was far from my first time.

Before the situation which was used to place me in segregation, an officer had confided in me that other C.O.s were profiling me and due to a long history at the institution of racial and religious discrimination and retaliation

Le'Taxione (a.k.a. YoYo)

against me and other Black and Latino inmates, I had filed many official misconduct reports in an attempt to not only exercise my rights, but to also eradicate the differential and bigoted treatment that I'd been subjected to.

While in segregation, I was told that the consensus among the administration was to transfer me out because I was not suitable for that facility. I found this ironic for this was a closed custody facility (meaning that inmates deemed violent and who had behavior problems were housed there.) Here, I'd been infraction free for almost three years, had the highest number of custody points given to those that stayed out of trouble, was programming and had been given the privileges of having extended family visits, where my family could come in and we'd spend two to three days in a trailer together. Yet, I was not suitable for that institution.

Ajali had done all that she could to secure my right to be back in the general population. She contacted outside representation from the Nation of Islam in hopes of securing support for me, to no avail. I was ashamed when her pleas fell on the deaf ears of most of those who I'd represented to her as my brothers and comrades in the struggle. I'd fought for the rights of the Nation of Islam to congregate and worship behind these steel curtains for ten years, but at the time that I need our outside sponsors they were not there for me. Once I got out of segregation I would re-evaluate my position as it related to the Nation.

I retained another attorney to represent me in this matter. I could no longer watch as Ajali cried about me being in segregation and not being able to touch me.

I continued to write my memoirs while in segregation and I made great progress on the book during that time. I told Ajali that sometimes people think that they are doing something to you when they are really doing something for you.

Original Diamond Boy

My attorney contacted the administration and I was released back into the general population. Justice has never been free...there is always a price to pay.

Definitely to be continued...

Black Rose

The precious seed that didn't need much to succeed
Rotated in the earth's soil and pushed its way upward, finding life in the midst of weeds...
Reaching towards the sky seeking to be kissed by the sun and sustained
But the deprivation of light introduced it to pain...
Petals eventually shriveled, leaves withered and the lack of water made the stem dry
But under the most adverse conditions it refused to die
Everyday people passed by and unwittingly spat, but the moisture from their mouths restored the flowers strength
Now in full bloom, gaze upon the beauty of this rare black rose, the stem alive and strong with protruding thorns for its foes
I am the precious seed that didn't need much to succeed
Spat on by humanity, yet flourished in the midst of weeds.

Conclusion

The Black Rose is a befitting poem to end this first part of "Original Diamond Boy: Psychology of a Gang Banger". The "precious seed that didn't need much to succeed" is descriptive language that captures the reality of our youth that languish in lower socio-economic environments, not only across America, but all over the world. The reality of environment is that it has the ability to change a person into that which is prevalent in itself.

I was raised in the projects, which is another name for experiment. And the experiment was to house low income families in designated geographical locations and in doing so a designated area became a bed of despondency. Despondency is the mother of all social ills.

The projects across America have become a haven of drugs, robbery, prostitution, violence, and despair, creating in its inhabitants a self defeatist survival of the fittest mentality that perpetuates capitalism to the detriment of family and community.

Our youth, being the products of impaired homes, for the most part, adopt surrogate fathers and mothers through the most ancient form of socialization (now erroneously called "ganging") and though this is a normal peer activity, the wanton violent aspect of f it is not.

Le'Taxione (a.k.a. YoYo)

What we are witnessing in the fabric of violent gang behavior is the effect of a social order and its institutions' failure to prepare its youth for the trials, tribulations, and adverse circumstances that they must face in their developmental journey from male to man or from female to woman.

The parental structure too must bear the culpability, for it is the parental structure's obligation to foster, nurture and cultivate the life in its charge. Instead, out of the need to support the family structure, financially, that obligation has been tendered to the schools, making them the second primary stewards of life

Impaired homes must be mended. Fathers must begin to shoulder the responsibilities inside and outside of the home. Parents must become more active in not only their children's education, but also in their developmental process preparing them for life's trials and tribulations. Then and only then will the normal social interaction erroneously called "ganging" return to it's primordial state of existence where our youth can socialize with their peers and engage each other in organic conversations that address the needs of our communities instead of engaging each other in the toxic conversations that propagate the selfish desires of the individual.

*Watch for
    Le'Taxione's next book...*

GIDEON:
The Futures Past

**A struggle between the wisdom of the past
And the frustration of the present**

Chapter 1

I was born Gideon Washington in Tulsa, Oklahoma in 1908. My mother, Betty and her brother, David were the children of Thomas and Mary, who were slaves, owned by Thomas Washington; hence our last name.

It was customary in those days for slavemasters to give their slaves their last names which denoted that the slaves were their chattel property. My father would tell me that although the slaves were freed in 1865, his father and mother chose to sty on the plantation. I guess by that time, they'd become mentally enslaved.

It's like having an animal chained up in a designated area all of it's life and then one day setting it free and because it has been chained in that specific area, it refuses to move.

As soon as my father could put together enough money to leave Virginia where his parents were slaves, he moved to Tulsa and met my mother. There they started a family and there is where I was born. Though in 1908 slavery had been abolished for over 40 years, racism was still rampant and opportunities for black people in Tulsa was limited.

In 1948, just as my father had done previously, I'd saved up enough money doing menial work to leave Tulsa in search of an opportunity to realize the American dream. I ended up in a little town called Fresno located in central California. Fresno was best known for its agricultural opportunities but the West Side, where the masses of Black people resided, had it's own flare and exhibited the trappings of any major city.

I was 48 years old when I took up residence in West Fresno. I bought me a truck and began selling produce off of it to the residents of west Fresno. I'd learned that the large majority of Black people in west Fresno relied on government assistance called welfare and since they were the most in need, I provided my services to them exclusively. When they were in between checks I'd allow them to start a line of credit and this brought me into direct contact with the occupants of the government subsidized housing projects and I established lifelong personal relationships with the occupants.

They all called me Gideon and when I'd drive through the projects, the children would run up to my truck and I'd give them penny candy before collecting their parent's debts. I loved providing this service to the community while at the same time making a living. The parents respected me and cherished my service and the children loved me. I was a long way from home, but the inhabitants of west Fresno made me feel like family.

Though I'd made many friends with many families, there was a particular family that I was very close to – the Williams family. The Williams family consisted of Garnett Williams, his wife Artha Mae Williams and their children.

Garnett and Artha Mae were also from Tulsa and though I didn't know Garnett well, I knew Artha very well because we lived in the same neighborhood in Tulsa. I'd heard stories about Garnett. They used to say that he was mean as a snake and just as deadly. I came to find out that that description was accurate. It was rumored that Garnett had shot (and some people even say killed) a policeman in Tulsa. It was rumored that that was why they lived in Fresno. All of that aside, they were very respectable people and the fact that we all was from Tulsa gave us a natural foundation on which to build a relationship.

Garnett had a daughter named Mzazi who'd grown up and married a city slicker that people called Rip. Garnett didn't approve of the marriage and that was made evident in our porch conversations. Rip was a light skinned Puerto

Rican who Garnett would always refer to as "that piss colored boy". Like any father, he didn't think that Rip was good enough for his daughter Mzazi. Whether he was right or wrong was neither here nor there because Mzazi loved the "piss colored boy".

Rip and Mzazi had children together which further complicated the posture that Garnett had taken concerning Rip. While he didn't like Rip, his grandchildren YoYo, Duce and Soldier Boy were from Rip's loins and he loved his grandchildren to death. I could see the sparkle in his eyes when he spoke of them and his granddaughter Ben.

Mzazi and Rip were as different as night and day. Mzazi was interested in education and Rip was intrigued by the allure of the streets and all of the accoutrements it had to offer. They resided in the projects known as Pole Cat Alley. When I'd drive the truck through the projects, it was customary for Rip to come out and conduct business with me until his quest for fast money got him sent to prison.

I'd seen it so many times on my route and it broke my heart every time. Black men's aversion to work and or lack of work led them to chase the allure of fast money and always landed them in prison. Rip was no exception to this fact and his children would be no exception to the single parent home in the black community which seemed to become the norm.

I'd always check on Mzazi and her children when I'd come through. Garnett had asked that I do so and I'd taken a special interest in Mzazi's son, YoYo. He was the oldest of Mzazi's boys so naturally I felt that it would soon be his responsibility to take on the role of the man of the house. His age didn't negate this fact because many times on the plantation the father would be separated from the family and when that happened, as it did in most instances, the eldest son would assume the role of the father. I'd watched this play out in my life and as I grew older, I observed this reality become woven into the fabric of the Black family's reality.

YoYo was very bright. Garnett used to say that one day he would be a genius, but I could see that he was changing. He used to be the first child to run up to my truck but after Rip went to prison, it seemed as though he became more recluse, reluctant to interact as freely as he once did. This alarmed me and I expressed my concern to Garnett one day while sitting on his porch reminiscing about Tulsa.

"Garnett, I'm concerned about YoYo. He used to be the first one to run up to the truck, but now he just looks at me from a distance."

"Don't you fret about YoYo Gideon. He's going through some changes about his father being in the clink. He growin'. He'll get over it directly."

Though Garnett spoke indifferently about the situation, I could see the concern on his face. That's how Garnett was, he would never allow another man to hear him express deep concern. It was almost as if he thought that was the manly thing to do and Garnett was a man amongst men.

I decided that I would address YoYo the next time that I saw him and I did.

I'd usually drive through Pole Cat Alley on the 1st and 15th of the month. This was when the single mothers received their welfare checks and they had directed me to come through on those days to square their debts. It was the first of July, 1973. I'd been in business since 1950 and had saved enough money to buy me a brand new cherry red truck with all the bells and whistles. I should have been retired but I never drank, smoke or used any drug…not so much as an aspirin and I was strong as an ox. Besides, who would provide my service to Black people if I retired?

I remember the day very clearly. It was Fresno hot and

as it always was at the first of the month, the mood was jovial amongst all. I drove up and all of the children made a bee line towards the truck…all except YoYo.

After I'd given all of the children penny candy and squared their parent's debts, I got back in the truck and just before I pulled off I hollered out to YoYo..

"YoYo!"

"What?" he replied.

"Come here for a minute."

He reluctantly walked towards the truck, kickin' up the dust that served as grass on the project lawns.

"What you doin' youngsta?" I asked.

"Nothin" he replied.

"Why you don't come to the truck with the other kids no mo?"

"I'm not a kid no mo Gideon."

That's crazy talk YoYo…of course you a kid."

He simply turned and walked off…

About the Author

Le'Taxione is a student of the human condition and a specialist in the mentality that causes destructive gang violence; wielding the pen to enrapture the mind much like an artist wields a brush. On these pages, he paints a picture of the psychology present in the development and growth of a gang banger and ultimately a picture of his transformation.

Never denouncing the gang, he now utilizes his own life experience to change the violence prevalent in gang culture in a productive and sustainable way - "from the inside out"™.

Original Diamond Boy: Psychology of a Gang Banger is the next in a series of literary pursuits, all focused on the gang lifestyle, mentality and culture and all pointing towards a transformation, experienced by Le'Taxione, and possible for all those who suffer from the destructive mentality evident in today's gangs

In addition to his experiential knowledge of the miscreant aspects of the gang mentality, Le'Taxione is a scholar of a wide array of various disciplines, including psychology, sociology, religion, biology and physiology. In this work, he brings to bear his extensive studies and his own life experience to the illuminate the psychology of the gang member; an illumination necessary to aid the gang member and ultimately the community in the quest for healing and transformation. Just as in "The Nine Steps To Empowerment Process" (N'STEP)™, a gang violence prevention/ intervention curriculum which he also authored, his work is based on the premise that to change the actions, one must change the thought process that drives such action.

ALSO BY Le'Taxione (a.k.a. YoYo)

Nine Steps to Empowerment Process (N'S.T.E.P.)

For years we have tried to address the violent behavior present in the gang culture with recreational escapism, legislation and incarceration. Realizing that violent gang behavior is a manifestation of the gang member's thought process, N'S.T.E.P. speaks directly to the violent gang mentality. By making the gang member cognizant of why he or she acts out in violence, N'S.T.E.P. seeks to ameliorate the destructive gang behavior and to affect positive and productive change in the gang member's thought process – leading the gang member back to the honorable and protective elements which were present at the inception of the gang.

The 9 Steps to Empowerment Process is an innovative and effective gang violence prevention and intervention curriculum that targets the psychological effects of the traumatic gang experience which in turn gives rise to violent and counterproductive gang behavior. N'S.T.E.P. juxtaposes the proven elements of Post Traumatic Stress Disorder with the violent gang experience and proposes a solution for what results – Post Traumatic Gang Syndrome (PTGS). N'S.T.E.P. posits that PTGS is a psychological conditioning that is nurtured by societal conditions and brought about by violent gang experiences which become incessant memories. These memories are then triggered and relived by the gang member every time that he or she experiences a perceived threat.

N'S.T.E.P. is that which diagnoses the problem, addresses its elements and its causes and finally proposes the fix. It is the answer to the gang violence which plagues our communities and disrupts its health and productivity.--"N'S.T.E.P. to me is not only a place to gain knowledge…and to get different outlooks concerning gang life and everything that comes with it, it is also a place of acceptance, no matter what "hood" you are from, or even if you are not from one at all...where no one will discredit or judge you because of the way you look, act, or because of what allegiances you may or may not have...N'S.T.E.P. has taught me many things as well as given me many different outlooks on life...The lesson I value the most is self-awareness. I'm 19 years old and a member of a Gangster Disciple Nation called F.O.L.K.S. I am also a student of N'S.T.E.P…, but first I am a man. My street name was "Bully", in prison, I'm branded "888278", but through N'S.T.E.P., I've gotten to know and love me, Lyndale Galloway."

- Lyndale Galloway, Gangster Disciple

**Learn more at:
www.outskirtspress.com/9-STEPS**

CPSIA information can be obtained
at www.ICGtesting.com
Printed in the USA
BVHW031935120620
581302BV00001B/13